THE
HISTORY
OF THE
FUTURE

THE
HISTORY
OF THE
FUTURE

DAVID A. WILSON

McArthur & Company
Toronto

Published in Canada in 2000 by
McArthur & Company
322 King Street West, Suite 402
Toronto, ON M5V 1J2

Canadian Cataloguing in Publication Data

    Wilson, David A., 1950
      The history of the future

    ISBN 1-55278-169-0

    1. Forecasting - History. 2. Prophecies. I.Title.

    CB158.W54 2000   003'.2'09   C00-931361-3

Design & Composition by *Mad Dog Design Connection Inc.*
Cover Compostion, Design & F/X by *Mad Dog Design Connection Inc.*
Printed in Canada by *Transcontinental Printing Inc.*

The publisher would like to acknowledge the financial support of
the Government of Canada through the Book Publishing Industry
Development Program (BPIDP) for our publishing activities.
The publisher further wishes to acknowledge the financial
support of the Ontario Arts Council for our publishing program.

10 9 8 7 6 5 4 3 2 1

CONTENTS

To

Colin Eastwood,

Ann Dooley, and

Mariel O'Neill-Karch

for their part in the history of my future.

ACKNOWLEDGMENTS

THINK OF THIS AS A TRAVEL BOOK, ranging backwards and forwards through real and imaginary time, rather than across different lands. The concept behind the trip came from Professor James A. Leith of the History Department at Queen's University, Kingston. One winter's afternoon, back in the late 1970s, he suggested that the history of the future would be a great subject for a book, and the idea sort of stuck. I don't know whether he would have tackled it in quite the same way, but I'm grateful that he set the wheels in motion. I thank him for the inspiration, and hope he likes the results.

As any traveller knows, the journey is made more enjoyable and interesting by the people you meet on the road who point you in different directions and suggest various sites to visit. Among them I thank Bob Malcolmson, Nick Rogers, Keith Walden, Dan Donovan, Ann Dooley, Simon Jones, and Michael Jursic. The way was also smoothed by earlier travellers who mapped out important parts of the route: they include Norman Cohn, Gordon Leff, Marjorie Reeves, Keith Thomas, Paul Boyer, Eugen Weber, and Frank and Fritzie Manuel. If this short book prompts people to read their bigger and better ones, it will have served its purpose.

No journey is complete without a good set of pictures, and I thank Erica Sweeney for tracking down the illustrations that accompany and enliven the text.

Finally, a special word of appreciation to those who read the manuscript and improved it with their perceptive comments and their wide range of knowledge. I particularly thank Rosemary Shipton, Elizabeth Schoales, Richard Raiswell, and, with love and affection, the clairvoyant and charming Madam Zsuzsa.

In the end, though, I followed the advice Sean O'Casey gave to one of his biographers: "Write your own damn book and never mind the Criticonians." Here it is, then: my own damn book.

·1·

Prophetic Fallacies

Throughout the past, we have been fascinated with the future. "There is no nation whatever," wrote Cicero in the year 45 BC, "however polished and learned, or however barbarous and uncivilized, which does not believe it possible that future events may be indicated, and understood, and predicted by certain persons."[1] He knew what he was talking about: if you threw a brick into a crowd of Romans, the chances were that you would hit a soothsayer.

This is no less true today than it was back then. We have Jack Van Impe Bible-thumpers, New Age psychics, sophisticated scientific futurologists, stock market seers, horoscope readers, Faith Popcorn predictors – a veritable plethora of prognosticators. And how many of us, products of a rationalist society that has supposedly shaken off its superstitions, still think twice before walking under a ladder?

No matter how the future has been envisaged, its power to grip and engage the imagination has been an enduring feature of the human condition. "The desire of penetrating into futurity," commented Joseph Lomas Towers in 1796, "is a passion congenial to the human mind."[2] For religious figures such as Bishop Thomas Newton, history was simply a record of biblical prophecies that had already occurred; the future, by the same logic, consisted of prophecies that had yet to be fulfilled.[3] For others, the future could be discerned in folkloric divinations, astrological charts, or the lines on your forehead. By the eighteenth century the future was increasingly seen in terms of progress, the triumph of technology and reason over nature and passion – a view that would eventually be challenged by those who came to recognize the immense destructive potential that lay within technological change.

This book explores the changing character of our continuing fascination with the future. It is limited, if that is the right word, to the place of the future within Judeo-Christian cultural traditions, and particularly within the English-speaking world that straddles the Atlantic. Here is a summary of what lies ahead. After a general discussion of prophecies in this chapter, chapter 2 looks at medieval and early modern images of the future: we enter into the world of apocalyptic cults, bogus Christs, revolutionary monks, anarchical "Free Spirits," and millenarian megalomaniacs.

From here, we switch in chapter 3 into folkloric approaches to the future. Most of our sources on folklore come from the eighteenth and nineteenth centuries, but they describe popular values, customs, and beliefs that go back at least to the Middle Ages. The focus is on the ways in which people used folklore, magic, witchcraft, and astrology to assert some kind of influence over an uncertain and precarious future: to change the weather, safeguard the animals, prevent or cure illnesses, figure out who you were going to marry, work out ways of doing in your enemies, and ensure the victory of your favourite football team.

We move in chapter 4 into revolutionary political movements during the seventeenth and eighteenth centuries: the English Civil War, the American Revolution, and the French Revolution. Rather than providing a blow-by-blow account of what happened and why, this chapter looks at the place of prophecy within revolutionary ideas and actions. Once a revolution began, there were always people who "discovered" that it was fulfilling ancient prophecies. Not only that, but the very act of revolution generated new expectations and hopes of a better future that boosted morale and inspired people into action. A strong religious sense of apocalyptic change permeated supposedly secular revolutionary endeavours: revolution, as we shall see, was frequently fuelled by revelation.

With the Age of Revolution came new dreams of utopia. We meet Louis-Sebastian Mercier, the author of the world's first secular futuristic utopia, in chapter 5. He takes us to Paris in the year 2440, where science, reason, and order prevail: an enlightened monarch plays chess and other rational games with his virtuous male subjects in their tobacco-free, alcohol-free, caffeine-free shops and houses, while their wives concentrate on pleasing their husbands, doing the chores, and bringing up the babies. We also look at two other prominent French revolutionary writers: the Comte de Volney, who escaped the guillotine by fleeing to the United States, and the Marquis de Condorcet, who escaped the guillotine by dying in prison. Clearly, a Government Health Warning should be attached to all utopias – and applied not only to the manufacturers but also to the consumers.

The book briefly examines some of the major and most interesting utopian writers of the nineteenth century. Instead of trying to provide a comprehensive guide to utopian thought, I have focused on a few writers whose work exemplifies broader changes in approaches to the future. One of them is Mary Griffith, who envisaged a world in which technological progress and women's social and economic (but not political) equality ushered in a golden age of religious piety, sobriety, peace, and order. Another is Edward Bellamy, who maintained that the industrial unrest rocking America during the 1870s was actually preparing the way for a democratic socialist paradise, in which everyone by the year

2000 would work for the state and commit themselves to the common good. And a third is H.G. Wells, who did more than any other single writer to popularize the notion of eugenics, or selective breeding, as the key to future perfection.

These are not worlds in which most of us would like to live, except for one thing. In all utopias, whether secular or religious, and whatever the differences among them, one common feature stands out: there are no lawyers.

As we move in chapter 6 into the first half of the twentieth century, the most violent period in the entire history of humankind, utopias collapse into rubble. Even before the First World War, there was a growing sense that the rationality, order, and functionalism associated with earlier utopian visions could actually produce a world in which initiative, spontaneity, and artistic creativity would all become stifled and that the very notion of progress was an illusion. These nagging doubts were clearly expressed by Jules Verne, whose futuristic image of Paris in the early 1960s, written in the early 1860s, hit remarkably close to home. There was also an increasing awareness of the terrors of technology. This view was reflected in the novels of H.G. Wells, who was the first person to predict the nature and consequences of nuclear warfare – even though he managed to convince himself that everything would work out for the best in the long run, with an enlightened elite of scientists and intellectuals rescuing the world from ambitious and power-hungry politicians.

After the First World War, images of the future become darker and darker. In 1920–21, during the early years of the Russian Revolution, Yevgeny Zamyatin wrote the first dystopian futuristic novel. Simply entitled *We,* it described a world in which the collective state had obliterated individualism, and near total order had been achieved at the price of virtually all freedom. The same theme was taken up, less successfully, by Ayn Rand, whose general level of compassion was roughly on a par with that of Wells.

Much more impressive than Rand's work was Aldous Huxley's *Brave New World.* Huxley took the central Enlightenment premise that the human mind was infinitely malleable, and the late-nineteenth-century obsession with eugenics, and transformed them into a dystopic vision in which selectively bred human automatons were programmed from birth to be happy and functional members of an ultra-rational social order. But by far the blackest and bleakest dystopian novel came from George Orwell, whose *Nineteen Eighty-Four* drew on the nightmare of totalitarianism, dictatorship, propaganda, mind-control, and torture to present the possibility of a future where power and oppression became ends in themselves, and where all progress would be "progress towards more pain." It is a book that makes your blood run cold, precisely because it is so closely attuned to the world in which it was written.

Again, my discussion of dystopia concentrates on a few key figures rather than making a wide sweep through the sources. I have opted for depth over breadth, on the assumption that writers such as Verne, Wells, Zamyatin, Huxley, and Orwell reflect and reinforce more general patterns in our changing perspective on the future.

As we move closer to the present, I have sketched out in chapter 7 some of the main characteristics of modern North American images of the world to come. One strand of thought, stretching back to the nineteenth century, takes an optimistic view of technological change and looks forward to greater and greater progress. Against this background, fears about nuclear war, global terrorism, and environmental degradation produce a sense of catastrophe, which has found expression in everything from the religious right to Hollywood disaster movies. Meanwhile, the feminist movement during the 1970s produced the first utopian images of the future that had been seen in over fifty years — although these promises were counterbalanced by a close awareness of the destructive and dystopic potential that exists within the modern world.

Finally, in chapter 8, I discuss the so-called scientific futurologists of the 1950s and beyond who may have convinced themselves that they can predict the future, but should convince no one else. I also make a few comments about what happens when prophecies and predictions fail – as they usually do. This is a kind of "Tips for Prophets" section: a good prophet always has the chance of bouncing back, provided the right strategies are adopted.

That's what lies in store. Now, here's what you *won't* find in this book. There isn't much on Marxism; in fact, Nostradamus gets more space than Marx. Reams have already been written on Marxist philosophy, and, in any case, Nostradamus now seems to be more influential than Marx. Nor will you get much on the current crop of clairvoyants, since this book is more about the *history* of the future than about present predictions. And you should not expect a lot about science fiction, largely because this subject is so large that it deserves a book in itself. My approach is unapologetically geo-centric: only predictions about the planet Earth are considered, and the future of space exploration and colonization is completely ignored. The strange new twenty-third-century world of the Starship *Enterprise,* with its Russian officer who thinks that Leningrad still exists, and its captain who believes that "one to the fourth power" is more than one, will have to wait for a sequel.

If you were expecting these things and you've already paid for this book, there's only one thing for it: march down to your local bookstore and demand your money back. Otherwise, stay tuned.

• • •

Immense intellectual effort went into prophecies and predictions. Medieval scholars developed concordances and mind-bending theories of numerology as they attempted to decode the hidden messages within biblical texts. They had fierce arguments about the significance of the "little horn" of the beast with ten horns in the Book of Daniel, or the identity of the "woman clothed with the sun" in the Book of Revelation.[4]

In modern times there have been equally intense attempts to uncover the true meaning of that more recent predictive system, Marxism. Karl Marx believed that the key to understanding the future lay in a rigorous scientific study of the past, and he dismissed religious prophecies as so much mumbo-jumbo. Yet the outlines of his world view bore an uncanny resemblance to the very Judeo-Christian eschatology that he had repudiated. In the Old Testament there is God, the Fall, the prophets, the chosen people, and redemption. In Marxism the categories are strikingly similar. For God we have history; for the Fall we have capitalism; for the prophets we have Marx and Engels; for the chosen people we have the proletariat; and for the redemption we have communism. Perhaps it is not entirely coincidental that Marx came from a long line of rabbis.

Medieval prophecies and Marxist predictions had something else in common as well: for all the erudition and intellectual sophistication that went into them, they turned out to be dead wrong. Brilliant philosophical superstructures were erected on false assumptions. Precisely what was false about these assumptions remains a matter of lively debate. Within the Christian tradition the central case against predicting the Second Coming has rested on the seemingly unequivocal words of Christ: "But of that day and that hour knoweth no man, no, not the angels which are in heaven, neither the Son, but the Father."[5]

Those Christians who remain more prophetically minded have found various ways of wriggling out of this caution. Some have argued that Christ really meant that no man could know the day and the hour without the aid of the divinely inspired scriptures.[6] Others have taken the ingenious position that although Christ argued that no man shall know the day or the hour, people could still figure out the year or the month.[7] From this perspective it was relatively easy to explain the failure of previous prophecies to materialize: either they were based on misinterpretations of the Bible or they had simply yet to come true.

For deists and atheists, in contrast, the false assumptions were more basic: the real reason for prophetic failure was that the Scriptures invented God, rather than that God invented the Scriptures. The first person to transmit such ideas to a popular audience was the eighteenth-century Anglo-American democrat and deist Thomas Paine. In his *Age of Reason,* which sets out to show that the Bible was spurious and attempts to shock readers into their senses, Paine ridiculed the entire notion of prophecy. "Upon the whole," he wrote, "mystery, miracle and prophecy are appendages that belong to fabulous and not true religion"; they were calculated to overawe the superstitious multitude and corresponded to "fortune-telling, such as casting nativities, predicting riches, fortunate or unfortunate marriages, conjuring for lost goods, etc." The whole thing, in his view, was nothing more than a gigantic system of fraud.[8]

Yet Paine's own ideology was itself based on a form of faith in the future – the belief that reason, science, and progress would produce an enlightened, prosperous, and broadly egalitarian society of property-owning democrats. And when Paine made specific predictions – as he did about the supposedly inevitable fall of the English financial system – he turned out to be just as wrong as the prophets whom he had mocked.[9]

So it was, on a larger scale, with Marx's prognostications about the collapse of capitalism. Marxism also rests on an act of faith. It is based on an arational wager that human life, or history, has a meaning – that there is an objective order of reality in which humankind moves through class struggle from the realm of necessity into the realm of freedom. With its emphasis on class relations and its acute sense of the relationship between socioeconomic change and human consciousness, Marxism has provided many insights into historical analysis. As a guide to the future, however, it is on a par with palm-reading or inspecting the entrails of a chicken.

Ironically, prophets never foresee the way in which their own prophecies will be twisted and turned by those who come after them and act in their name. The most influential medieval prophetic writer, Joachim of Fiore, would have been astounded by the uses to which his followers put his prophecies, all the more so since the world was already supposed to have spiritually transformed itself when many of those followers got going. Paine would probably have gagged had he learned that his political prophecy about America's ability to "begin the world over again" would be used by Ronald Reagan (or his scriptwriters) to justify the Star Wars program during the Cold War. Similarly, Marx would perhaps have stayed in bed had he known what Joseph Stalin would do with his writings – or at least one hopes.

Other supposedly scientific predictions have turned out to be equally unreliable. In 1798 Thomas Malthus wrote his brilliantly argued *Essay on Population,* which predicted "epidemics, pestilence, and plague" as population growth pressed against limited resources.[10] Population, he said, expanded geometrically, while food production increased arithmetically. Humankind would be forever trapped by this inexorable law of nature. There is no denying that the population explosion is one of the most serious issues facing the world today; in 1999 the global population burst through the six billion mark, and it continues to climb. Even so, things have not turned out quite the way Malthus anticipated. The use of contraceptives, the application of technology to food production, and the inverse relationship between living standards and the birth rate contradicted the moral and logical underpinnings of his theory, as applied to the "First World" of Europe and North

America. And the undoubted food crises of the Third World are too complex to be contained within a Malthusian framework.

Contemporary economists and social scientists do not have a good track record either. Just as medieval prophets built impressive intellectual structures on false biblical premises, modern economists have constructed complicated mathematical microeconomic models on assumptions that exist only in their own minds: that there is perfect competition, that there is perfect knowledge, that there is perfect rationality. The predictions are equally perfect, as long as they are not applied to the real world. More generally, Seymour Martin Lipset's research indicated that at least two-thirds of the forecasts made by American social scientists between 1945 and 1980 were wrong.[11] As John Kenneth Galbraith once remarked: "Economists don't predict the future because they know; they predict because they're asked."

This, then, is the basic point: the future is, for the most part, unknown territory. We can make guesses and assess probabilities, but we can never actually know. Prophecies and predictions tell us little or nothing about what will actually happen. Rather, they tell us a great deal about the fears, hopes, desires, and circumstances of the people who peer into their own future and imagine what it will be like.

In this sense, it is useful to contrast interpretations of the future with interpretations of the past. All history is "contemporary history," wrote the Italian philosopher Benedetto Croce.[12] We view the past through the prism of the present; each generation reinterprets the past according to its own preoccupations, and the angle of vision shifts with the passing of time. But the historian, inescapably, has to deal with sources and has to make hard decisions about how to select, arrange, and evaluate the available evidence. The writing of history becomes a dialogue between past and present, in which each informs and influences the other. Among other things, this exchange creates awkward problems for those who would like to press the past into the service of their own political or social movements. Charismatic figures might talk about returning to a golden age of equality, harmony, and justice, which might be projected onto pre-Norman England or early Celtic civilization, but there are always some pesky historians around to argue that Saxon England was actually a pretty nasty place or that the Celts did not practise free love under the People's Mistletoe. Even worse, such historians are usually able to back up their arguments with evidence.

The future, in contrast, suffers from no such problems. In the future, anything goes. The problem of evidence simply vanishes, and the vacuum can be filled according to each generation's own concerns and needs. In the future you are free: the only limitations are those of your imagination, and your imagination is itself shaped by the society in which you happen to live. From this perspective, Croce's words can be turned upside down: "All future is contemporary future."

●●●

But although the future is much more malleable than the past, not all prophets enjoy an equal success rate. As a general rule, the vaguer your prophecy, the better chance you have of being taken seriously. It is a good idea to avoid specifics, such as the date of the end of the world. Everyone has been wrong so far, and should someone eventually get it right, there will be nobody around to appreciate the call anyway. If you must insist on date-setting, it is best to select a year well outside your own life span or that of your listeners. Otherwise, you could wind up like the Reverend William Sedgwick, who rushed into London in 1647 with the breathtaking news that the Second Coming would take place in two weeks. For the remaining fifteen years of his life he was known as "Doomsday Sedgwick."

Another case in point was the Princeton-educated Presbyterian minister David Austin, who had a vision in February 1796 that the millennium would begin on the last Sunday of May. On the day in question his church was packed with people who were wailing and weeping and trembling with anticipation. When it became clear that nothing was going to happen, they became increasingly restive; in the end, they turned on him and threw him out of the church. In this respect, Austin's experience echoed that of the Lutheran pastor Michael Stiefel 263 years earlier. Stiefel had prophesied that the Day of Judgment would occur at 8.00 a.m. on October 9, 1533; when the time came and went without incident, members of his congregation took matters into their own hands and decided to have a Day of Judgment of their own. They tied him up, dragged him to nearby Wittenberg, and, in the best Lutheran tradition, sued him for damages. Austin, at least, escaped that fate. He wound up in New Haven, where he made plans to help American Jews return to the Holy Land, and thus get the divine schedule back on track.

The most famous example in American history, though, was that of William Miller, the Baptist farmer from upstate New York who calculated from the Book of Daniel that the Second Coming would occur in 1843. Spreading the news through newspapers, tent meetings, and aggressive publicity, Miller attracted thousands of followers, many of whom relinquished all their possessions in anticipation of the great day. When the year passed without incident, the figures were hastily reworked and the date was changed to October 22, 1844. It was the arithmetic that was wrong, not God. But October 22 came and went like any other day, heralding the Great Disappointment and an equally great falling away. Subsequent American evangelists learned the lesson well: for the most part, they have wisely refrained from specifics about the Second Coming.

Not only should you be vague about dates, but your prophecies should be as obscure as possible. The great advantage here is that later generations will then be able to interpret your prophecies in the light of subsequent events, read their own meanings into your words, and prove you right time and again. Take, for example, the vision of Nahum the Elkoshite in the Old Testament: "The chariots shall be with flaming torches ... and the fir trees shall be terribly shaken. The chariots shall rage in the streets, they shall justle one against another in the broad ways: they shall seem like torches, they shall run like the lightnings."[13] No one had a clue what this meant until the early twentieth century, when suddenly everything became clear: Nahum, in the seventh century BC, had foreseen the coming of the railway, with trains that roared through the American forests and pierced the darkness with their headlights.

But Nahum pales in comparison with Nostradamus, the sixteenth-century physician and astrologer who has become, arguably, the most famous prophet in the modern world. He was something of a cult figure during the hippy days of the 1960s, remains an inescapable presence in supermarket lineups, and has recently been elevated into the ranks of the Arts and Entertainment television biography series, along with such illustrious figures as Winston Churchill and Benjamin Franklin. "Thousands of years after his death, the prophecies of Nostradamus continue to amaze," gushed the program's presenter, even though Nostradamus actually died less than five hundred years ago. The assumption seems to be that Nostradamus lived sometime in the remote, vague, and distant past and that authenticity increases with antiquity. The program provided a platform for a host of true believers, who explained how Nostradamus had predicted Napoleon (the first Antichrist), Hitler (the second), the assassination of John Fitzgerald Kennedy, Neil Armstrong's moon landing, and the *Challenger* space shuttle disaster. Nostradamus, for some reason, was particularly preoccupied with events that would take place in America.

Nostradamus was the perfect prophet. His prophecies were

couched in "dark and cryptic sentences," contained in a series of apparently impenetrable quatrains. As such, they became a kind of Rorschach test for his readers. It may not be entirely coincidental that his interpreters have always been wise after the event, giving Nostradamus's prophecies a retrospective justification. This is how it works. You take a quatrain that reads:

> An emperor will be born near Italy
> Who will cost the empire very dear. When they
> See the people who ally with him, they will say
> He is less a prince than a butcher.

You then juxtapose this verse with another quatrain that appears much later in Nostradamus' works and states that the villages of "Pay, Nay, Loron will be more fire than blood." From here, you conclude that the emperor in question is obviously Napoleon. Obviously? Well, Napoleon was indeed born near Italy, and if you rearrange the letters of the villages, you get "Napolyon Roy," which in turn becomes "Napoleon the King." *Quod erat demonstrandum.* The beauty of this system is that no one could possibly have figured it out until after Napoleon became emperor of France.

In fact, every time Nostradamus' interpreters have attempted to use his quatrains to foresee the future, they have fallen flat on their faces. At the turn of the century one enthusiastic interpreter used Nostradamus to predict that Canada would soon become a utopia of 93 million people, with Americans desperately trying to get in. (Not that you needed Nostradamus to make such extravagant predictions; a Canadian imperialist, writing in 1887, told his readers that "the valley of the Saskatchewan, according to scientific computation, is capable of sustaining 800,000,000 million souls.")[14] More recently, in 1994, another commentator pointed to the quatrain that ran:

She who was cast out will return to reign,
Her enemies found among conspirators.
More than ever will her reign be triumphant.
At three and seventy death is very sure.

He took this to be a prophecy about Charles and Diana (another of Nostradamus' apparent obsessions) and concluded that Diana would be welcomed back into the royal fold, where she would live happily until she reached the age of seventy-three.[15] The Nostradamus industry, it is clear, is much better at predicting the past than predicting the future.

There is an even better way to make sure your prophecies come true, although it is not entirely ethical: back-date your prophecy to make it appear as though you have foretold events that have already occurred. The classic case is nothing less than the Book of Daniel itself, one of the foundation texts of the apocalyptic tradition. Apparently dating from the sixth century BC, during the Babylonian captivity of the Jews, the Book of Daniel prophesied with unerring accuracy the events of the next four hundred years. It promised the faithful that they would eventually prevail over their enemies and enjoy everlasting life with God.

Daniel's prophetic powers appear less impressive, however, when you realize that the book was really written around 167 BC by an author who cleverly pretended that he had found an ancient manuscript from the days of Nebuchadnezzar. At the date of its actual composition, the Jews were being persecuted by Antiochus Epiphanies of Syria and their future looked bleak. By making it appear as though Daniel's prophecies had repeatedly been proven right in the past, the author lent increased credibility to Daniel's promise of deliverance in the future and offered hope to a suffering people. If this was forgery, it was forgery in a good cause.

The same pattern has repeated itself throughout history. During the Irish revolutionary movement of the 1790s, for example, the country was awash with prophecies, many of which had been specially manufactured for the moment. In 1796 a senior figure in the government complained about "the vast number of emissaries constantly going through the country" who were carrying "songs and prophecies, just written, stating all late events and what is to happen, as if made several years ago, in order to persuade the people that, as a great part of them has already come to pass, so the remainder will certainly happen."[16]

One such prophecy was supposed to have been made by the Irish Saint Columcille in 1412. In 1790, it ran, there would be "a Rebellion against the French King"; in 1794 there would be "No Religion observed in France"; by 1797 the forces of Antichrist would wage war on the righteous; and at the end of the decade the "Remnants of all Nations" would unite "to be one Religion & Bannish war from the Earth and Man shall live in Friendship and Love as long as God pleasures."[17] Columcille had actually been dead for more than eight centuries in 1412. The whole thing had been invented during the mid-1790s to boost revolutionary morale at a time of intense fear, uncertainty, and hope.

On occasion, this creative approach to prophesying was pressed into narrow commercial ends rather than higher political purposes; here, prophet-making converged with profit-making. This is what happened with Mother Shipton, a prophetess who was said to have lived in York between 1488 and 1561. During the late nineteenth century the publication of her four-hundred-year-old prophecies caused something of a sensation:

> Carriages without horses shall go,
> And accidents fill the world with woe.
> Around the world thoughts shall fly
> In the twinkling of an eye ...
> Under water men shall walk,
> Shall ride, shall sleep, shall talk.

In the air men shall be seen,
In white, in black, in green;
Iron in the water shall float,
As easily as a wooden boat.
Gold shall be found and shown
In a land that's now not known ...
The world to an end shall come,
In eighteen hundred and eighty one.

She may have stumbled at the last fence, but her record up to then appeared impeccable.

The only trouble is that Mother Shipton did not actually make any of these prophecies. On the contrary, they were all invented in 1862 by an enterprising scoundrel named Charles Hindley, who later admitted to the fact. There is not a shred of evidence that any such person as Mother Shipton ever existed, except in the minds of a series of enterprising con-artists. Her only biography was penned in 1667 by a "wild and dissipated gambler," Richard Head, who was motivated by a desperate need to recoup his losses and relied on nothing but his vivid imagination. Mother Shipton was "in all likelihood, a wholly mythical personage," according to the *Dictionary of National Biography*, which normally restricts its entries to people who actually lived.[18]

• • •

Prophecies work best when they are indefinite, obscure, and retrospective, but they are also tightly connected to specific places and times, to an ever-shifting here and now. "Where is the centre of the world?" runs an old Irish proverb. "Here, where you are standing." Prophets throughout the ages have been convinced that the ground on which they stood was the most important place in the world and that their own epoch was a pivotal period in the unfolding of human history. The arrogance of place meets the arrogance of time, and local events become charged with cosmic significance. Even those writers who were acutely aware that all ages had fallen victim to the parochialism of the present could not resist the pull themselves. The seventeenth-century English radical John Tillinghast could ridicule in one breath his predecessors who had connected biblical prophecies with their own particular time and argue in the next that the millennium was due to occur within the next two years.[19] Throughout a wide variety of cultures and over a wide range of time, people have fervently believed that God has chosen them for his special mission and that the fate of humanity hinges on their particular actions.

This was certainly true for the followers of Girolamo Savonarola, a Dominican friar who emerged as the prophet and protector of Florence during the troubled year of 1494. The French had invaded Tuscany and were threatening to destroy the city; meanwhile, the local oligarchs ousted the ruling Medici family from power. Savonarola's negotiations with the French paved the way for their peaceful departure, and the political instability created by the coup gave him the elbow room he needed. His message was powerful and appealing: the French invasion had been prophesied in the Book of Revelation and heralded the dawn of a new era, in which the Florentines were destined to play a special role. The decisive battle with Antichrist was beginning. By establishing a true Christian polity, Florence would rejuvenate the world and prepare the way for the Second Coming.

The response was remarkable. Florentines had long believed that their city had a divine destiny and that they were a chosen people. Now, it seemed, all the prophecies were finally being fulfilled. For more than three years Savonarola presided over the public life of the city: public games, traditional festivals, and "immodest" clothes were all banned, as part of the effort to make Florence the spiritual centre of the world. In the end, though, everything fell apart. Economic crisis interlocked with intense political factionalism to send the entire structure crashing down. The pope, who had the quaint notion that Rome, rather than Florence, was Christianity's central city, had Savonarola excommunicated. By April 1498 Savonarola's enemies had taken over Florence. Savonarola was captured and "confessed" under torture that he was not in fact a prophet. When they kept on torturing him anyway, he retracted his confession. "If I must suffer," he said, "I wish to suffer for the truth ... God, you are giving me this penance for having denied You. I have denied You, I have denied You, I have denied You out of fear of the torments!"[20] Shortly afterwards he was burnt at the stake as a heretic.

It is a long way, geographically, temporally, and spiritually, from Florence in the Renaissance to Nova Scotia during the American Revolution. Yet, in the remote fishing villages of the north Atlantic, we can find an equally powerful sense of mission and destiny, the same conviction that this particular place and time were central to God's divine plan. In Nova Scotia the millennial impulse came from New England settlers who had arrived during the early 1760s, bringing with them the belief that colonial America was a "City upon a Hill" that would serve as a religious model and source of inspiration for the rest of the world. During the American War of Independence, between 1775 and 1783, these "Nova Scotia Yankees" found themselves torn between New England and Britain and began to experience something approaching a collective identity crisis. "The whole province," commented one contemporary in 1777, "is in Confusion, Trouble & Anguish."[21]

At this point, enter a charismatic preacher named Henry Alline, who single handedly triggered a religious revival that swept through the outports. His message: the war was God's punishment for New England's backsliding and Britain's corruption. God had delivered the New Englanders in Nova Scotia from the conflict and given them a special mission to rejuvenate the world.

Far from being a divided and peripheral people, Alline told them, Nova Scotians should see themselves as "the salt of the earth, the light of the world and as CITIES ON HILLS"; they were, in short, "a people highly favoured of God." And to prepare for the millennium, they should establish an egalitarian and puritanical society, unblemished by cursing, swearing, and drunkenness, free from the debaucheries of "Stage Plays, Balls and Masquerades," and where people would read the Bible instead of "Tragedies, Comedies, Romances, Novels and other profane histories." Nova Scotia has manifestly failed to follow Alline's advice, but his religious revival, with its implicit eye on the Second Coming, was enormously influential in its day.[22]

What is particularly interesting about these examples is that in two radically different contexts, the same themes appear. In both fifteenth-century Florence and eighteenth-century Nova Scotia we find communities steeped in the belief that they were God's chosen people. In both cases it took an external political crisis to trigger imminent expectations of a total religious transformation. And that transformation was associated with a renunciation of the flesh and a celebration of the spirit. As it turned out, though, the transformation proved to be temporary and the mundane prevailed over the millennial.

Precisely because so many prophecies are vague, they are capable of almost endless adaptation. American evangelists have shown more ingenuity than most in this matter. During the mid-nineteenth century some of them came to believe that all the biblical prophecies about Israel were really coded references to the United States. What kind of evidence was produced? Well, argued J.T. Philpott in 1864, Joseph's son Manasseh had thirteen children, just as there had been thirteen colonies. Even more strikingly, five of those children were female, just as five of the colonies had female names: Maryland, Virginia, North Carolina, South Carolina, and Georgia. Therefore, Israel was really America, and the chosen people were actually Americans. The logic, as they say in Russia, was as clear as chocolate. It was on a par, in fact, with the contemporaneous calculations of the unforgettable Fountain Pitts, which proved that the Book of Daniel had foretold the Declaration of Independence right down to the day and the minute of its signing – at quarter to three in the afternoon.[23]

Sometimes, local place names were incorporated into the quest to pin down the site of the Second Coming. During the English Civil War, in the same year that King Charles I was beheaded, a rope maker named William Franklin announced that he was Christ and that the millennium was imminent. He took as his text the 105th Psalm, verse 23: "Israel also came into Egypt; And Jacob sojourned in the land of Ham." The land of Ham, he convinced himself, must refer to Hampshire, in the south of England. He and his lover, a born-again brothel keeper, moved to Hampshire, where they attracted a following of over five hundred people, including a local minister. For the next year they identified various unpopular figures in the county as the agents of Antichrist, until the authorities put a stop to their activities by throwing Franklin in jail. After a while, he admitted he was not Christ after all.[24]

If Franklin's followers believed that the millennium would begin in Hampshire, the eighteenth-century Irish member of parliament Francis Dobbs was equally certain that it was about to occur in Armagh, the religious capital of Ireland. In a speech to the Irish House of Commons in June 1800, he argued that the two central preconditions for the Second Coming were "the fall of the Papal power" and "a very high degree of infidelity." With the French Revolution's attack on Catholicism and its abolition of the Christian calendar, he said, there could be no doubt that these conditions had already been met. Christ, it was clear, was due to arrive any day now. The exact location of his return could be inferred from the Book of Revelation, which foretold that the

Messiah's army would be playing harps, would be clothed in white linen, and would assemble at Armageddon. Could it be mere coincidence, he asked, that Ireland was famous for both its harp music and its fine linen? "And I believe the word Armageddon in the Hebrew tongue," he continued, "and Ardmah or Armagh in the Irish, means the same thing. At all events, there is a great similitude in their sounds."

Dobbs's speech was not a success. According to his editor, it was greeted in the House with "apparent levity." But the context, as always, is crucial. Dobbs delivered this speech in the aftermath of the violent Rising of 1798 and during the debate over a union between Ireland and Britain. He was strongly opposed to an Act of Union, but was fighting a losing battle. One of the themes of his speech was that Ireland would always be an independent nation in the eyes of God, no matter what the politicians said or did. Another was that the terrible sufferings of the previous decade would soon give way to a period of great joy. "He [Christ] is now about to establish a kingdom founded in justice, in truth, and in righteousness," Dobbs said, "that shall extend from pole to pole, and which shall place this hitherto wicked and miserable world upon the highest pinnacle of human happiness and human glory." The future, in his view, offered a glorious compensation for a miserable past.[25]

• • •

What are the social and political functions of the future? For a defeated or a dispersed people, the future can be a great source of hope and comfort. No matter how bad things are now, how bleak is the situation, in the end your people will triumph and live in peace, prosperity, and harmony. Such a perspective reaches right back to the Jewish apocalyptic tradition, with its message that, for those who hang in there, everything will work out in the end. It also glissades into the modern secular notion of progress, which promises that technological, economic, social, and political change will produce a more enlightened, rational, and just society. This idea found expression in the first futuristic utopias that were written in the late eighteenth century.

Closely allied with the future-as-hope motif is the view of the future as a time of revenge, when the oppressed will rise up and destroy their oppressors, along with any rival ethnic and religious groups that might be blamed for their misfortune. This view also has biblical precedents. The Book of Ezekiel, for example, promised that the forces of evil would be hammered by "hailstones, fire and brimstone," and prophesied that the beasts of the field would "eat the flesh of the mighty, and drink the blood of the princes of the earth."[26] A similar note was struck in the New Testament: "He shall have judgment without mercy," wrote James, "that hath shewed no mercy."[27] Such reasoning and such feelings have recurred repeatedly throughout history; only the targets have changed. The biblical warrant for vengeance has been applied by the poor against the rich, Christians against Jews, Catholics against Protestants, and Protestants against Catholics.

Typical of the genre was the prophetic vision of the radical Protestant John Maxilimian Daut in 1712. In a speech delivered before the Senate at Frankfort, he reported that the Almighty had shown him "a city of abominations in a trance, that was full of murder and idolatry," had revealed that the city was Rome, and had promised to punish its inhabitants for defiling the inheritance of Christ. "I will send famine, plagues worse than Egyptian, and a flaming sword, the fierce messenger of my relentless wrath, upon your murderers," God had told him. "O Rome, Rome! I will consume thee to ashes upon the earth, before the eyes of the whole world – Rome, like Sodom, shall be utterly burnt with fire – she shall sink like a millstone in the sea, and her smoke shall rise up for ever and ever."[28]

Less typical, but equally heartfelt, was the vision of a modern

American evangelist that a limousine full of ultraliberal church-men would go hurtling into oblivion when the driver, a "true Christian," was suddenly scooped into the skies to meet Christ at the moment of Rapture. It was no coincidence that the true Christian was the limousine driver, for in this view of the future the poor and humble get even with the rich and proud. Nor is it surprising that many people who articulate such a future have themselves been marginalized or silenced by the dominant social order. These prophecies happen most frequently in times of crisis and revolution, when the world is being turned upside down. "Not only men but women shall prophesy," asserted Mary Cary during the English Civil War; "not only superiors but inferiors; not only those that have university learning but those that have it not, even servants and handmaids." She was convinced that the millennium would begin within the next twenty years and that it would usher in a new era of social justice and women's equality.[30] Through prophesying, women could acquire a voice and an audience that would otherwise have been unthinkable. Along with Mary Cary, this prominence applies to women like Joanna Southcott and Mother Ann Lee, who emerged during the revolutionary turmoil of the late eighteenth century. It is also true for women who lived much earlier, such as the twelfth-century prophetesses Elisabeth of Schonau and Hildegard of Bingen. Elisabeth justified her prophetic preaching by arguing that men had grown lazy, and that the Lord had accordingly filled women with the Spirit of God and the gift of prophecy. Hildegard, contending that she lived in an "effeminate age" in which men were increasingly behaving like women, implied that an exasperated God had given women masculine powers of prophecy so they could carry on his work. To both of them, their direct line with God ensured that any men who questioned their prophetic abilities did so at their peril.[31]

The future can also function as a source of fear, as a warning of what will happen unless you change your ways. This theme can be found in the earliest Jewish prophetic texts, where the future was frequently viewed as a threat; if you don't smarten up, the people were told, you can be sure that terrible things will happen to you. Throughout the history of Judeo-Christian civilization, the same message became a religious staple, as preachers warned their flocks of the dire consequences of sinful behaviour. In colonial New England, Puritan ministers developed the "jeremiad," as it became known, into a veritable art form. If their sermons had been the only source available to subsequent generations, historians would have concluded that Puritan America had more fornicators per square yard than any other place on earth.

During the twentieth century, the future-as-warning theme has become closely connected with a more general reaction against the pieties of progress and has been powerfully articulated in the dystopian novels of writers such as Huxley and Orwell. Here, the general approach has been to isolate a disturbing social or political trend, magnify it, and project it onto the future. Beneath the surface of their pessimism, though, lies an undercurrent of hope. Through the act of publicizing such dark potentialities, the writers hope to prevent the future they are describing.

In strange juxtaposition to these dystopian images is the increasingly influential approach to the future as a source of entertainment. The adventure novels of Jules Verne pointed the way, and popular American magazines of the 1920s and 1930s carried on the tradition. It was a future of amazing gadgets, incredible stories, and seemingly unlimited possibilities. "Extravagant Fiction Today, Cold Fact Tomorrow," ran the motto of *Amazing Stories,* the magazine founded in 1926 by Hugo Gernsback, the founding father of science fiction. While a minority of writers were agonizing about the future of humanity, most people, it seemed, were content to lie back and enjoy it.

Such an approach would not have amused the prophets of old,

who had reputations to protect and images to maintain. When Merlin met the British king Aurelius, Geoffrey of Monmouth reported in the twelfth century, the king "received Merlin gaily and ordered him to prophesy the future, for he wanted to hear some marvels from him." But Merlin refused to become a kind of performing prophet for the amusement of the court. "Mysteries of that sort," he replied, "cannot be revealed, except where there is the most urgent need for them. If I were to utter them as entertainment, or where there was no need at all, then the spirit which controls me would forsake me in the moment of need." And that took care of that.[32]

In recent times, the consumerist future-as-entertainment outlook has itself become the object of dystopian fears, most notably in the work of the English television playwright Denis Potter. His *Cold Lazarus* depicts a high-tech, violent, and amoral society that is governed by the crassest commercial instincts of Hollywood. In this future, entertainment is politics and politics is entertainment. The emancipation of the passions has propelled us into a world of voyeuristic escapism, where the values of pornography and profit reign supreme. For Potter, the future as entertainment has become the future as warning.

Underlying all these different views of the future is a shared sense of its critical importance to the present. This dimension is something that is easily missed by historians, but was readily apparent to the French sociologist Gabriel Tarde. "It seems to me neither more nor less conceivable," he wrote, "that the future, *which is not yet,* should influence the present than that the past, *which is no more,* should do so."[x] As the present turns into the past, the imagined future emerges as a significant cause of what becomes our actual history.

At first sight, this argument appears like something out of *Alice through the Looking Glass,* where the Queen is living backwards and remembering things that happened the week after next. But it is not quite as bizarre as it seems. Most human activities, after all, are deeply influenced by our expectations and hopes about the future. The farmer who sows the seeds in the spring operates on the assumption that there will be a crop to harvest in the late summer. The athlete who is training for a triathlon will adopt a schedule that is conditioned by the date of an event *which is not yet*. Without a sense of the probable consequences of our actions, we would be fumbling in the dark; without hope, we would succumb to blind despair.

Concern for the future well-being of our families has been another important spur to political and social action in the present. "You are wrestling with the Enemies of the human Race," leading English radicals informed their supporters in 1796, "not for yourself merely, for you may not see the full Day of Liberty, but for the Child hanging at the Breast."[34] The unprecedented entry of the "common people" into politics at the end of the eighteenth century was motivated at least in part by their concern for those who would come after them. Similarly, the migrants who crossed the Atlantic from Europe to North America during the nineteenth century often did so because they wanted a better life not only for themselves but for their children. The historian Bruce Elliott, in his study of the Irish in Canada, has concluded that immigration is best understood as a "strategy of heirship"; the primary object of the exercise, in his view, was to provide land and security for the next generation.[35]

It is equally apparent that hopes and expectations about the future have exerted an enormous influence on a wide variety of reformist and revolutionary movements. The campaigns to abolish slavery and to prohibit alcohol in the United States, for example, were pushed forward by Christians who believed in the possibility of perfection and were preparing the path for the Second Coming. In different contexts, the quest for perfection could have horrific consequences. Religious extremists such as the

Anabaptists of sixteenth-century Munster launched a reign of terror against broadly defined "sinners" to create the New Jerusalem. Secular extremists such as the French Revolution's Robespierre could talk of the need to destroy equally ill-defined "corrupt" elements of society to create the Republic of Virtue. In modern times, guerrilla organizations such as the Irish Republican Army have justified revolutionary violence on the grounds that the future is on their side, that they are moving with the grain of history. Conveniently, this defence has placed their Loyalist guerrilla enemies into the role of knee-jerk reactionaries who are doomed to defeat, and whose own violence cannot be justified.

Time and again, the promise of a better future has been used to condone or create immense sacrifices – and often immense bloodshed – in the present. The fact that fascist and communist regimes have thrived on such logic is well known; less obviously, some of the most revered figures of the late eighteenth-century democratic revolution adopted a strikingly similar stance. Consider, in this respect, Thomas Jefferson's response to an American diplomat's criticisms of French Revolutionary violence: "The liberty of the whole earth was depending on the issue of the contest, and was ever such a prize won with so little innocent blood? My own affections have been deeply wounded by some of the martyrs to this cause, but rather than it should have failed, I would have seen half the earth desolated. Were there but an Adam and Eve left in every country, and left free, it would be better than as it now is."[36]

Nor was it isolated to Jefferson. When Wolfe Tone, the Irish revolutionary, was exiled to America in 1795, he commented that "the lives of Thousands and Tens of Thousands are a cheap purchase" for the establishment of a government like that of Pennsylvania.[37] Another radical immigrant, the English scientist and millenarian Joseph Priestley, contemplated a civil war in the United States to rid the country of its supposedly "pro-English" elements. "Many lives, no doubt, will be lost in war, civil or foreign," he wrote; "but men must die; and if the destruction of one generation be the means of producing another which shall be wiser and better, the good will exceed the evil, great as it may be, and greatly to be deplored, as all evils ought to be."[38]

When weighed in the scales of future perfection, even "deplorable evils" became acceptable. This was the kind of argument that incensed people like Edmund Burke, the counter-revolutionary liberal conservative: "I have no great opinion," he wrote, "of that sublime, abstract, metaphysic reversionary, contingent humanity, which in *cold blood* can subject the *present time,* and those whom we *daily see and converse with,* to *immediate* calamities in favour of the *future and uncertain* benefit of persons who *only exist in an idea.*"[39]

One can see Burke's point: considerable suffering has been inflicted upon humanity in the name of the religious millennium or the political utopia. But this is only one of many ways in which the future can work. It has inspired a broad range of cults and communities, ranging from masochistic medieval Flagellants and anarchical Free Spirits to the Branch Davidians and the Heaven's Gate movement of the 1990s. And it has also been channelled into constructive courses, through reform movements that have grounded themselves in the art of the possible rather than chimerical dreams of perfection.

Even when they are wrong, predictions can have benign consequences. If the more alarmist environmentalists of the 1970s and 1980s were to be believed, the world would already have run out of natural resources and we would now all be freezing in the dark. But such warnings stimulated a new environmental movement that has acted as a countervailing force to the untrammelled exploitation of our natural resources. This is not to deny that such exploitation continues apace, or that the energy crisis may simply have been deferred. Nevertheless, warnings about the future can change the present in positive ways, opening up the possibility of changing the future itself. A recent example concerns the dire predictions about the catastrophic consequences of the Y2K bug: they did not materialize partly because they were made in the first place. There is a lot to be said for the self-destructing prophecy.

Whether the future is seen as a source of hope or a form of threat, an inspiration or a warning, something to be embraced or resisted, it has always permeated our sense of the present. On the one hand, we cannot live without some sense of the future. Circumstances may change, historical contexts may change, but the hunger to know the future is with us always. On the other hand, most prophets and prognosticators have got the future wrong; the ones with the best results are those who have faked them. Almost all successful prophecies, remarked Francis Bacon more than four centuries ago, "have been impostures, and by idle and crafty brains were combined and feigned after the event passed."[40] Because the desire to know is so strong, the potential for deception – and for self-deception – is particularly high. And because the future is so important, we should refuse to suspend disbelief when people pretend or purport to see into it.

They can't.

· 2 ·

THE AGE OF THE SPIRIT

JIM JONES BELIEVED THAT HE WAS GOD, and he was not alone. In 1978 he led his followers from the People's Temple in San Francisco into a remote part of Guyana, to a settlement they called Jonestown. Here they prepared themselves for the "great day," which they knew was coming soon. Death would not be death; rather, it would release them from the miseries of merely human life, elevate them to a higher spiritual level, and save them from the wrath that God was about to pour over the world. The decisive moment came in November, when an American senator and members of the media arrived on a fact-finding mission. After ambushing the visitors and murdering as many as possible, Jones and his followers said farewell to this world, drank cyanide punch, and committed probably the greatest mass suicide in history. By the time it was over, more than nine hundred of them were dead.

Fifteen years later, near Waco, Texas, an equally charismatic figure known as David Koresh gathered his followers together at a place they named Mount Carmel, to await the arrival of Antichrist and the battle of Armageddon. He had been born as Vernon Howell and brought up as a carpenter. Now he was spiritually reborn as the Angel of the Apocalypse, whose coming had been foretold in the Book of Revelation. Koresh and his followers called themselves the Branch Davidians, armed themselves to the teeth, stocked up on food, and prepared for the Last Days. At the end of February 1993 the forces of Antichrist appeared in the form of the United States Bureau of Alcohol, Tobacco, and Firearms, whose agents raided the community. For the next fifty-one days there was an increasingly tense standoff, which ended under controversial and disputed circumstances with a fire that killed seventy-four people.

Since then, other apocalyptic religious cults have briefly flared through public consciousness before expiring in orgies of violence. Among them was the Order of the Solar Temple in Switzerland and Quebec, with its largely middle-class members who believed that the New Age was approaching, drove a stake through the heart of a six-month-old boy in the belief that he was Antichrist, and collectively destroyed themselves in 1994. There were the members of the Heaven's Gate collective, who associated the apocalypse with the arrival of the Hale-Bopp comet and believed that a spaceship travelling in its tail would rescue the faithful. Thirty-nine of them committed suicide in 1997. Other recent cults include Shoko Asahara's Aum Supreme Truth, which combined apocalypticism with chemical terrorism when its members sprayed the Tokyo subway system with sarin gas, and Monte Kim Miller's Concerned Christians, who hoped to trigger the Battle of Armageddon in Jerusalem and rise again after the Second Coming.

These cults seemed to come out of nowhere, with their authoritarian, power-hungry, and bizarre leaders, who claimed to act under divine inspiration or to have become divine themselves, and their deluded or brainwashed followers, who were desperately seeking some kind of meaning in a materialistic, pointless, and lonely late twentieth-century world. In fact, such cults are the latest expressions of an apocalyptic tradition that runs right back to the Middle Ages and beyond. The same patterns, with charismatic leaders and fanatical followers preparing for the apocalypse, have recurred repeatedly throughout history.

It is almost like watching the same play over and over again, where nothing changes from generation to generation but the actors. Almost – but not quite. As the context changes, so does the script. The contemporary cults, for example, employed techniques of recruitment, isolation, sleep deprivation, and indoctrination that were far more sophisticated than those of their predecessors. And, tragic as they were, the activities of these cults have actually been considerably less destructive than those of their pre-modern counterparts. Apart from anything else, most of the recent violence has been turned inwards rather than outwards. Mass suicide has loomed larger than mass murder – at least, so far.

This chapter discusses the medieval and early modern roots of this enduring apocalyptic tradition. Be warned, though: much of what follows is pretty grim stuff.

• • •

Central to the apocalyptic tradition is the notion of the millennium, as drawn from the Book of Revelation, chapter 20, verses 1–10. An angel would come down from heaven and cast Satan into a bottomless pit. This act would set the stage for the Second Coming, after which Christ would rule with his resurrected martyrs for a thousand years – the millennium. At the end of this period Satan would briefly escape and wreak havoc throughout the earth. His army, however, would be devoured by heavenly fire, and the devil would be thrown forever into the lake of fire and brimstone. Then would come the Last Judgment, the end of history, and a new heaven and a new earth.

Early Christianity was permeated by millenarian expectations, which were heightened by Christ's own words, as reported in the gospels of Mark and Matthew: "There be some standing here," he told his disciples, "which shall not taste of death, till they see the Son of Man coming in his kingdom."[1] At the same time, the notion of Christ's thousand-year reign was broadened to incorporate not only the resurrected martyrs but all Christ's faithful followers. The millennium, it was believed, would happen soon and would embrace the entire Christian community.

The only trouble was that the Second Coming stubbornly failed to materialize. Something was clearly wrong: the gap was growing between expectations and reality, and explanations were imperative. In effect, Christianity was experiencing the same crisis that besets all movements whose prophecies do not come true. The answer, in this case, was to maintain that apocalyptic texts should be understood in allegorical rather than literal terms and to push the millennium further and further into the future.

This solution fitted well with the changing organizational character of Christianity. By the fourth century, with the conversion of the Roman Empire, Christianity had evolved from a persecuted sect into an established religion. Under these circumstances, the practical tasks of ensuring long-term institutional stability became more important than preparing for the apocalypse – especially when all previous predictions about the Second Coming had proven to be false.

And this is where St. Augustine came in. He ingeniously associated the thousand-year reign of Christ with the emergence of the existing Christian church and reminded his readers of Jesus' words that no one would know the time of the Second Coming. It was better, then, to concentrate on the church in the here and now, rather than bother with futile speculations about things that were known only to God. Augustine's arguments carried the day and rapidly hardened into the orthodox Christian position.

Nevertheless, beneath the carapace of Augustinian authority, millenarianism proved remarkably resilient and would repeatedly break out in times of acute stress and uncertainty. One index was the number of self-proclaimed resurrected Christs who kept cropping up throughout western Europe. In the late sixth century Gregory of Tours (who himself believed that the world would end between 799 and 806) reported that a couple claiming to be Christ and Mary had emerged during a "great famine" in southern France and attracted a following of some three thousand people – including a few local bishops.

This so-called Christ, Gregory wrote, "foretold the future and announced that disease would come to some, to others losses and to others health." The apocalypse met Robin Hood: Christ and Mary demanded that people worship them, robbed from the rich, and gave to the poor. In the end they assembled outside the town of Puy and sent in messengers, who danced naked in front of the bishop and announced the arrival of the Messiah. The bishop, apparently "amazed" by such behaviour, sent out a party of "strong men," who confronted the false Christ and "cut him into bits." Mary was tortured until she confessed that the whole thing had been a fraud. But their grisly fate did not stop similar figures from arising: "many appeared," commented Gregory, "who attracted poor women to themselves by trickery and influenced them to rave and declare their leaders holy, and they made a great show before the people."[2]

Another indicator of popular millenarianism was a general willingness to interpret strange and unexpected circumstances as a sign of the end times. Just as the Hale-Bopp comet triggered the Heaven's Gate suicides in 1997, the appearance of Halley's comet was widely interpreted as a harbinger of doom over one thousand years earlier, in 989. Unusual calendar configurations also provoked intense anxiety. According to one tradition the world would end when the feast of the Annunciation fell on Easter Monday. The dates actually coincided in 992, sending out shockwaves of fear over the next three years. Similarly, in Ireland, it was believed that general mayhem would ensue when the feast of John the Baptist fell on the Friday of a leap year. When this happened in 1096, "the men of Ireland were seized with great fear" and only staved off the apocalypse by prolonged fasting and prayer.[3]

There is also some evidence to suggest that the year 1000 occasioned apocalyptic expectations. During the 990s, reported the French chronicler Raoul Glaber, the eruption of Mount Vesuvius, the Great Fire of Rome, and the outbreak of plague and famine were all taken as signs that the world was coming to an end. Nevertheless, the year 1000 was just one candidate among many for the Second Coming. And when nothing happened (because of a sudden show of piety in the form of church building and repairs), Glaber himself simply shifted the date to 1033, a thousand years after Christ's crucifixion.[4]

The millenarian impulse received a further boost with the Crusades, which began at the end of the eleventh century. Official attempts to drive the "infidels" from the Holy Land were accompanied by unofficial popular campaigns to purify society at home, in preparation for the thousand-year reign of Christ. The principal targets were the Jews, who had long been demonized as agents of Antichrist. From York in England to the banks of the Rhine, they were massacred in their thousands. While mainstream Christians focused on the conversion of the Jews, a messianic minority viewed them as enemies of God who deserved nothing less than annihilation. There were also vociferous denunciations of rich clergymen, who were identified as Satan's minions. The corrupt, the complacent, and the comfortable, in this view, should be cleared out of the church, and the values of spiritual poverty should replace those of material wealth. Then, and only then, would the way be clear for the Second Coming.[5]

Running through all this speculation was the popular and powerful myth of the Last World Emperor, a warrior-king who would destroy all manifestations of Antichrist, liberate Jerusalem from the infidels, and establish a Christian golden age. Historians have traced the legend of the Last Emperor back to Byzantium. It became Christianized during the fourth century, with the conversion of the Roman Empire, and fitted perfectly with the new status of Christianity as the religion of the rulers. A Christian king could now present himself as the agent of God's will – and reap the benefits. The myth proved to be infinitely adaptable: it could be applied to just about any emperor you cared to choose, including those who had already died. Belief in the resurrection of the Last Emperor turned out to be at least as strong as belief in the resurrection of Christ. During the First Crusade, for example, there were rumours that Charlemagne, emperor of the Romans, had returned from the dead to lead the march on Jerusalem and fulfil his divine destiny as the scourge of the infidels.

So, by the twelfth century, we have a popular and persistent millenarian tradition characterized by self-proclaimed messiahs, ferocious anti-Semitism, anger at the worldliness and wealth of the church, and faith in an authoritarian figure who would establish a golden age after saving Christendom from its internal and external enemies. It is against this background that we have to place the mystical writings of a contemplative monk from central Calabria, a man with a face like a dried leaf, who transformed medieval concepts of the future and gripped some of the greatest minds of subsequent generations. Richard the Lionheart sought his advice, Dante regarded him as a great prophet, Savonarola was inspired by his writings, artists from Boticelli to Kandinsky adopted his symbolism, Columbus charted a spiritual map that drew on his writings, Nostradamus was an admirer, and Yeats' poetry echoed his images. Some historians have related his thought to Nazi notions of the Third Reich; others have connected him with Marxism.[6] His name was Joachim of Fiore.

•••

At the heart of Joachim's philosophy was the notion, communicated to him in a vision in 1183, that "the whole understanding of truth is to be found in the Trinity."[7] The history of the world, he believed, was progressing through three great ages whose character corresponded to that of the Father, the Son, and the Holy Spirit. Within each age, there were seven periods, which matched the mysterious book with seven seals that appeared in Revelation.

Joachim also maintained that the Old Testament provided a model for all subsequent history. The same patterns that had characterized the lives of the sixty-three generations before Christ, in Joachim's view, would recur during the sixty-three generations following the crucifixion. Each generation, he estimated, lasted for thirty years, so the entire span of human history would be played out, from start to finish, in 3,780 years. Had he been right, the world would have come to an end in 1890.

The Age of the Father, according to Joachim, had been hatched in the twenty-one generations between Adam and Abraham, and became fully formed during the remaining forty-two generations between Abraham and Christ. This was the age of fear, submission, and suffering: it was the age of the flesh, symbolized by married men, and the age of knowledge without wisdom.

In the final twenty-one generations between Elijah and Christ, though, the Age of the Son had emerged in embryonic form, to be born through Christ's death. This was the age of faith, service, and action: it was the age of the flesh and the spirit, symbolized by the priesthood, and the age of partial wisdom. It would last for forty-two generations, and, since each generation was counted as thirty years, the Age of the Son was destined to end in the year 1260.

Even as he wrote, Joachim believed, the ground was already being prepared for the third age, the Age of the Spirit. It had been incubated twenty-one generations after Christ, through the life and example of St. Benedict, and would be brought fully into existence through the agency of spiritual monks. These monks

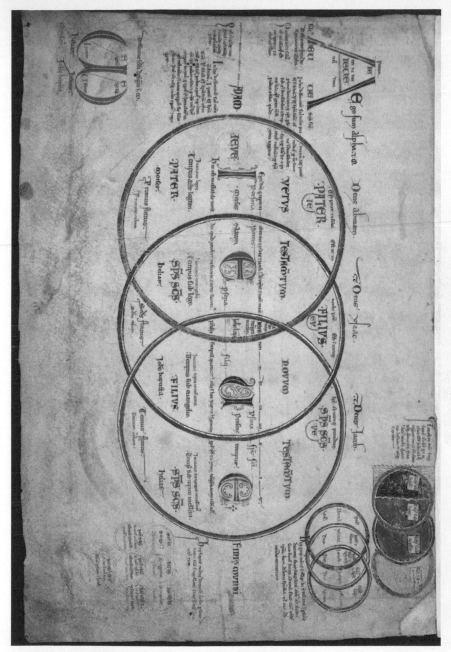

"Trinitarian Circles", from the LIBER FIGURARUM,
*composed by Joachim or one of his disciples around 1200. A visual
representation of the past, present and future, as history moved
through the three ages of the Father, the Son and the Holy Spirit.*
©Corpus Christi College, Oxford University, MS.255A, f.7v

would be assisted by the Angel of the Apocalypse, who carried the seal of the living God and would defeat the forces of evil. Their efforts would culminate in the age of love, freedom, and contemplation: it would be the age of spiritual fulfilment, symbolized by monks, and the age of complete wisdom. It would last for twenty-one more generations, until the end of time, the Second Coming and the Last Judgment.

Pulsing through this chronological framework, and providing yet another level of insight into the past, present, and future, were the patterns of seven that Joachim derived from his reading of the Book of Revelation. He was convinced that the book with seven seals encompassed the totality of history: each seal represented a specific phase within each age, and the sixth and seventh seals were characterized by acute conflict and persecution, in an intensifying series of crises. Since the Age of the Son was drawing to a close, and the sixth and seventh periods were about to begin, it was clear that turbulent times lay ahead. "One thing we can say with certainty," he wrote: "The sixth period will be worse than the previous five periods, and the seventh period will be worse than the sixth, and both will be filled with the evil doings of the dragon of the Apocalypse."

The dragon in question, from the Book of Revelation, had seven heads and was widely taken to symbolize the forces of Antichrist. The sixth head, Joachim told Richard the Lionheart in 1191, was Saladin, the Muslim leader who held the Holy City and was the target of the Third Crusade. But Saladin was only the warm-up act for the final head, who would be none other than Antichrist himself. Antichrist had already been born in the Roman Empire, Joachim believed, and would appear to the world as a false prophet. Between 1200 and 1260, he predicted, the righteous would suffer terrible persecutions, before the spiritual monks and the Angel of the Apocalypse finally prevailed. Antichrist would make a brief reappearance at the end of the third

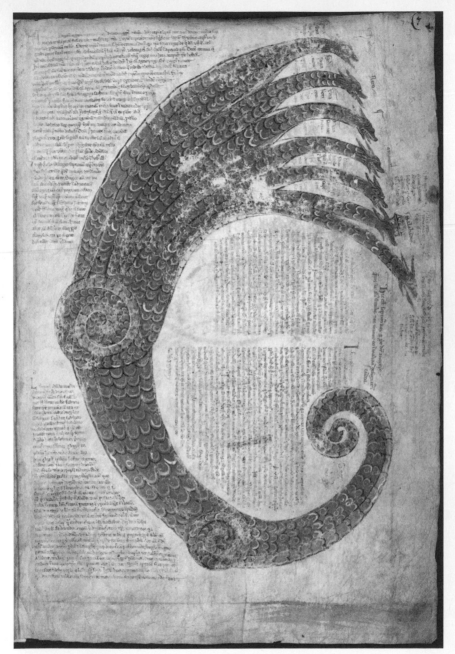

"The S7-headed Dragon", from the LIBER FIGURARUM;
*Joachim's vision of the manifestations of Antichrist. The sixth head,
wearing a crown, represented Saladin; the seventh head, belonging
to Antichrist himself, was expected to appear before 1200.*
© Corpus Christi College, Oxford, MS.255A, f.7r

age, only to be crushed forever by the risen Christ.[9]

For Joachim's contemporaries and immediate successors, all this detail raised difficult and disturbing questions. It was clear they were moving into a pivotal phase of history, but the *dramatis personae* remained unknown. Who, exactly, were these spiritual monks who would lead the world into the Age of the Spirit? Joachim had spoken of two orders of spiritual men: one consisted of preachers and the other of hermits. How were they going to take on and defeat Antichrist?

And how could you be sure of Antichrist's true identity? On one thing everyone was agreed: Antichrist was a slippery customer who would present himself as a man of God. How, then, could you distinguish between the Angel of the Apocalypse, God's agent of change, and the Antichrist who masqueraded as God's agent of change? And how could you be sure that Antichrist had not wormed his way up the church hierarchy to become none other than the pope himself?

On the answer to such questions hinged your own role in the cosmic struggle between Good and Evil. And in the attempt to find out, much blood would be spilt and many lives would be lost.

• • •

As time wound down to 1260, Joachim's followers knew that Antichrist was out there somewhere and that the Angel of the Apocalypse would soon be marching out to meet him. The key player in this unfolding drama was Frederick II, the ruler of Germany and Sicily, who was embroiled in a series of escalating struggles with the papacy for power and territory. There was, however, one problem: it was not at all clear whether Frederick was acting for or against God, whether he was the Angel or the Antichrist.

Frederick, of course, was inclined to encourage the former interpretation. His supporters in Germany and Sicily portrayed him as the Emperor of the Last Days, who would purify the church and reclaim the Holy Land. His capture of Jerusalem in 1229 provided more grist to this apocalyptic mill. Brother Arnold of Swabia, a Dominican monk, argued in 1248 that Frederick was on a divine mission to destroy Antichrist, soon to be revealed as the pope, and was destined to fulfil Joachim's prophecies about the impending Age of the Spirit.

Strange to say, the pope in question, Innocent IV, did not share this view. In fact, he was so furious with Frederick that he put the whole of Germany under the interdict: all Christian services were withheld from the population, who were now perched on the edge of eternal damnation. Similarly, the Italian Joachites perceived Frederick as the embodiment of evil. To them, his appearance was living proof that Antichrist had arrived right on cue, in the final periods of the Age of the Son, just as Joachim had prophesied. As Italian Joachites locked horns with their German counterparts, in the countdown to 1260, the apparently universalist philosophical system of their master was splintering along national and political lines.

Then, in 1250, Frederick ruined everything by the inconsiderate and selfish act of dying. To make matters worse, the supposedly fateful year of 1260 passed without incident, except for the emergence of bands of flagellants who whipped their flesh into pulp for thirty-three-and-a-half-day periods (one day for each of Christ's years on earth) in anticipation of the Age of the Spirit. Neither the Antichrist nor the Angel of the Apocalypse had appeared, and the world in 1261 seemed pretty much like the world in 1259.

What to do? When in doubt, push back the dates and elongate the time frame. For the next three centuries the Age of the Spirit would be perpetually postponed. The immediate fall-back date was derived from the Book of Daniel: "Blessed is he that waiteth, and cometh to the thousand three hundred and five and thirty days."[10] According to traditional interpretations of biblical prophecy, a day symbolized a year. From this basis, it was relatively straightforward to push back the Age of the Spirit to 1335, at which point Antichrist would get what was coming to him, and the Angel of the Apocalypse would carry the day.

Even the death of Frederick, awkward as it was, did not prove insuperable. Italian Joachites, who associated Frederick with the Antichrist, were fond of quoting the description of the Beast in the Book of Revelation: "And I saw one of his heads as it were wounded to death, and his deadly wound was healed: and all the world wondered after the beast."[11] The meaning of this passage now seemed clear: although Frederick appeared to be dead, he would be reincarnated to persecute the faithful. Meanwhile, from the other side of the spectrum, Frederick's admirers happily invoked popular myths about the resurrection of the Last Emperor and eagerly awaited their hero's return.

In Germany fake Fredericks arose with the same frequency as bogus Christs. The myth of the resurrected emperor proved durable, tough, and flexible: it might be used to challenge or confirm the legitimacy of existing kings, and it could be employed to express dreams of social equality, ethnic purity, and national glory. Such views clearly fed the imagination of one early fifteenth-century writer, who prophesied that a new German emperor would chastise the church, exterminate the Jews, subjugate the Slavs and Hungarians, take over the papacy, and prepare the way for the Day of Judgment.

Broadly similar sentiments were also expressed by the anonymous author of the *Book of a Hundred Chapters,* who in 1510 penned one of the most bloody-minded portraits of the future ever written. This individual, from somewhere in the Upper Rhine, had been told by God that the resurrected Frederick would reign over a millennium of peace and plenty. The German emperor, on this reading of the future, was going to upstage the role traditionally assigned to Christ. To clear the ground the world must be purged of sin – a state that could not, of course, be achieved without killing sinners. Frederick and his followers, organized into the Brethren of the Yellow Cross, would expand eastwards and westwards, stoning, burning, strangling, and burying alive all the enemies of God. Such enemies were widely defined. They included all clergy, "from the Pope right down to the little students," who were to be killed at the rate of 2,300 a day for four-and-a-half years. While that purge was going on, the Brethren would also wipe out all merchants, money-lenders, shopkeepers, and lawyers. In the millennium, "all property shall become one single property," and the Germans would return to the communal way of life they supposedly had before the Romans came in and ruined everything.

The new regime would begin in five years' time, wrote the author, whose delusions included the belief that he himself was going to become the resurrected Frederick. The best that can be said for this deranged fantasy is that it languished in unpublished obscurity and that its author never tried to put it into effect. But it drew on a stock of eschatological hopes and hatreds that reached back to the Middle Ages, and that bear a disturbing resemblance to the Nazi ideology of the twentieth century.[12]

• • •

In the first half of the thirteenth century, eschatological hopes and fears were focused on Frederick's conflict with the papacy. During the late thirteenth and early fourteenth centuries, in contrast, the battle against Antichrist was increasingly conducted within the church itself. As the church grew in numbers, wealth, and privilege, it began to resemble a powerful corporation, defending its own position. This process was intensified during the struggle against Frederick II and his successors, when the church became still more centralized and was run very much like an empire – which, indeed, it had become. The result was a crisis of expansion,

in which the worldly power of the church increasingly contradicted the simple lives of Christ and his disciples.

Such developments did not go unresisted. Shortly after
Joachim's death in 1202, two new religious orders emerged, the
Dominicans and the Franciscans, which asserted the ideals of
apostolic poverty and attempted to get back to Christian basics.
Yet these orders themselves quickly ran into the same problems
facing the church as a whole: the demands of absolute poverty
conflicted with the organizational requirements of expansion. As
the orders acquired buildings, established libraries, and became
involved in church work, they developed an institutional infra-
structure that seemed to contradict their original spirit.[13]

The mendicant orders began to reproduce the very tensions
that had produced them in the first place. Within the Franciscans,
in particular, a group describing themselves as the Spirituals vig-
orously reasserted the original precepts of their founder, St.
Francis, and clashed with those who insisted on the need for stability and order. As the struggle intensified, many Spirituals came
to identify themselves with Joachim's prophecies and to see their
battle with the "carnal church" as part of the transition from the
Age of the Son to the Age of the Spirit.

This association made a lot of sense. Joachim had written that
two orders of spiritual monks would play a crucial role in defeat-
ing Antichrist and ushering in the third age. Shortly afterwards,
and quite independently, the Dominicans and the Franciscans
had been formed. Could their emergence be mere coincidence?
No, it was obvious that Joachim's prophecies were coming true
and that the future of the world rested on Dominican and
Franciscan shoulders.

The first person to make this connection, at least in writing,
was a young Franciscan named Gerard of Borgo. In 1254 he
argued that St. Francis was the Angel of the Apocalypse, that the
Franciscans were Joachim's spiritual monks, and that Joachim's

writings constituted a third testament for the third age. "And I saw another angel fly in the midst of heaven, having the everlasting gospel to preach to them that dwell on earth," ran the Book of Revelation. Gerard believed that this other angel was none other than Joachim himself, and that Joachim's "everlasting gospel" had rendered the Old and New Testaments redundant. This interpretation, of course, went far beyond anything that Joachim had claimed about his own writings. It was also a clear case of heresy. Gerard's writings were burned, and he spent the rest of his life in prison.[14]

Hard on his heels, though, came an even more influential Franciscan, Peter John Olivi. He warned his followers that Antichrist would appear in the form of a false pope, accompanied by a phalanx of corrupt bishops and abbots. God had appointed the Spirituals to overcome the forces of evil – not by force, but by exemplifying the true Christian ideals of meekness and poverty. At the very moment when Antichrist would seem victorious, he wrote, the spirit of St. Francis and Christ would suffuse the world and elevate humanity onto a higher plane. In this way, Olivi associated the worldly and corrupt church with Antichrist, assured his supporters that they would ultimately prevail, and reasserted the principles of poverty and passivity. But there was considerable potential here for revolutionary activism, as both the church authorities and his own followers understood.[15]

The fears of the authorities have to be placed in the wider context of popular grievances about the church. Although modern historians rightly point out that the church was not actually degenerating, there were enough abuses to aggravate and agitate large numbers of people, quite apart from the internal challenge posed by the Spirituals. In 1250, for example, a maverick monk from northern France, calling himself the "Master of Hungary," had condemned the clergy as hypocritical self-seekers, presented himself as the living Christ, and attracted a following of several thousand people. The Virgin Mary had personally told him to organize a crusade against the infidels, he said. As proof, he carried around the letter that Mary had given to him on the subject. This was a particularly nice touch, since it would be rather difficult to check the handwriting. Besides, the "Master of Hungary" had a nasty habit of killing anyone who questioned him. The man was almost certainly not a Joachite, but the anger that he articulated could easily attach itself to apocalyptic notions of the Age of the Spirit.[16]

Such manifestations of anti-clericalism, together with the apocalyptic language of dissent within the church, produced a vicious circle of repression and radicalization. Religious conservatives believed that the Spirituals were fanatical heretics who must be suppressed. Under the pressure of persecution, the Spirituals became more convinced than ever that the forces of Antichrist controlled the church. And the growing radicalism of the Spirituals appeared to confirm the original fears of the conservatives and to justify further repression.

By the late thirteenth century, with the Age of the Spirit now scheduled for 1335, the Spirituals were increasingly forced on the defensive. They were losing the fight to reform the Franciscan Order from within. Some left in disgust, while others were forced out. With nowhere else to go, they formed their own dissident communities and radical networks outside the church and linked up with lay sympathizers. Proliferating throughout southern and western Europe, and describing themselves as Beguins or Fraticelli, such groups combined evangelical poverty with Joachite expectations and embraced a bewildering variety of ideas and attitudes. Out of this culture of radicalism there emerged some of the most militant figures the medieval world had ever seen.

In the process, Joachist thought was pushed in hitherto unimaginable directions. Nowhere was this expansion more evident than in the "cult of Guglielma" that arose in Milan during the 1270s. Guglielma and her followers accepted Joachim's model of history based on the Trinity, but infused it with a form of revolutionary feminism. During the Age of the Son, they argued, the word of God had been incarnated in a man; during the Age of the Spirit, the word would be incarnated in a woman – none other than Guglielma herself.

Guglielma's death in 1282 did nothing to diminish her stature. She was confidently expected to rise again, sending down the Holy Spirit in tongues of flame and presiding over a feminized church. The pope and the cardinals would all be women; together, they would convert the infidels and establish a new world order. Rather than seeking equality in the church, Guglielma's followers wanted to seize power for themselves, invert gender relations, and inaugurate an era of feminized spirituality. The Age of the Spirit, in short, would be the Age of Women.[17]

Among the other radical variants of Joachism, one of the most striking was the Apostolic Brethren, led by a charismatic friar named Dolcino and operating out of Lombardy. In their view, history was moving through four stages: those of the fathers, the saints, the monks, and the Apostolic Brethren themselves. Time and again, though, human backsliding had spoiled God's work: the Age of the Saints had been subverted by the institutionalization of the church during the fifth century, just as the Age of the Monks had been undermined by the increasing worldliness of the Franciscans and Dominicans during the thirteenth. But now, with the Apostolic Brethren, everything would be different. There would be no more backsliding. The showdown with Antichrist was going to occur around 1304, Dolcino said, after which the Apostolic Brethren would lead the faithful into the Age of the Spirit.

This process would involve a thorough purging of the existing church, which was now completely under Antichrist's control. The agents of Antichrist were easy to identify: they were all those people who happened to disagree with Dolcino – rather a lot, as it happened. Dolcino expected they would all be cut down by the sword of God, with a little help from the king of Sicily. The pope, the hierarchy, and most of the priests would be wiped out, leaving the way clear for a spiritually regenerated order with the Apostolic Brethren at its core. As the crucial time approached, Dolcino led his followers into the mountains, from where they could watch the cataclysmic events in relative safety – not unlike the Branch Davidians many centuries later. But neither God nor the king of Sicily felt inclined to fulfil his historic mission. Backsliding apparently reached into high places and was not confined to humankind.

For much of 1304 the Apostolic Brethren waited. Nothing happened. For all of 1305 they waited. Still nothing happened. But then, in 1306, they got more than they expected. Pope Clement V, who did not take kindly to being characterized as Antichrist, organized a crusade against them. The fantasy violence of the Apostolic Brethren was countered by the actual violence of the church. The Apostles fought to the death, and Dolcino was burned at the stake as a heretic. Even then, his ideas persisted. There were reports later in the fourteenth century that his followers had infiltrated the Franciscans, and the Inquisition kept a sharp lookout for them.[18]

As the cycle of persecution and radicalization continued, the forces of religious conservatism found their most powerful champion in John XXII, who became pope in 1316. "Poverty is good," declared his papal bull of 1317, "but chastity is better and obedience best."[19] What this meant in practice became abundantly clear the following year when four Franciscan Spirituals were burned to death in Marseilles for heresy. In Narbonne, Olivi's tomb, which had become a place of devotion for the Spirituals, was destroyed and his remains removed. His writings would eventually be condemned. All this set the stage for still further repression. During the 1320s hundreds of Beguins perished in flames, as the church attempted to destroy Joachism and impose obedience

For the Spirituals, Beguins, and Fraticelli – indeed, for the whole network of apocalyptic movements that awaited the critical year of 1335 – it now appeared clear that Olivi's prophecies were coming true. The church had become the Whore of Babylon, and John XXII was the Antichrist whose coming had long been predicted. If you want to find heresy, one Beguin told his inquisitors, all you had to do was look in the mirror. It was the persecutors who erred in the faith, he argued, and the Beguins who were following the true Christian ideal of evangelical poverty.

The Age of the Spirit was at hand, and confirmation was coming in from every quarter. Most striking of all was the vision of a woman from Montpellier named Prous Boneta. As a child, Boneta had made a pilgrimage to Olivi's tomb. Later in life, after a Franciscan church service, she had been transported to heaven, where Christ had explained the present and foretold the future. Olivi, she learned, had already initiated the third age, and his writings were the new "everlasting gospel" of the Holy Spirit that had been described in the Book of Revelation.

Christ went on to inform her that God had withdrawn his grace from the church when it turned against Olivi. John XXII was indeed Antichrist, he revealed. And just as Christ himself had been crucified at the beginning of the Age of the Son, the persecution of Olivi and his followers represented a second crucifixion at the beginning of the Age of the Spirit. There was still more: Boneta herself, Christ said, would be at the heart of the new dispensation. At the beginning of time, a woman had been responsible for the Fall. Now, as time itself was about to be transformed, God had ordained that another woman would be responsible for the salvation of humankind by spreading the Holy Spirit to the faithful.[20]

Everything was falling into place. Antichrist had arrived right on schedule, the spiritual monks were enduring persecution, divine delivery was at hand, and the world would end in 1335. But then things started to go off the rails. Antichrist was supposed to perish in a cosmic struggle between the forces of good and evil; for some inexplicable reason, John XXII died peacefully in his bed in 1334. Then the supposedly crucial year of 1335 passed by uneventfully, just as 1260 had come and gone without any discernible difference to the condition of the world. In desperation, some of the Spirituals began to argue that John was actually the forerunner of Antichrist, just as John the Baptist had been the forerunner of Christ. But it didn't wash. No obviously evil figure arrived after him to fulfil their apocalyptic expectations. More revisions to the schedule were hastily improvised. The Age of the Spirit would begin in the 1360s, or the 1380s, or maybe even the 1410s: it was just a matter of figuring out the hidden meanings in the Bible and properly reading the signs of the times.

All these prophecies failed, of course, but in a sense that is beside the point. What matters is the regenerative capacity of the prophetic system itself. During the early thirteenth century Joachim's largely abstract and symbolic scheme was employed to defend or denounce the ambitions of Frederick II. By the late thirteenth and early fourteenth centuries it was adopted and adapted by Franciscan Spirituals, Fraticelli, Beguins, the cult of Guglielma, and the Apostolic Brethren to explain and justify their attack on the worldliness of the church. Refracted at various angles through the lens of Revelation, Daniel, Joachim, and the Joachists, the future remained very much a function of the present.

· · ·

Joachim's philosophy, then, had played a shifting but significant role in the central political and religious struggles of the medieval world. But the Age of the Spirit could also be interpreted in highly individualistic terms and pushed in the direction of mystical revolutionary anarchism. Shortly after Joachim formulated his view of the future, a group of radical intellectuals at the new University of Paris began to argue that the key to the New Age could be found in a seemingly innocuous verse in Paul's second epistle to the Corinthians: "Where the Spirit of the Lord is, there is liberty."[21] Those people who were infused by the Spirit of the Lord, it was argued, had moved onto a higher level than their flesh-bound brothers and sisters. When you had become the incarnation of the Spirit, you were by definition incapable of sin; once you were incapable of sin, you were no longer bound by the codes that restricted lesser mortals. The Spirit of the Lord was within you; there was liberty.

What this meant, among other things, was a total liberation from traditional teachings that condemned the lusts of the flesh, associated chastity with spirituality, and insisted that sex was an unfortunate duty that could only be performed within marriage for the strict purposes of procreation. Spiritual emancipation was associated with sexual freedom – much to the horror of the church. "O what boundless folly," exclaimed the abbot of St. Victor near Paris, "what abominable presumption, that an adulterer, a male concubine, one weighed down with infamy, a vessel of iniquity, should be called God!" "They committed rapes and adulteries and other acts which gave pleasure to the body," he continued. "And to the women with whom they sinned, and to the simple people whom they deceived, they promised that sins would not be punished."

There was also a strong messianic component to the movement, initially expressed in the belief that the pope and the church of Rome would be destroyed within five years. All this was too much for the bishop of Paris, who in 1209 attempted to snuff out the heresy: those who recanted would be imprisoned for life, and those who did not would be burned as heretics. Most refused to recant. "As they were being led to punishment," reported their medieval chronicler, "such a furious storm arose that nobody doubted that the air was being stirred up by the beings who had seduced these men, now about to die, into their great error."[23]

This, however, was far from the end of the story. The radical ideas emanating from Paris continued to pulse through the medieval underground, mutating into what became known as the Brethren of the Free Spirit by the fourteenth century, and even resurfacing during the seventeenth-century English Civil War. In keeping with its anarchical character, the Free Spirit movement proved notoriously difficult to pin down. It could be found within all classes of society, appealed equally to the men and women in unofficial religious communities throughout northwestern Europe, and branched out in a wide variety of different directions. Some Free Spirits revered Christ, while others abhorred him. Some espoused the values of poverty and work, while others revelled in wealth and luxury. What they had in common was a profound belief in their oneness with God. They saw themselves as individual manifestations of God's all-embracing spiritual essence, as people who had achieved perfection in this world and would be reabsorbed into the whole in the next. They were, in short, men and women who had become God.

For the most part the Brethren of the Free Spirit followed a separate course from that of Joachism. But the two traditions occasionally coalesced, with striking results. In late fourteenth- and early fifteenth-century Brussels, a shadowy cult known as the Men of Intelligence combined Joachim's prophetic framework with the conviction that the Age of the Spirit meant a total inversion of traditional Catholic notions of poverty, chastity, and obedience. Despite its name, the cult included women as well as men. Because they had become one with God, the Men of Intelligence claimed, they had attained the same blissful state that Adam and Eve had experienced before the Fall. The immediate future, they believed, would replicate the distant past.

One prominent member, Giles Cantor, claimed that he copulated in exactly the same way as Adam in the Garden of Eden and eagerly attempted to demonstrate this secret method on every possible occasion. To demonstrate their liberation, the Men of Intelligence walked around in the nude, ate and drank all they wanted, and demanded instant sexual gratification. Such an approach to life would probably attract no attention whatsoever in contemporary California, but it did not go down well in early fifteenth-century Brussels. The movement was condemned, and its leader saved his life only through a public recantation.

The Men of Intelligence were never more than an obscure sect. Much more influential, and far more frightening, were the Free Spirits who emerged within the Taborite movement in Bohemia during the winter of 1419–20. The Taborites were religious fundamentalists who believed that the Bible alone provided the basis of faith. As such, they wanted to abolish almost all church ceremonies, including masses, prayers, and singing, and to impose a rigid morality that punished fornicators, drinkers, and anyone who displayed "levity" in life.

Faced with violent persecution, the movement became increasingly millenarian in outlook. One faction, led by a former priest named Martin Huska, believed that the Second Coming would occur amidst a general holocaust between February 10 and 14, 1420. To prepare for the great day and escape the general conflagration, the faithful formed their own community of true believers. They called their new home Mount Tabor, after the place where Christ had supposedly foretold his Second Coming – hence their name.

Within this highly charged atmosphere, some Taborites began to view themselves as God's avenging army, whose mission it was to exterminate all sinners before the Second Coming. The sinners in question included lords, nobles, and knights, as well as the urban rich. The Taborites themselves held all property in common. Towns and cities were regarded as hotbeds of iniquity; Prague, in particular, was singled out as the birthplace of Antichrist. We should wash our hands in the blood of our enemies, urged one of their leaders (an alumnus of Prague University); anything less was a sure sign of sinfulness, which would itself be punished. After the world had been cleansed of evil, Christ would return to their own Mount Tabor and usher in the millennium. In this new world, which was also the third age, or the Age of the Spirit, there would be "no sin, no scandal, no abomination, no falsehood." "Women will give birth to their children without pain and without original sin," they declared, "... and children born in that kingdom, if they are of the kingdom, will never die, because death will no longer be."[24]

For a while the Taborites were able to hold their own and became a significant military presence in south Bohemia, but serious problems rapidly emerged. Eschatological expectations were dashed by Christ's failure to show up in February; commonality of property proved incompatible with the demands of food production; and the pressures of war contradicted the ideology of equality. Before long the Taborites were torn apart by their own contradictions. The dominant group constituted a "party of order," which elected a bishop, imposed taxes on conquered lands, and reintroduced a hierarchical social order. At the other pole stood an extremist core of some two hundred Free Spirits, known as the Adamites. In February 1421, a full year after the expected arrival of Christ, the Adamites were expelled from Tabor.

Believing that they had transcended normal human life and had become divine embodiments of the Age of the Spirit, the Adamites recoiled like a spring from the austere morality of the mainstream Taborites. "Wandering through forests and hills," reported one observer, "some of them fell into such insanity that men and women threw off their clothes and went nude, saying that clothes had been adopted because of the sin of the first parents, but that they were in a state of innocence. From the same madness they supposed that they were not sinning if one of the brethren had intercourse with one of the sisters, and if the woman conceived, she said she had been conceived of the Holy Spirit." They even rewrote the Lord's Prayer, it was said, so that it began with the words "Our Father who art in us."[25]

Acting on behalf of the millennium and convinced of their own divinity, the Adamites struck terror into the countryside. Blood, they said, must flood the world to the height of a horse's head. They swept down on villages, stealing everything they could lay their hands on and killing everyone they could find. Their argument was, in effect, a collective version of the one put forward fifty years earlier by Johann Hartmann, a Free Spirit from Germany: "The truly free man is king and lord of all creatures. All things belong to him, and he has the right to use whatever pleases him. If anyone tries to prevent him, the free man may kill him and take his goods."[26] For neither the first nor the last time in history, the most brutal violence had found the highest spiritual justification.

In the end the Adamites were hunted down, captured, tortured, and burned to death by their Taborite enemies. Thirteen years later, in 1434, the Taborites were themselves defeated. For the next two centuries the Free Spirits disappear from the historical record. The sudden revival of their ideas during the seventeenth-century English Revolution, however, suggests the persistence of a significant invisible tradition. More apparent, though, was the populist apocalyptic tradition that had characterized the early stages of the Taborite revolution. It would repeatedly break out into action over the next hundred years, rising to a new and terrifying climacteric in the German town of Munster during the 1530s.

• • •

There was a certain trajectory to the emergence and course of popular revolutionary apocalyptic movements.[27] For one thing, they generally occurred in regions that already had an underlying millenarian tradition. For another, they were almost always precipitated by a crisis or a series of multiple crises. These could take the form of natural disasters, such as widespread disease or famine, or they could arise out of major political, religious, and social conflicts.

As customary patterns of behaviour collapsed, as the established authorities could no longer cope, and as there was a general breakdown in order, a charismatic leader would arise, proclaiming the imminent arrival of the millennium. He (and it usually was he) would present cosmic solutions to immediate grievances, hold out the prospect of revenge where there was anger, offer hope where there was despair, and promise a total, transformative deliverance where there was fear and insecurity. Eventually, there would be a revolutionary bloodbath, in which the forces of order would prove themselves to be at least as vindictive as their millenarian opponents. Inevitably, the millennium would fail to materialize at the expected time. And, usually, the charismatic leader would die a horrible and public death, as a state-sanctioned warning for the others.

Such it was in the first stages of the Protestant Reformation, when the break with Rome opened up the political space for popular apocalyptic movements. This was not something that the leaders of the Reformation, such as Martin Luther and Jean Calvin, either anticipated or welcomed. In their view, revolutionary millenarian violence was wrong on two counts: it usurped the functions of God by assuming that human actions could speed up the Second Coming; and it discredited the Reformation by associating Protestantism with fanaticism.

Accordingly, the Lutherans and Calvinists watched with horror the rise of radical sects such as the Anabaptists, who maintained that all true Christians had to be rebaptized, identified Luther himself as the Beast of the Apocalypse, and argued that direct action could hasten the millennium.[28] In 1534 and 1535 that direct action occurred in Westphalia, in the town of Munster.

Munster has become the classic case in the revolutionary millenarian textbook.[29] All the ingredients were there – escalating political conflicts between the town's guilds and its religious rulers, natural disasters in the form of the Black Death and crop failure, and sharp increases in taxation. In this tense social environment, a charismatic Anabaptist preacher named Bernt Rothmann attracted a large following and effectively turned Munster into a magnet for Anabaptists throughout northwestern Europe.

Among the thousands of religious radicals who streamed into the town, overwhelming its fifteen thousand inhabitants, were the Dutch followers of Melchior Hoffmann, who had prophesied that the millennium would occur exactly 1,500 years after the death of Christ. The air was charged with millenarian expectations, which were intensified by the presence of a besieging Catholic army at the gates. God would destroy the world at Easter 1534, it was believed, and only the Anabaptists of Munster would be saved.

Extreme conditions produced extreme leaders. Jan Matthys and Jan Bockelson, both from the Netherlands, organized the defence of the town, expelled all its Catholics and Lutherans, and inaugurated a religious reign of terror that imposed a Christian communist regime. Private property was abolished, money was forbidden, and all books except the Bible were banned. The Anabaptists ransacked the cathedral, destroying its ancient manuscripts in the process. Shortly afterwards the order went out that all books must be brought to the town's bonfire and publicly burned. When Easter came, Matthys led a handful of men out against the besieging forces. He was convinced that he would receive God's protection and confidently expected the Second Coming. He was wrong: they were all hacked to death in a matter of minutes.

At this point, the leadership passed to Bockelson, who ratcheted up the terror by several notches. Henceforth, the death penalty would be imposed for offences such as lying, slander, avarice, and quarrelling. In effect, Bockelson could kill anyone he wanted, for whatever reason he wanted. In line with the biblical precept to "increase and multiply," he now insisted on polygamy. Those who criticized the new doctrine, including wives and husbands who refused to be unfaithful to each other, were executed. The enemy continued to press at the gates, but Bockelson resisted their attacks. Flushed with success, he proclaimed himself the Messiah of the Last Days. The millennium had officially arrived: Bockelson was the new Christ, destined to rule over the New Jerusalem, now expanded to include not only Munster but the entire world.

The rest of the story is almost too surreal to be believed. Bockelson set up a throne in the marketplace, wore a crown, carried a sceptre, dressed in the robes of royalty, and appointed a court of two hundred admirers who wallowed in luxury while the rest of the population shivered and starved. Like the Free Spirits before him, he believed that he had become divine and could live life in extravagance precisely because he had transcended temptation. Meanwhile, the execution of sinners continued apace. Women, in particular, were singled out for such crimes as refusing to have sexual relations with their husbands or for mocking the New Jerusalem.

As the siege tightened and people were reduced to eating rats, Bockelson forced them to participate in dramatic pageants to celebrate the glorious new era in human history. In the final days of his reign, with the corpses piling up in communal graves, he began personally to behead anyone who contravened his codes or attempted to escape from the city. Not that escape offered an attractive option: almost all the fugitives were killed by the besieging army. On June 24, 1535, that army eventually broke through

Munster's defences. Most of the Anabaptists were killed, and those who surrendered were offered safe passage out of the city, only to be massacred almost to the last person. Bockelson, though, was left alive. For the next six months his captors led him around on a chain, before taking him back to Munster, publicly torturing him to death, and leaving his body to rot in a cage that hung from a church tower. That cage is still hanging there today.

What are we to make of this story? In part, Bockelson's draconian measures could be seen as a pragmatic, calculated response to the pressures of the siege – keeping people's spirits up through dramatic performances, imposing authoritarian control to organize the defence of the town, bestowing privileges to a loyal elite who would willingly enforce his will, and so on. But it clearly goes far beyond that; indeed, there would not have been a siege in the first place without the millenarian takeover of the town. The behaviour of Matthys and Bockelson could also be viewed in psychological terms, characterized by paranoid delusions, psychotic actions, and the acting out of sadistic and misogynist fantasies.

At some level, Matthys and Bockelson truly believed that they were carrying out God's will and that they had divine powers. Why else would Matthys have marched out with two dozen men against an entire army on the very day that the Second Coming was supposed to occur? It seems equally clear that their followers were true believers. Through the means of terror, they hoped to create a classless, egalitarian society.

A collective rage was at work here, a rage borne of scarcity, disease, insecurity, and fear, and a rage that became a disease itself. The anger of the poor against the rich, the anger of men against women, the anger of the humble against the proud, the anger of despised artisans against learned intellectuals – all that anger became channelled into the comforting simplicities of a black-and-white religious ideology which held out the illusory promise of utopia, with disastrous consequences.

One might think that the memory of these events would have permanently inoculated subsequent generations against such revolutionary millenarian fantasies. After the example of Munster, it might reasonably be asked, how could anyone ever have anything to do with charismatic figures speaking in certainties, spouting simplicities, and promising utopia? Yet it has happened over and over again: before, with the popular crusades, false messiahs, last emperors, Free Spirits, Taborites, and Adamites; and afterwards, with the killing fields of the twentieth century and the persistence of contemporary killer cults. It is not a picture that is conducive to optimism about our species.

Those who forget the future, it seems, are condemned to repeat it.

· 3 ·

THE FUTURE IN FOLKLORE

IN BILL FORSYTH'S FILM *Local Hero,* Macintyre, a Texas business-man, arrives in a remote Scottish village to buy up the land and build port facilities for North Sea oil tankers. The longer he stays in the village, though, the more he falls in love with its way of life – the relaxed pace, quirky characters, and communal values that are sharply contrasted with the crass commercialism of the mod-ern world. But the villagers are not quite what they seem. Unbeknownst to Macintyre, they want to make as much money as possible from the deal and live in luxury under the sun. Macintyre yearns for the imagined values of the villagers; the vil-lagers yearn for nothing less than his kind of wealth.

Beneath the humour lies a serious point. There is, in human nature, a marked tendency to idealize the opposite. Those of us who live in an urban, industrial, materialistic, and individualistic culture are particularly prone to romanticize the rural, agrarian, spiritual, and communal way of life we have left behind. Such a sentiment is reflected in the popularity of such television pro-grams as *Northern Exposure* or *Hamish Macbeth,* in which an urban outsider comes to appreciate and identify with the values of a rural community. It also helps to explain the current popularity of all things Celtic. Ireland, in particular, has become the mythic community that America never had but always wanted. And the idealization of the "other" also lies behind nostalgic views of the pre-industrial past.

There was, in fact, little to be nostalgic about. For most people, most of the time, the past has not been a pleasant place. Life, like Hobbes' state of nature, was all too often nasty, brutish, and short. The death rate was high, and the infant death rate was astronomical. A baby born in the picturesque and prosperous rural village of Clayworth, England, in 1679 was less likely to survive its first year than was a baby born in the worst slums of industrial Glasgow two centuries later.[1] Diseases such as smallpox, typhus, and the dreaded Black Death raged through medieval and early modern Europe. There were few doctors: only the rich could afford them, and they probably did more harm than good anyway. Hospitals were more likely to kill than cure. Standards of hygiene were abysmal, and a putrefying smell pervaded the air. Fires were a constant threat. In an age long before insurance, they swept through wooden houses, sometimes destroying whole towns and leaving their inhabitants totally destitute.

Behind these immediate threats, people struggled against the brutal dominion of nature. Everything depended on sowing, planting, and reaping the crops, on keeping the animals alive and healthy, and on producing enough hay to feed the livestock over the winter. "It was only when the farmers had their hay cut and dried," observed one historian, "that the future of civilization was assured."[2] Bad weather was more than an inconvenience: it was potentially lethal, as were the crop failures that struck with alarming frequency. Most people lived just above the subsistence line, and if there was any increase in the price of bread, they would go under.

In short, it is hard to imagine a more insecure, fragile, and precarious environment. No wonder people desperately needed not only to comprehend their future but also to control it. And this is where folklore came in.

• • •

Despite the differences among them, pre-industrial European societies shared a network of popular beliefs, rituals, and customs that were intended to predict and prepare for future events, protect communities from misfortune, and bend the future in more benign directions. Take the crucial question of the weather. It was widely believed that certain days and dates contained the key to the coming year's climate. If Christmas Day fell on a Sunday, for example, you could stop worrying and take your ease, since the year would turn out fine. The twelve days of Christmas were also important indicators of what to expect over the next twelve months: if the weather on the first day was dire, you could expect a grim January, and so on. In medieval England, rain on Saint Swithin's Day (July 15) meant forty days of wet weather. This belief was eventually transmitted to Ireland, where it was much more likely to come true.[3]

But while such beliefs could provide a general guide to the year's weather, they could not actually alter it. In emergencies, other methods were required. When storm clouds gathered on the medieval horizon, church bells rang out in darkening skies and villagers formed holy processions through the first showers of rain. This assertion of religious values and communal solidarity would, it was hoped, ward off the evil spirits in the air, protect people and animals from the elements, and save the crops by changing the weather.[4]

A wide variety of calendar customs could also be employed to safeguard the community from the vagaries of the future. These customes were particularly evident in the folklore of Scotland and Ireland, where many pre-Christian rituals persisted right up to the nineteenth century. Traditionally, the Celtic year was divided into two halves: the winter began at Samhain, which evolved into Halloween, and the summer started six months later at Beltain, which eventually became May Day.

The summer and winter were again divided in two: the mid-winter festival of Imbolc took place on February 1, while the mid-point of the summer was the festival of Lughnasa on August 1. Within this organization of time, the critical moments occurred between the dualities, in the interstices between the seasons, when it was neither winter nor summer. For it was in these cracks in time that mysterious and powerful supernatural forces were released, for good and for evil. If you could somehow tap into these forces, you might be able to turn them to your own advantage.[5]

Such opportunities arose particularly at Beltain, which was also the time when the summer grazing began. The cattle were taken from the barns to graze in the hills, amid rituals that were designed to preserve the stock. The "driving of the cows" was accompanied by incantations that invoked Christian and pagan figures, such as Mary the Virgin, Fionn mac Cumhall, and the "king of the sun," to shield and shelter the animals from "evil deed and quarrel, from evil dog and red dog." When they reached the hilltops, the cattle were driven through bonfires in a further act of purification and protection for the coming year.

At the same time, symbolic offerings were made to the deities who were associated with particular animals. In a typical Beltain ritual from eighteenth-century Scotland the herdsmen began by heating a mixture of eggs, butter, oatmeal, and milk over an open fire, and then spilt some of the contents on the ground, to appease the spirit of the land. After that, they divided their oatmeal cake into nine pieces. Each person faced the fire and threw his piece over his shoulder, as a gift to the spirit that protected the horses, sheep, and other animals. The ritual was then repeated, this time to propitiate potential predators, such as the fox, the crow, and the eagle. Finally the men turned their attention to spirits of a different kind, as they passed around the whisky until all the bottles were empty.

In some cases, the customs were clearly modern versions of ancient sacrificial rites. Elsewhere in Scotland, the men at Beltain made a fire, baked a cake, and divided it among themselves. One piece was covered in charcoal and put in a hat with the rest. After the men were blindfolded, they each drew out a piece. The man who got the charcoal piece was supposed to be sacrificed to Belinus, the Celtic god, whose good will was essential for a bountiful future. There was, however, an escape clause. If the man jumped six times over the fire, it was assumed that Belinus would be satisfied. Fifteen hundred years earlier, the herdsmen did not hold with such soft liberal attitudes: the man would most likely have been roasted in the fire, rather than allowed to leap over it.[6]

If Beltain was traditionally associated with safeguarding the livestock, Lughnasa was closely connected with harvesting the corn. Named after Lug, the Celtic "god of each and every art," and Nasad, the Gaelic word for "games" or "assembly," the festival went back well over fifteen hundred years and lingered longest in the Gaelic areas of Scotland and Ireland. By holding the assembly, the community hoped and expected to secure a successful harvest, along with peace and plenty in the coming year. People ignored the festival at their peril: "there comes from neglect of it," wrote one Celtic bard, "baldness, weakness, early greyness, kings without keenness or jollity, without hospitality or truth."[7]

The reaping itself, it was said, should always take place on a Tuesday. The same held true for ploughing and sowing, earlier in the year. At dawn the farmer would face the rising sun, cut a handful of corn with his sickle, and turn with it three times following the sun's path. All the while, he and his family would be singing blessings to the god of the harvest. Through such actions, the farming community attempted to assert some degree of control over the unpredictable forces of nature, and thus over their own collective and individual future. When the reaping was over, the men would gather together and throw their sickles high in the air. They could tell from the way the sickles struck the ground who among them would stay single, get married, become sick, or die over the next twelve months.[8]

...

The supernatural forces that poured through the cracks in time could also reveal personal fortunes, provided the correct rituals were followed. A typical example at Samhain was the practice of placing three saucers, containing, respectively, water, meal, and earth, before individuals who were blindfolded. If they put their hand in water, they would live beyond the year; if they put it in meal, they would live long and prosper; but if they put it in the earth, they would not live to see the next Samhain. This custom was transmitted from rural to urban Ireland, and survived into the twentieth century as a Halloween game. It appears in James Joyce's *Dubliners,* where it was transmuted into a cruel trick played by children on a vulnerable and lonely single woman.[9]

Marriage prospects were a major preoccupation. The world of folklore was crowded with young women desperately trying to find out if, when, and whom they would marry. The young men, in contrast, seemed totally uninterested in such matters. There were various methods of identifying the man you would marry. According to one tradition, a girl who placed garments in front of the fire at Samhain would see an apparition of her future husband in the shadows that were cast. Another ritual was associated with the first full moon of the new year and involved gathering herbs by its light, while repeating this rhyme:

Moon, moon, tell unto me,
When my true love I shall see?
What fine clothes am I to wear?

How many children shall I bear?
For if my love comes not to me
Dark and dismal my life will be.

The woman then cut three pieces of turf with a black knife, tied them up in her left stocking with her right garter, and placed them under her pillow. That night, it was said, all her dreams would come true.[10]

At May Eve, the future could be found in the flowers, as a rhyme from Islandmagee illustrated:

Ye yarrow, yarrow I pull thee –
And under my pillow I'll put thee
And the first young man that speaks to me,
Will my own true love be.

Elsewhere, it was believed that a pod containing nine peas had special powers. If you placed it on the lintel of a door, the first unmarried man who walked underneath it would be your marriage partner. It was also possible to foretell your fate by suspending the yoke of an egg in water. If it rose to the surface, you would be married; if it sank, your marriage prospects sank with it. Something similar took place at Salem in 1692: the notorious witch trials began after the girls in the Reverend Samuel Parris' kitchen suspended egg yokes in water to "see what trades their sweethearts should be of," only to find instead "a specter in the likeness of a coffin."[11]

Marriage was supposed to offer emotional and economic security. To be single was a sign of failure, and to be single and female was seen as a kind of living death. This view was literally reflected in a divination ritual from Guernsey in the Channel Islands. To find out her future, a woman would visit a sacred well for nine mornings, fasting and in silence. On the ninth morning, if she were lucky, she would see the face of her future husband in the water. But if, instead, she saw a grinning skull looking back up at her from the water, it meant that she would stay single for the rest of her life.[12]

In most of these rituals, the young woman was trying to discover her preordained fate. She might be able to see the future, but she could not actually alter it. Nevertheless, according to some folkloric accounts, there were also rituals in which she could take a more active role in the process. These rituals were not always for the squeamish, however. The primary ingredients, in one such account, were a freshly buried corpse and a sharp knife.

To explain: You're a young woman and there's a young man you are after, but he's not interested in you. You've tried being nice to him, yet you've got nowhere. How can you make him change his mind? First, go the nearest cemetery and find yourself a corpse whose skin has yet to decay. Next, take the knife and start peeling the skin from the side of one foot. The trick is to make a continuous band of skin, coming up the outside of the leg from the foot, continuing up the side of the body, going over the head, along the other side of the body, and down the other leg. Now comes the awkward part. Carefully proceed up the inside of the leg, and back down the inside of the other, until the strip of skin meets the point at which it began.

Having done this, you wait until the man you're after is sleeping. You creep up to him and tie the skin around him while he's still asleep. If he wakes up while you are doing it, too bad for him, for he will die within twelve months – if you cannot have him, at least no one else can either. And if he stays asleep, he's in your power. When he awakes in the morning, he will be hopelessly in love with you, if a little uncomfortable.

That, at any rate, is the story the Reverend Caesar Ottway was told, and believed, during the mid-nineteenth century. Whether it reflects reality is another matter altogether. For centuries the Irish have taken a secret delight in feeding preposterous stories to outsiders. They did it with Gerald of Wales just after the Norman Conquest of Ireland, and they are still doing it with visiting anthropologists, folklorists, and journalists to this day. Seeing how far you can stretch the skin of credulity is an ancient Irish art form. So the story might not be true – but it certainly ought to be.[13]

If marriage figured prominently in folkloric divinations, so too did the state of one's health and general well-being – something that is not surprising in societies with only rudimentary medical knowledge, few doctors, and no social insurance. Precisely because people were so vulnerable to illness, and had so little control over their own health, they turned for help to the world of magic. By unlocking the supernatural forces within nature, they hoped not so much to predict the future as to change its course.

Again, some of the methods were not for the fainthearted. It was widely believed, for example, that the human corpse had curative powers. The hand of a dead person was supposed to be especially effective – preferably the left hand, and ideally the left hand of an unbaptized infant. Since the left hand was supposedly "sinister," and an unbaptized infant had not been claimed by God, it would seem that malevolent forces were being used for benevolent purposes.

Whether or not that was the case, getting hold of a dead person's hand was not an easy task. The most common approach was to visit the house where a dead person was lying and hold the hand close to you during the wake. In some cases, a body would be disinterred and the left hand sliced off. The hand would then be used for a variety of purposes, such as stirring the milk to produce more and better cream. Public hangings afforded another opportunity. In 1795 a French visitor to Ireland described an execution he had witnessed in Dublin: "My horror was intensified," he wrote, "by seeing many men and women carried to the scaffold in order to have applied to them for the cure of various diseases the still throbbing hand of the just executed criminal."[14]

Not only the hand but also the head of a dead person was supposed to possess curative powers. The best remedy for a raging toothache was to drink water from a human skull: if that didn't cure you, nothing would. Epilepsy could be cured by taking nine pieces of a dead man's cranium, grinding them into powder, dissolving them in herbs, adding milk, and swallowing a teaspoon each day until there was nothing left. If you did not take the entire dosage, it was believed, the owner of the skull would be after you in short order. There was also a link here between preventive medicine and magical medicine. If you wanted to ensure that you never got epilepsy in the first place, you were supposed to pierce small pieces of a skull and wear them around your neck to ward off the demons.[15]

All these cures and precautions were enacted against the background of a landscape that was itself charged with magic. There were trees that could protect you from misfortune, stones that could speak, and wells that could cure the sick. One tree in County Cork was said to prevent people from drowning. To ensure a safe voyage, emigrants would chip off pieces and include them with their baggage. By the middle of the nineteenth century the whole tree had disappeared, carried piece by piece across the Atlantic. Certain stones knew the future and would prophesy if you approached them correctly. You had to turn around them three times following the direction of the sun and never ask them the same question twice. In many local legends, that particular restriction explains why the stones have become silent today. Some idiot in the past broke the taboo and ruined it for everyone.[16]

Stones with holes in them were often the route to a healthier future. Children with measles or the whooping cough were passed through the holes to be cured. At Ardmore in County Waterford thousands of people each December crawled face down through St. Declan's Sacred Stone, knocked their backs against it three times, and walked bare-kneed over the rocks. If they followed this procedure three times and made sure they were wearing their own clothes, they freed themselves from the agony of back pains. Similar rituals were associated with such places as St. Tecla's Well in Wales. There, people were dipped three times in the well, walked around it three times sun-wise, recited the Lord's Prayer, and made an offering to appease the water spirit. Through such methods, anything from rheumatism to blindness could be healed.[17]

A deeply ambivalent view of the future runs through such beliefs. On the one hand there is a considerable degree of fatalism, reflecting a reality in which nature controls human life more than human life controls nature. The weather, the harvest cycle, and the state of one's health were largely matters of chance. On the other hand there is the notion that humankind can alter the future, reflecting a refusal to become mired in helplessness. Folkloric divinations, customs, and rituals walked the knife-edge between passivity and activism, between the terrifying reality of vulnerability and the comforting illusion of security. But the illusion of security could in itself provide peace of mind, a security of the spirit. And in this sense, perhaps, the magic actually worked.

There was one area, though, in which there was no room for illusions – the inescapable reality of death. This was something that mythological and folk traditions confronted head on: "deaths," commented Alwyn and Brinley Rees, "are preordained; and the contingent causes are but the agents of pre-existent and precognizable destinies." According to one Irish folktale, there was a time when "everybody knew the exact time when he would die" and, consequently, stopped bothering with life once it was known that death was imminent. When the Almighty cottoned on to what was happening, the story continued, he soon put a stop to that little game, and that is why none of us knows today. But the omens are out there, for those who know where to look and listen – an apple tree blossoming out of season, a hen crowing like a cock, or, best known of all, the cry of the banshee, the supernatural messenger of death.[18]

The banshee gets a very bad press these days. She is often seen as an evil figure whose wail brings on death to anyone unfortunate enough to hear it. Nothing could be further from the truth – in fact, such an image is a classic case of shooting the messenger. The banshee almost certainly originated as a guardian spirit who wept for people who were about to die. In most (but not all) accounts, she shared and articulated the family's grief, as did the "keening woman" who sang laments after the death of a loved one. The banshee and the keening woman were closely connected in the folk tradition.

Contrary to modern beliefs, the person on the brink of death never actually heard the banshee's cry. It came instead as a warning to close friends and relatives, to prepare them for the worst. At a time when someone was desperately ill, when friends and family were suffering the intolerable anguish of uncertainty, the banshee's cry would help them accept the painful reality of death. The banshee was essentially benevolent: by confirming the inevitable, she turned anxiety into resignation. This, too, could be a form of comfort.[19]

•••

But there was also a dark side to divinations: supernatural forces were sometimes invoked to inflict future misery on real or imagined enemies. A classic example in the Celtic tradition was St. Elian's Well near Colwyn Bay in Wales. Normally, wells were associated with the ability to heal the sick. St. Elian's, in contrast, was used for curses rather than cures. During the eighteenth and nineteenth centuries thousands of people visited the well each year to wreak vengeance on their enemies, in a kind of pilgrimage of vindictiveness. Once there, they would scratch the initials of their intended victim on a "cursing stone," or pebble, and throw it into the water. The spirit of the well would then ensure that the person in question would suffer or even die

Not surprisingly, the "curse of the well" struck terror into its targets – so much so that one enterprising well-keeper made a handsome living by removing the curse for a suitable fee. After receiving his money, he told the victim to walk three times sunwise around the well while reading aloud from the Bible. The well-keeper then drained the water, took out the offending pebble, and gave it to the victim, who was instructed to read from the Book of Job and the Psalms for three consecutive Fridays. It was a fascinating mixture of Christianity, paganism, and profiteering.[20]

The key point is that magical power was ambivalent and could be used for good and for evil purposes. The belief in magic assumed not only that occult forces could be manipulated but that specific individuals who understood magical techniques could harness supernatural forces to transform the world to their advantage and to foretell the future. Virtually every village in early modern Britain and Ireland, and by extension in colonial America, had a magical expert who was known as a "cunning man" or "wise woman." These "cunning folk" acted as healers, diviners, and fortune tellers and were usually respected, appreciated, and valued in their local communities – although the church frequently frowned on their activities.

Their methods might be rooted in local lore, or might be folk versions of ancient and complex systems of divination. Among the former were techniques for predicting the future from the croaking of frogs or from watching the way that grains moved on a hot hearth. Among the latter were predictions based on facial characteristics, such as the moles on your face or the lines on your forehead. These methods reached back to respectable medieval theories of physiognomy and anticipated the nineteenth-century preoccupation with phrenology, which assumed that an individual's future could be decoded from the shape of the skull. Some of the greatest intellectuals of the nineteenth century, such as the Irish archbishop Richard Whately, visited phrenologists and took their prognostications very seriously indeed.[21]

Complex systems of numerology, drawn from antiquity, also filtered down to the folk level. Local magicians would inscribe a circle in which different segments represented different fortunes, calculate the numerical equivalent of a person's name, and see where the numbers fitted in the circle. In Ireland and Scotland, folk divinations and remedies were often based on the number nine, which had been associated with magical powers in ancient Celtic mythology.[22]

A major component of popular magic was the secret book, containing the hidden knowledge of the cunning man or wise woman. In a pre-literate or semi-literate society, the written word could in itself appear to possess magical powers. It is no coincidence that many of the self-proclaimed Christs we encountered in the previous chapter carried around letters of reference from the Virgin Mary or the Archangel Michael. And there was, of course, a sense in which access to the written word conveyed special knowledge and greater power – a person's influence in the community was directly related to his or her ability to read and write. When the power of literacy was allied to the power of the occult, the results could be formidable. Time and again cunning folk impressed their friends and neighbours with books that supposedly contained the keys to the future.

As long as the cunning men and wise women restricted themselves to benevolent activities, they were generally accepted within the community and tolerated by the authorities. When things went wrong, though, the cunning folk could easily become the focus of popular fears. If, for example, a wise woman administered herbal medicine to a sick person and the person died shortly afterwards, it might be assumed that she had used her magical powers for negative purposes. And from here it was a short step to accuse the woman of witchcraft.

There were, broadly speaking, two definitions of witchcraft in the early modern Anglo-American world. The official religious position was that a witch was a woman who had rejected God and embraced Satan's law and authority. She had made a compact with the devil, exchanging short-term gain for long-term pain, and had aligned herself with Antichrist. In the folk tradition, though, the witch was more likely to be associated with a species of occult criminality. Popular fears clustered around the ability of the witch to control the future for malevolent purposes. If someone – usually, but not always, a woman – had a history of using threatening language, and if these threats were followed by misfortune, it seemed likely that witchcraft was at work.

The classic case, of course, is Salem, where both definitions were in full operation. Particularly revealing, in this respect, was the testimony against Martha Carrier from nearby Andover. Another accused witch had "confessed" that she and Carrier were part of a witch's coven, making a pact with Satan and riding over Massachusetts on a "stick or a pole." Almost immediately, stories started to surface about Carrier's wilful malevolence and her supernatural powers. One of her neighbours recalled that, seven years earlier, he had been threatened by Carrier in the course of a quarrel. Shortly afterwards, two of the neighbour's "large lusty sowes" disappeared: one was never seen again, and the other was found "dead ... with both Eares cut of[f]" near Carrier's house. At the same time, one of his cows, which had given good milk twice a day, suddenly dried up. "I did in my Conscience believe then ... and have so done ever since," he told the court, "... that Martha Carrier was the occasion of those Ill accidents, by Meanes of Witchcraft, she being a very Malicious woman."[23]

"Malicious women" were particularly vulnerable to accusations of witchcraft: even the vaguest curses and threats could be taken as evidence of supernatural malevolence. One woman, for example, told a farmer named Henry Batchelor that some of his cows would die, some would live, and some would be indifferent. It is hard to get a prediction much looser than that, except perhaps in modern-day horoscopes. And sure enough, a year later, Batchelor was testifying in court that as she had spoken, so it had come to pass. His cows, he was convinced, had been bewitched.[24]

Among other things, the Salem witch trials revealed the world of popular magic that existed beneath the official Puritan culture of New England. At least two of the accused, Samuel Wardwell of Andover and Dorcas Hoar of Beverly, were cunning folk who told fortunes. On July 6, 1692, the Reverend John Hale informed the court:

> Dorcas Hoar ... had a book of fortune telling. About twenty-two years agoe she manifested to me great repentance for the sins of her former life and [said] that she had borrowed a book of Palmistry and that there were rules to know what should come to pass. But I telling her that it was an Evill book and an Evill art[,] shee seemed to me to renounce or reject all such practices.

But "fourteen yeares agoe last spring," Hale continued, his daughter Rebecca told him that she had seen a book with "many streaks and pictures, by which Hoar ... could reveale and work witchcrafts ... I called to minde that book of Palmistry ... I asked Thomas Tuck if he knew Goody Hoar to have a book of fortune-telling and he said yea shee had."[25]

It is all there – the mysterious book that apparently conferred magical powers; the view of the Christian minister that all supernatural forces not controlled by the church must necessarily emanate from Satan; the fears of the fortune teller that the minister might actually be right; her ultimate decision to continue practising magic in secret; and the easy way in which palmistry could be connected with witchcraft. In the end, Dorcas Hoar, the wise woman of Beverly, managed to escape execution; the governor of Massachusetts put a stop to the trials while she was still in prison. Samuel Wardwell, the cunning man of Andover, was not so fortunate: he was found guilty of witchcraft and brought to the scaffold on September 22, 1692. As he professed his innocence to the assembled crowd, he began to cough from the smoke of the hangman's pipe. The last thing he heard was the taunts of the girls who had initially accused him, as they cried out that he was choking on the words of the devil.[26]

• • •

While folk magic at the village level often had a tense and uneasy relationship with civic and religious authorities, the more sophisticated art of astrology remained very much part of the mainstream during the early modern period. The tenant farmer with a problem would visit the local wise woman or the cunning man; a monarch, such as Elizabeth I or Charles II, would head straight for the nearest astrologer. With an intellectual pedigree that stretched back to the Babylonian empire, astrology assumed that the movement of heavenly bodies played a critical role in shaping human destinies. Just as astronomy could project, within limits, the future path of the Sun, Moon, planets, and stars, astrology claimed to show how such movements affected the future patterns of society and the individual fortunes of daily life. Astronomical projections were quantitative; astrological predictions were qualitative.

As Keith Thomas has pointed out, one of the reasons for astrology's appeal was that it seemed to fit the dominant assumptions about the way the world worked. God must have put the heavenly bodies up there for a reason, and there was no doubt they affected life on Earth. Plants and flowers reached towards the Sun, and without the warmth of spring and summer the land would have remained barren and infertile. The Moon controlled the tides, and it seemed reasonable to assume that it exercised a similar pull on the moisture within the human body. During the twelfth century, Gerald of Wales explained that the Moon "is to such an extent a source and influence on all liquids, that according to her waxing and waning she directs and controls not only the waves of the sea, but also the bone-marrow and brains in all living things as well as the sap of the trees and plants."

Because the brain was supposed to contain more moisture than any other part of the body, the human mind was regarded as being particularly vulnerable to lunar movements. In 1660 one astrologer declared that a child born at the full Moon would never be healthy: such beliefs are also reflected in the use of words like *lunatic* and *moonstruck* to describe insanity. If the Sun and the Moon exerted such a decisive influence on life on Earth, it was a short step to the position that the planets and stars also affected human behaviour.[27]

Apart from anything else, astrology offered an explanation for the sheer diversity of human personalities: the answer lay not in hereditary or environmental differences, but in the conjunction of the stars and planets. This notion, too, is reflected in our language. When we describe someone as being *mercurial* or *saturnine,* we are unconsciously adopting an astrological vocabulary in which volatility is associated with the planet Mercury, and a gloomy temperament with Saturn. Character traits were supposedly conditioned by the state of the sky at the moment of birth: as the map of the heavens changed from year to year, so too did your personal prospects.

Not surprisingly, then, people flocked to astrologers in times of stress or uncertainty. A parade of the usual suspects passed through the offices of prominent seventeenth-century English astrologers such as Simon Forman and William Lilly. Women who were torn between two lovers wanted to know which one they should choose; maidservants wanted to know if they might marry their masters; widows wanted to know if they should remarry; single women wanted to know if their boyfriends would work out. Single men wanted to know if their girlfriends loved them, how much money they might bring to a marriage, and "whether they were really whores." Married men wanted to know if their wives were having affairs, and about the paternity of their children. Meanwhile, illegitimate children wanted to know how they could track down their parents. Couples wanted to know which one would live longer, and the date of birth and sex of their future children. And so it went. The astrologer, it seemed, functioned as a cross between an oracle and a guidance counsellor.[28]

More generally, astrologers also attempted to predict natural disasters, so that people could at least prepare for events that remained beyond human control. During the early 1660s, for example, John Gadbury compared the history of London's plagues with the position of the stars, to see if any connections could be detected. Having found what he was looking for, he confused these forced correlations with an equally dubious cause-and-effect logic to conclude that future plagues could be predicted through astrological analysis. The result, he maintained, was nothing less than a collective horoscope of London. To clinch the case, he argued that such methods had enabled him to predict the Great Plague of 1665. He made this claim, it should be noted, after the event.[29]

Other astrologers used similar techniques to forecast the outbreak of fires and the state of the weather. And even as late as the nineteenth century, equally dubious logic was applied to the business cycle. W.S. Jevons, one of England's leading economists, found correlations between sun-spots and trade depressions, suspected there was a causal relationship, and offered a predictive model to guide people through booms and slumps.[30] Jevons was not, of course, an astrologer – but sometimes astrologers and economists are much closer than they appear.

Astrology was also used for political purposes, especially during times of crisis such as the English Civil War. What we have here is a gigantic Rorschach test written in the sky: the stars could always be relied upon to support all the partisan predictions that emanated from Earth. Royalist astrologers such as George Wharton argued that the conjunction of the planets during the 1640s was such that King Charles I would be "unexpectedly victorious and successfull in all his Designes." Their republican opponents, including William Lilly, drew exactly the opposite conclusion from the same astronomical evidence.[31]

One of the key texts, on the republican side, was Sir Christopher Heydon's early seventeenth-century *Astrological Judgment,* which maintained that the Sun represented the king, the planets represented the nobility, and the fixed stars represented the people, "amongst whom some excel others." From these assumptions, Heydon suggested that the appearance of a nova in 1604 would brighten the prospects of the people, while the solar eclipse of the following year portended the end of the monarchy[32]. By the time of the Civil War some forty years later, it seemed that these predictions were finally coming true.

Following the same reasoning, Lilly pointed out in 1645 that there would be another eclipse of the Sun on August 11, which was also the date of the king's birthday. The conclusion appeared clear: the king was doomed to defeat. And when the royal army suffered a major defeat that year, it seemed that Lilly had made the right call – a view that the execution of Charles I four years later apparently confirmed. On the other hand, the restoration of the monarchy in 1660 threw all these assumptions into reverse. It could now be argued that the royalists had got it right after all, despite a few local difficulties about timing and the separation of Charles I's head from his body.

The most common vehicle for astrological predictions was the almanac, which came into its own during the seventeenth century. Almanacs charted the phases of the Moon and the movement of the planets, made long-range weather forecasts, warned of natural disasters, predicted personal and political changes, and suggested propitious times for action. Thus in 1666 a group of republican revolutionaries in England timed an attempted coup for September 3, on the basis of astrological calculations in a popular almanac. (They must have got their arithmetic wrong, because they were all caught and arrested.) The people of England, commented one observer in 1652, were "alarmed and even half dead with prophecies." Not surprisingly, almanacs were the first secular books to outsell that other great work of prophecy, the Bible.[33]

Precisely because of their popularity, and a growing conviction that their predictions were grounded on false premises and flawed logic, the almanacs became increasingly vulnerable to satirical attacks. By far the most effective was that of Jonathan Swift, who in 1708 took on the leading astrologer of the day, John Partridge. Writing under the pseudonym of "Isaac Bickerstaff," Swift composed a spoof almanac, which purported to defend the "noble Art" of astrology from those "gross Impostors" who prophesied in its name. One of the common tricks of these charlatans, Bickerstaff noted, was to make their predictions so general as to be meaningless: "they are such," he wrote, "as will equally suit any Age, or Country in the World." Against these abuses, Bickerstaff claimed that all his predictions had come true and declared that all his new ones would prove just as accurate. And with that, he got down to business.

Some of Bickerstaff's prophecies were wonderfully vague: "On the 15th [of May]," he wrote, "News will arrive of a very *surprizing Event,* than which nothing could be more unexpected." But others were very specific – including the prediction that "*Partrige* [sic], the Almanack-Maker ... will infallibly die upon the 29th of *March* next, about eleven at night, of a raging Fever." This was only the first round of the joke. Shortly after March 29, Bickerstaff put it about that Partridge had indeed died, four hours before the appointed time. At first, ran the account of the death, Partridge had simply ignored the prediction, on the grounds that "Mr. *Bickerstaff* spoke altogether by guess, and knew no more what would happen this Year than I did myself." "I am a poor ignorant Fellow, bred to a mean Trade," Partridge was supposed to have said; "yet I have Sense enough to know, that all Pretences of foretelling by Astrology are Deceits."

It wasn't long before others got into the act. One writer, pretending to be Partridge, wrote an indignant reply, complaining that he could not persuade anyone that he was still alive. The undertaker mistook me for my brother, "Partridge" complained. When I tried to convince him otherwise, he simply said that I was out of my mind with grief and promised to come back in the morning. The sexton came round to inquire about the funeral sermon. "Why Sirrah, says I, you know me well enough; you know I am not dead, and how dare you affront me after this Manner? Alack-a-day, Sir, replies the Fellow, why it is in Print, and the whole Town knows you are dead." Another person upbraided him for standing and "frightening Folks at your Window, when you should have been in your Coffin this three Hours." Meanwhile, his wife was "almost run distracted with being called Widow *Partrige.*" "Now how can any Man of common sense," Partridge supposedly asked, "think it consistent with the Honour of my Profession, and not much beneath the Dignity of a Philosopher, to stand bawling before his own Door — Alive! Alive! Ho! The famous Dr. *Partrige!* No Counterfeit, but all alive!"

The real John Partridge did not see the funny side. Bickerstaff, he wrote, was "an *Impudent Lying Fellow.* But his Prediction did not prove true: What will he say to excuse that?" Swift, though, got in the last word. After lamenting that Partridge was demeaning the "Republick of Letters" with such intemperate language and apologizing to his readers for predicting that Partridge would die at eleven when he "actually" died at seven o'clock, Bickerstaff set out to prove that his prophecy had indeed come true. Virtually all the people who read Partridge's latest almanac, Bickerstaff wrote, "would lift up their Eyes, and cry out, betwixt Rage and Laughter, *They were sure no Man* alive *ever writ such damned Stuff as this.*" "But now," he concluded, "if an *uninformed* Carcass walks still about, and is pleased to call itself *Partrige;* Mr. *Bickerstaff* does not think himself any way answerable for that."[34]

• • •

Swift's satire reflected and reinforced a more general intellectual repudiation of astrology. By the end of the seventeenth century the scientific revolution had eroded the underlying assumptions of the astrological system. The Earth was just another planet revolving around the Sun, the stars had no discernible purpose, and the connection between heavenly bodies and earthly events seemed more a matter of faith and hope than reason and logic.

Beyond that, science appeared to offer a new and more effective means of control over the environment. By challenging received wisdom, emphasizing empirical reasoning, and disseminating "useful knowledge," the new scientists of the seventeenth and eighteenth centuries believed that nature could be harnessed for the general good and that humankind would at last be able to control its own destiny. The application of scientific methods to agricultural production pointed towards liberation from the tyranny of the harvest cycle. Similarly, medical advances promised to reduce the degree of human pain, suffering, and disease. And with the possibility of control, the social functions of folklore became less pressing. Science was replacing magic.

This transition was not accomplished quickly or easily, nor was it ever complete. When itinerant eighteenth-century Newtonian lecturers such as Benjamin Martin toured England to popularize the new science, they frequently encountered a wall of hostility. "There are many places," commented Martin in 1746, "so bar-

barously ignorant, that they have taken me for a magician; yea, some have threaten'd my life, for raising storms and hurricanes."[35] This hostility was not quite as superstitious as it seems. Although the methods of magicians and scientists were obviously antithetical and mutually exclusive, their ultimate goals were similar.

The cunning folk, squeezed between religious opposition and scientific disdain, eventually disappeared from rural villages, which were themselves being transformed beyond recognition. Witchcraft was increasingly dismissed by secular and religious authorities as the product of popular credulity and ignorance. During the eighteenth century the kind of events that had triggered the Salem witch trials were more likely to culminate in religious revivalism. The initial behaviour may have been the same, but the interpretation placed upon it by adult community leaders had become very different.

Meanwhile, the various rituals associated with appeasing evil spirits and protecting crops and livestock either faded out or lost their original significance: the outward forms may have continued, but the inner magic withered away. The almanacs that had been so popular in early modern times persisted well into the eighteenth and nineteenth centuries, and sometimes became vehicles for radical political views. By the twentieth century, though, they had lost their central place in popular culture. Astrology continues to attract adherents, and horoscopes remain regular features of our daily newspapers. But, Nancy Reagan notwithstanding, our political and social leaders do not generally consult astrological charts before deciding whether to embark on a particular course of action.

And yet, for all that, the world of folklore, ritual, and magic still permeates the present. This approach to the future cannot simply be consigned to the past. Fortune tellers, palmists, diviners, New Age witches and healers, tarot card readers, numerologists, and astrologers are with us still and show no signs of giving up the ghost. The cunning folk, it seems, are making a comeback. In part, this revival can be seen as a reaction against the hubris of scientific rationalism and the formal structures of organized religion. But it also reflects the inescapable and sometimes intolerable uncertainties of the human condition. No matter how much influence we may exert over our environment, we can never control it completely. There can be no guarantees about the future. And as long as this is the case, fortune tellers and folk rituals are likely to flourish.

The last word, in this respect, goes to Nick Hornby, who in his book *Fever Pitch* describes how he began using rituals during the 1970s to help his soccer team, Cambridge United, win its matches. On the way to a game, one of his friends bought a sugar mouse, bit its head off, and accidentally dropped it in the road, where it was immediately run over by a car. That afternoon, against all expectations, Cambridge United won the match. And so, before every home game, Hornby and his friends would buy sugar mice, bite off their heads, and throw them under the wheels of passing cars. It worked: Cambridge United went undefeated at home for months. Hornby also supported Arsenal and, to help that team win, he would follow other rituals, such as entering the ground through the same turnstile or wearing lucky socks for the game:

Nothing (apart from the sugar mice) has ever been any good. But what else can we do when we're so *weak*? We invest hours each day, months each year, years each lifetime in something over which we have no control; is it any wonder then, that we are reduced to creating ingenious but bizarre liturgies designed to give us the illusion that we are powerful after all, just as every other primitive community has done when faced with a deep and apparently impenetrable mystery?[36]

·4·

REVOLUTION AND REVELATION

AT THE BEGINNING OF 1792 Thomas Paine sat down at his desk, gazed through his window, and composed the conclusion to the second part of his *Rights of Man,* the book that would shake the traditional world to its core and become a political bible for republicans and democrats throughout the Atlantic world. One of the so-called common people, who had been a corset maker, grocer, and excise officer before exploding onto the political scene as the author of *Common Sense,* the best-selling revolutionary pamphlet in colonial America, Paine wrote in a style that was incisive, clear, often humorous, and sometimes lyrical. "I had some turn, and I believe some talent, for poetry," he once remarked; "but this I rather repressed than encouraged, as leading too much into the field of imagination."[1] Now, as the goose-quilled pen moved across the page, he let the imagination and the poetry take over, with results that were memorable and moving:

> It is now towards the middle of February. Were I to take a turn into the country, the trees would present a leafless winterly appearance. As people are apt to pluck twigs as they walk along, I perhaps might do the same, and by chance might

observe, that a *single bud* on that twig had begun to swell. I should reason very unnaturally, or rather not reason at all, to suppose *this* was the *only* bud in England which had this appearance. Instead of deciding thus, I should instantly conclude, that the same appearance was beginning, or about to begin, everywhere; and though the vegetable sleep will continue longer on some trees and plants than on others, and though some of them may not *blossom* for two or three years, all will be in leaf in the summer, except those which are *rotten.* What pace the political summer may keep with the natural, no human foresight can determine. It is, however, not difficult to perceive that the spring is begun.[2]

The coming of a new world order, based on the principles of liberty, equality, and fraternity, would be as normal, natural, and inevitable as the change of seasons. It was, Paine declared, "an age of revolutions, in which every thing may be looked for."[3]

Such optimism is perfectly intelligible in the context of the time. It really did seem that the days of hereditary rule, aristocratic power, economic oppression, and religious establishments were numbered and that things would never be the same again. The American Revolution had pointed the way: "We have it in our power to begin the world over again," Paine had written in *Common Sense,* telling his readers what they already knew in their bones. "The birthday of a new world is at hand, and a race of men, perhaps as numerous as all Europe contains, are to receive their portion of freedom from the events of a few months."[4]

And then, shortly afterwards, the French Revolution shattered the *ancien régime* in the heart of continental Europe. Against the background of domestic turmoil, external attack, and increasing terror, France lurched leftwards from the constitutional monarchy of 1789 to the revolutionary republic of 1792. The political, social, and moral order would be rebuilt from the ground up.

Time itself was to be transformed: according to the new calendar it was no longer 1792 but Year I of the republic. And the French revolutionaries wanted to export their revolution to the rest of the world. Even before the declaration of the republic, they had proclaimed their intention to launch a "universal crusade for liberty."[5]

Taken together, events in America and France revolutionized the very concept of revolution itself. Originally the word denoted a circular movement, as in the revolution of a planet around the Sun. When applied to politics, it had meant turning back to the right starting point. Revolution, in this sense, was synonymous with restoration. By the late eighteenth century, though, this definition had become obsolete. "What were formerly called revolutions," wrote Paine, "were little more than a change of persons, or an alteration of local circumstances. They rose and fell like things of course ... But what we now see in the world, from the revolutions of America and France, is a renovation of the natural order of things, a system of principles as universal as truth and the existence of man, and combining moral with political happiness and national prosperity."[6]

The change in meaning signified a radically new way of looking at the political future. During the century before the American and French revolutions, cyclical theories of social and political change had prevailed. The body politic was frequently compared to the human body, as it proceeded through the stages of infancy, youth, maturity, and old age. If this were the case, then all societies must eventually deteriorate and die. Such a view was paralleled by historical theories that traced social development through the four stages of hunting, pasture, agriculture, and commerce. With commerce, it was believed, came luxury, vice, corruption, and selfishness. This moral decline would produce political degeneration and culminate in social collapse. Behind these attitudes lay a dark and fearful view of the future.

All these traditions were challenged by political radicals like

Thomas Paine and his apostles, who wanted to make a clean break with the past, replace cyclical theories with a linear approach to social and political change, and inaugurate a future of unlimited progress. "Are we forever to walk like beasts of prey, over the fields which [our] ancestors stained with blood?" asked Irish democrats in 1791. "In looking back, we see nothing but savage force, savage policy ... But we gladly look forward to brighter prospects; to a people united in the fellowship of freedom; to a parliament the express image of the people; to a prosperity established on civil, political, and religious liberty."[7] Once the political system had been democratized, everything would be easy: humankind could look forward to a future of universal peace and prosperity, friendship, and cooperation, in a broadly egalitarian society of small property owners, where productive and virtuous citizens would come into their own. Political revolution would usher in a kind of secular millennium.

At first glance, this secular millennium had little in common with its religious counterpart. Many democratic revolutionaries were deists who rejected all forms of "revealed religion"; the French Revolution was fiercely anti-Catholic; and modern notions of progress emphasized the power of human reason rather than divine intervention. Yet traditional religious forms of thought proved remarkably persistent and continued to resonate at both the subconscious and conscious levels. Paine in 1792 was almost certainly not a Christian, but his imagery of the "political summer" was strikingly similar to the words of Jesus when his apostles asked him about the Second Coming: "Now learn a parable of the fig tree; When his branch is yet tender, and putteth forth leaves, ye know that summer is nigh: so likewise ye, when ye shall see all these things, know that it is near, even at the doors."[8] Similarly, the French revolutionaries who rejected Christianity nevertheless drew on its methods as they attempted to proselytize their cause and create a new republican man for the republican future.[9]

But it was not only a question of Christian forms being filled with secular content. Many people who lived through the revolutionary period were convinced that events in America and France were charged with cosmic significance, that the biblical prophecies were finally coming true, and that the end of the world was at hand. From this perspective, the subjective beliefs of secular revolutionaries were less significant than their objective place in the Divine Plan. Democrats who were infidels and deists were actually following a script that had been written by God. Revolution had converged with revelation.

One of the best examples of this process comes from the American Revolution. In a Thanksgiving sermon delivered at Danbury, Connecticut, in November 1775, the Reverend Ebenezer Baldwin tried to make sense of the troubled times through which the colonies were passing. Seven months earlier American minutemen at Lexington and Concord had fought against British soldiers, firing the shot that was heard around the world. Britain and the colonies were in a state of undeclared war, but most colonists had not yet embraced the idea of independence. In the course of his attempts to reassure the colonists that they were right to resist British policies, Baldwin told his listeners that the colonies were destined to become "a great and mighty Empire; the largest the World ever saw, to be founded on such Principles of Liberty and Freedom, both civil and religious, as never before took place in the World; which shall be the principal Seat of that glorious Kingdom, which Christ shall erect upon Earth in the latter Days."[10]

The more Baldwin thought about it, the more it made sense. The population of the Thirteen Colonies, he estimated, was around three million, and was doubling every twenty-five years. Projecting these figures into the future, and allowing for a gradual reduction in the rate of growth, he predicted that the population of America would reach 192 million in 1975. By this time, he wrote, "the American Empire will probably be in its Glory." Unlike other empires, which had been built on conquest and despotism, America would be governed according to the principles of civil and religious liberty. Meanwhile, across the Atlantic, the kingdoms of Europe would be sinking under the "Weight of Tyranny, Corruption and Luxury." By the late twentieth century, it seemed, America would be the last remaining area of freedom in the world.

With this scenario in mind, Baldwin then turned his attention to the work of biblical scholars such as William Lowman, who had calculated from Daniel and Revelation that the millennium would begin on or about the year 2000. It seemed highly unlikely, to say the least, that Christ would want to return to vice-ridden Europe. On the contrary, the obvious choice for the site of the Second Coming would be the American Empire. "Since it is in the last Ages of the World that America is to enjoy this prosperous State, and as this is the Time, in which Christ's Kingdom is to be thus gloriously set up in the World," Baldwin concluded, "I cannot think it chimerical to suppose, America will largely share in the Happiness of this glorious Day, and that the present Scenes are remotely preparing the Way for it." In this way, a struggle for power between the American colonies and the British Empire became transformed into an event of transcendent significance.[11]

Nor was Baldwin's position isolated or exceptional. Patriotic sermons during and after the War of Independence constantly connected the American Revolution to the millennium and portrayed American patriots as God's chosen people. Secular variations on the theme insisted that the fate of humanity hinged on the outcome of the war with Britain, and viewed the American Revolution as an equally transcendent ideological conflict between democratic republicanism and hereditary power.

In both cases, religious and secular, this apocalyptic outlook had deep roots in the English Revolution of the seventeenth century. American ministers during the 1770s presented variations on a millenarian theme that their Puritan ancestors had played during the 1640s. And, as one American loyalist argued in 1776, Paine's revolutionary arguments echoed "the enthusiasm of *Fifth-monarchy* men, and their rudeness too." The Fifth Monarchy Men were among the most militant millenarians that the seventeenth-century English Revolution had produced.

If we are to understand the power of prophecy during the American and French revolutions, we need to go back to the strange world of Ranters, Muggletonians, and Fifth Monarchy Men that England's Puritan Revolution had summoned to the surface more than a century earlier.

• • •

The English Civil War that broke out in 1642, pitching the forces of Parliament against those of Charles I, was primarily a political rather than a religious conflict. But the breakdown in social order, together with the unprecedented nature of political change, took the lid off popular apocalyptic traditions and gave them a greater sense of immediacy and urgency.

Despite the horrors of early sixteenth-century Munster, millenarian ideas had continued to circulate throughout Europe and cropped up in the most unlikely places. In 1556, for example, there had been reports from Germany that a message – in German, of course – announcing the imminent end of the world had been seen in the sky. Or again, some three decades later, fishermen in the North Sea caught two herrings that had the word *Vici* inscribed on their backs. The fish were duly taken to the king of Denmark, whose advisers concluded that the herrings were really the two Last Witnesses of the Book of Revelation: "And I will give power unto my two witnesses, and they shall prophesy a thousand two hundred and threescore days, clothed in sackcloth."

God, it appeared, was literally writing on Nature.[12]

In sixteenth-century England, popular prophets were commonplace. Among them was London's William Hacket, who claimed to be the Messiah, attracted "a great multitude of lads and young persons of the meaner sort," and prophesied that England would be struck by plagues unless the people changed their ways. He was not a man to be crossed: he not only bit off the nose of one of his enemies but ate it as well. This behaviour marked a significant departure from the original Christ's injunction to turn the other cheek.

Hacket came to the attention of the authorities in the summer of 1591, when he told a large crowd of followers that Queen Elizabeth was not the true monarch and called for revolution. He was immediately arrested, tried for treason, and sentenced to death. Right up to the last moment, Hacket believed that God would step in with a miracle and allow him to escape. Probably remembering Hacket's penchant for noses, however, God decided to let things run their course.[13]

Such prophesying cut right across class lines. While Hacket preached in Cheapside to the "lower orders," the university-educated minister Ralph Durden told his congregation that the English monarchy represented Antichrist and that he himself had been chosen by God to rule over the world for a thousand years. His true identity, he said, had been revealed by the birthmark on his thigh, which supposedly matched the description of the messianic king in the Book of Revelation: "And he hath on his vesture and on his thigh a name written, KING OF KINGS, AND LORD OF LORDS." The authorities found neither the logic nor the message compelling and threw him in jail.[14]

The views of Hacket and Durden – and there were many others like them – illustrate the way in which revolutionary sentiments could be expressed through the medium of millenarianism. As the conflict between king and Parliament intensified during the 1620s and 1630s, radical opposition was frequently articulated in apocalyptic language. A classic case was that of Lady Eleanor Davis, who in 1625 heard a "Voice from Heaven" telling her that the world would end in 1644. Subsequent readings of the Book of Daniel convinced her that Charles I was destined to be overthrown. At the time, she was declared insane and thrown in Bedlam. After her release she went on a rampage at Lichfield Cathedral and declared herself Primate of All England. Her enemies made an anagram of her name: "Dame Eleanor Davis" became "never so mad a ladie." But her prophecies acquired retrospective validation after the Civil War began in 1642 and Charles I was executed seven years later. The minor detail about the world ending in 1644 was quietly overlooked.[15]

By re-evaluating Eleanor Davis' prophecies in the light of later events, her admirers were following a familiar path. Just as historians implicitly assume the inevitability of an event and then reason backwards to identify its causes, prophecy believers assume that events in their own time have been preordained and reinterpret earlier predictions in the light of later experiences. In both cases the past is seen through the prism of the present, the role of chance and contingency in the historical process is downplayed, and the possibility that things could have been different is either foreclosed or dismissed as idle speculation.

During periods of great turmoil, such as war or revolution, this tendency is particularly strong. Despite their very different approaches to the past, the historian and the prophecy believer share a common need to show how the present fits into the broader scheme of things and to impose a sense of order on apparently random events. Eleanor Davis may have been mad, but her prophecies made sense to many people who lived through the Civil War and needed to convince themselves that the trauma of their times was connected to a higher purpose.

This was, in fact, a common response to revolutionary crises.

In seventeenth-century England and in the later Age of Revolution, it is possible to detect recurring patterns of prophecy. First, during the early revolutionary stages, retrospective prophecies play a key role, as people seek both explanation and validation for radical and apparently unprecedented change. Second, the revolutionary process itself generates its own prophecies, which provide the vital function of boosting morale, for without hope or the expectation of success the revolutionary movement cannot be sustained. And third, ultra-radical sects emerge with the explicit aim of fulfilling the prophecies and making the millennium happen.

During the English Civil War, one of the best examples of the retrospective prophecy was George Wither's epic poem of 1628, *Britain's Remembrancer.* No one paid much attention to it until the early 1640s, when the English Revolution was gathering momentum. It would be more accurate to say that the English Civil War made Wither's reputation than that Wither actually prophesied the Civil War. In his poem, Wither had written that Britain was sinking fast in godlessness, factionalism, corruption, and profanity. Unless there was repentance, he argued, things were going to get very, very nasty. God would turn the rivers into "streames of ever-burning Pitch" and make the fields barren; the villages would be deserted and the cities would turn into "heaps of rubbish"; the people would be scourged by scorpions and serpents; sweet melodies would be replaced by "hideous cries, and howlinges of despair"; the women would lose their beauty and become deformed – and so the poem continued, for hundreds upon hundreds of lines.

In the course of these prophecies, Wither listed ten signs of God's growing impatience: they served as warning lights, which would be ignored only at great peril. Among these signs it was the last two that appeared particularly relevant to the Civil War years. The ninth sign was the growth of religious disunity, which would tear the country apart. And the tenth was that the people would become enslaved by their king:

> The last black *signe* that here I will repeat,
> (Which doth to kingdomes desolation threat)
> Is when the hand of God Almighty brings
> The people, into bondage, to their Kings.

In 1628 Wither had held out the hope that God's vengeance could be avoided if the people would only change their ways. Now, in the early 1640s, it seemed clear that their ways had stayed the same and the bitter harvest was coming in.[16]

As the revolutionary crisis intensified, new prophecies proliferated with remarkable rapidity – bringing in the second stage in the pattern of predictions. Of the 112 pro-Parliament ministers who published works between 1640 and 1653, almost 70 per cent were millenarians. They included people like Nathaniel Homes, who told the House of Commons in 1641 that they were the "promised people" who stood as "leaders and examples to the Christian world to pull down that part of Antichrist that is yet standing." The following year Stephen Marshall delivered another sermon to the House of Commons in which he praised the "poor and offscouring of the world," argued that the rich were all too often the agents of Antichrist, and eagerly anticipated violence: "If this work be to avenge God's church against Babylon, he is a blessed man that takes and dashes the little ones against the stones."[17]

Virtually all good English Protestants agreed that "*Rome* is the Seat of *Antichrist*." The more radical figures, though, believed that the Church of England was tainted with Romanism, and thus part of Antichrist's dominion. "Wee have need of zeale," wrote the Presbyterian Thomas Brightman in 1644, "to the intent wee may attaine to a full reformation. Wee hang as yet by Geometry, as it were, between heaven and hell; the contagious steaming of the Romish soggie lake doth in a deadly manner annoy us." But the days of Antichrist would soon be over. "For now is the last act begun of a most long and dolefull Tragedy, which shall wholly over-flow with scourges, slaughters, destructions; but after this Theater is once removed, there shall come in room of it a most delightfull spectacle of perpetuall peace, joyned with abundance of all good things." The Presbyterians, Brightman believed, were in the vanguard of this march towards the millennium. Their struggle against Charles I and the Church of England was paving the way for the Second Coming, which he expected to occur in 1686.[18]

Such messages were part of a wider popular apocalyptic mood. During the 1640s we find a steady stream of labourers who claimed to be the Son of God, ready to usher in the millennium. They competed for attention with a clutch of women who claimed to have conceived through the Holy Ghost and said they were about to give birth to the returned Messiah. "Within these twelve years," wrote one millenarian in 1653, "there have been ... many in this land ... calling themselves Christs and prophets and Virgin-Maries and such like."[19]

Millenarian views were particularly powerful within the parliamentary army, where otherwise scattered and isolated apocalyptic attitudes came together in concentrated form. When the royalist Edward Symmons visited a group of imprisoned parliamentary soldiers in 1644, they left him in no doubt about their motivation. We "took up arms against Antichrist and popery," they told him; "for 'tis prophesied in the *Revelation,* that the Whore of Babylon shall be destroyed with fire and sword, and what do you know, but this is the time of her ruin, and that we are the men that must help to pull her down?"[20]

With these men we come to the third stage in the prophetic trajectory – the emergence of ultra-radical millenarian sects whose mission was to put prophecy into practice. Among these sects were the Ranters, who stepped right out of the Free Spirit tradition of the Middle Ages. Believing that they had become one with God, they wanted to bring about nothing less than a total revolution that would destroy the bishops, the aristocracy, and the king. In its place, they would create a very different and most unusual kind of world.

One such figure, Abiezer Coppe, has left us with a vivid picture of his spiritual conversion. He had been rejected by everyone, he wrote: "the wife of my bosome loathed me, mine old name was rotted, perished; and I was utterly plagued, consumed, damned, rammed, and sunke into nothing." Then, two terrible thunderclaps, followed by a blinding light, announced the presence of the Lord, who told him that he would drink of a bitter cup and then receive eternal glory. He was immediately flung into "the belly of hell," with the "very blacknesse of darknesse." Through all this terror, though, he carried with him "a little spark of transcendent, transplendent, unspeakable glory."

As he resurfaced, Coppe saw visions, heard voices, and became one with the spirit. The visions and voices told him there would be blood on the hypocritical heart and vengeance throughout the world. God was the Ultimate Leveller, who would cut down the rich, the mighty, and the proud, and destroy the "fat parsons, Vicars, Lecturers &c" who had been responsible for so much misery in the world. As Coppe told his story, his voice became indistinguishable from that of God: "I will plague your Honour, Pompe, Greatnesse, Superfluity, and confound it into parity, equality, community," he wrote; "that the neck of horrid pride, murder, malice, and tyranny, &c. may be chopt off at one blow. And that my selfe, the Eternall God, who am Universall Love, may fill the Earth with universall love, universall peace, and perfect freedome."

The service of God, Coppe wrote, consisted not only in "perfect freedome," but also "pure Libertinisme." The spiritual elite, who were angels in the form of men, were no longer bound by human laws and conventions. The Ranters preached and practised free love and developed something of an obsession with swearing and cursing. To demonstrate their spiritual liberation, they would let streams of obscenity flow from their mouths. When the godly swore, it was a sign that they had transcended human conventions. But when the ungodly and unregenerate swore, it was a totally different matter: the Lord would throw them into Hell and laugh at their destruction. "Well! one hint more; there's swearing ignorantly, i'th darke, vainly, and there's swearing i'th light, gloriously."[21]

So, the millennium would be full of spiritualized human beings living in peace, harmony, equality, love, and freedom, combining constant fornication with non-stop swearing and laughing loudly at the damned. But the damned proved notoriously difficult to define: the revolutionary anarchical outlook of the Ranters was conducive to intense factionalism. In this apocalyptic atmosphere, small-scale personal conflicts rapidly assumed cosmic proportions.

Thus a charismatic Ranter like John Robins attracted a devoted following in the 1640s, only to be denounced by a splinter group in 1651 as "the last great Antichrist or Man of Sin." The dissidents, Ludovic Muggleton and John Reeve, had received messages from God about Robins' secret identity. The following year God informed Muggleton and Reeve that they were the two Last Witnesses who would herald the Second Coming. (This was at least slightly more plausible than the earlier view in Denmark that the last witnesses were actually a couple of herrings.) The Muggletonians, as they became known, believed that they were the only true prophets to appear after Christ. From the year 300 to the year 1651, when God had spoken to them, there had been no true faith in the world. But the Age of Apostasy was over and the "approaching day of Christ's coming to judgment" was at hand.

To prepare for the great day the Muggletonians spent most of their time heartily cursing their religious rivals, who heartily cursed them back. "To the bottomless pit are you sentenced, from whence you came," the Quaker William Penn told Muggleton, "and where the endless worm shall gnaw and torture your imaginary soul to eternity." For some reason, God decided not to send his Son back to this atmosphere of Christian love and charity, and the Second Coming was delayed indefinitely. But the Muggletonians lived on and continued to attract supporters for another three hundred years. In late eighteenth-century London they were part of the cultural world that William Blake inhabited. Muggleton's more general notion that the Beast was "the spirit or seed of reason" resonated with Blake's own outlook.[22]

Among the myriad apocalyptic sects that proliferated during the English Revolution, by far the most significant were the Fifth Monarchy Men, who emerged in 1651. The context is crucial: two years earlier, millenarian expectations had reached a new pitch of intensity with the execution of Charles I and the establishment of a republic. Religious radicals had eagerly anticipated a Puritan social revolution that would prepare the way for the Second Coming. But it soon became apparent that neither Parliament nor Oliver Cromwell, the leading republican in the country, was prepared to move in this direction. For the radicals, the Great Hope was replaced by a growing sense of disillusionment, frustration, and anger.

Under these circumstances, many militant Puritans came to the conclusion that Cromwell was Antichrist and that the Beast from Revelation, with its mysterious mark of 666, had taken over the country. Gerrard Winstanley, the leader of the proto-communist Diggers, noted with dismay that the lettering of parliamentary coins added up to the dreaded 666. George Foster, who had strong Ranter sympathies, predicted that Parliament would fall in November 1650, exactly 666 days after the execution of Charles

I.[23] But Parliament did not fall. Unless drastic action was taken, England would be enslaved by the forces of darkness. And this is where the Fifth Monarchists entered the scene.

They took their name from the Book of Daniel, with its strange dream of four kingdoms that would wreak increasing havoc on the Earth, before being superseded by Christ's everlasting dominion. "The saints of the most High shall take the kingdom," Daniel was told, "and possess the kingdom for ever, even for ever and ever."[24] Traditionally, the four kingdoms had been associated with the Babylonian, Assyrian, Greek, and Roman empires, and the candidates for the fifth kingdom had ranged from the papacy to the king of Spain. But in the 1650s a group of millenarian revolutionaries, who followed such visionaries and prophets as Anna Trapnel and John Tillinghast, came to the conclusion that they were the saintly elite who were destined to possess the fifth and final monarchy.

There was no doubt they meant business. Based in London, with significant pockets of support in East Anglia and North Wales, the Fifth Monarchists attracted around ten thousand adherents, many of whom were prepared to use violence to destroy the wicked and to establish the Kingdom of Heaven on Earth. England, they believed, had been elected by God to save the world. The Fifth Monarchists, in turn, had been elected to lead England.

The entire political, social, economic, and moral order was to be turned upside down. There would be no king or aristocracy, Parliament would be abolished, and the Fifth Monarchists themselves would reign in the name of Christ. The unregenerate were to be dispossessed, the condition of the poor would be improved, and a tight moral code would be imposed. Crimes such as adultery, blasphemy, and the profanation of the Sabbath would be punishable by death, and the new order would be characterized by purity, sobriety, plain clothes, and seriousness of purpose. Some of the more militant members wanted to abolish laughter. There were strong echoes here of the Munster Anabaptists of 1534–35; indeed, a minority of Fifth Monarchists planned to replicate their program. Once England had been purified, the Fifth Monarchists intended to launch an international crusade that would destroy the forces of Antichrist – and, given their narrow definition of the righteous, that meant almost everyone else in the world.[25]

Within England, much of their animus was directed against Cromwell, who was seen as the betrayer of the revolution. Anna Trapnel prophesied that the Lord would "batter" Cromwell, and the Fifth Monarchists believed they were destined to take over the country in 1656. Tillinghast had arrived at this date from his reading of Daniel, which spoke of 1290 days of desolation, and of Revelation, which predicted that the end times would begin after 1260 days. As we have seen, a day was generally taken to symbolize a year. If the correct starting point could be ascertained, it would be a relatively simple matter to determine the date of the millennium. In Tillinghast's view the 1290 days in Daniel should be counted from the destruction of the Temple at Jerusalem in 366, while the 1260 days in Revelation began in 396, when the popes began to assume political power. Both lines of addition pointed directly to 1656.[26]

That was the year, then, in which the Fifth Monarchists were supposed to establish the millennium. According to Tillinghast, the rule of the saints would last forty-five years, during which time perfection would be achieved. This phase would pave the way for the Second Coming, when Christ would take over from the Fifth Monarchists and rule in person. Again, the chronology was derived from Daniel, who had said that those who waited 1335 days would be blessed. Taking the destruction of the Temple in 366 as the baseline, this reckoning meant that Christ would return in 1701.

Unfortunately for Tillinghast, reality refused to correspond to his computations. The revolution failed to materialize in 1656, and the Fifth Monarchists were left scrambling for explanations and alternatives. Tillinghast's starting points were manifestly wrong and an entirely new framework was required. Had not Revelation said that the Beast would rule for forty-two months? Could there be any doubt that Cromwell himself was the Beast? And did he not become the ruler of England in December 1653? Counting forty-two months forward, it seemed that Cromwell was going to get clobbered in June 1657, which became the next anticipated date of the millennium.

Once again, nothing happened. And when the month passed without incident, attention became increasingly focused on 1666, the year that contained the number of the Beast. For a few brief moments it seemed that the prophecy was finally coming true: the Great Plague, followed by the Great Fire of London, seemed to presage the apocalypse. But the plague did not distinguish between the Fifth Monarchists and the unregenerate, and the fire was not the prelude to a universal conflagration. The revised prophecies turned out to be as wrong as Tillinghast's original one.

By this time the Fifth Monarchists had been effectively broken as a political movement. Their ultra-radicalism, together with memories of Munster and fears of social instability, contributed to a conservative backlash that culminated in the restoration of the Stuart monarchy and the return of Charles II in 1660. Ironically, the millenarianism of the Fifth Monarchists had helped to create a future that contradicted everything for which they stood. And within the general anti-republican reaction, there was a deepening distrust of apocalyptic thought in general – a development that was reinforced by the rationalist values associated with the scientific revolution. Politically and intellectually, millenarianism was becoming marginalized in England.

It did not, however, die out. During the seventeenth century Antichrist moved across the Atlantic and the apocalypse became Americanized.

• • •

In colonial America the millenarian traditions that had been transmitted from England were less intense, but more widespread. The lack of a powerful church-and-state establishment reduced the potential for religious conflict, while the relatively open political and social environment enabled millenarian ideas to enter the mainstream. Before the mid-eighteenth century American millenarianism was conceived purely in religious and spiritualized terms. The religious leaders in New England believed they were on an "errand into the wilderness," where they would establish communal Christian utopias and become a model for the rest of the world. From here, it was a short step to the position that Americans were on a mission for the millennium. Before long, some of the leading ministers in Massachusetts began to speculate that the Second Coming might take place in the New World, and more particularly in New England.

During the 1750s, with the strategic and military struggle between the American colonies and New France for control of the continent, this millenarianism became increasingly politicized. Combining an early form of American imperialism with a strong sense of religious destiny, Calvinists in New England looked to a future in which God "extends his empire from the *Eastern* to the *Western* Sea, and from the River of Canada to the Ends of *America*." But the French were expanding westwards from their base in Canada, and God's Chosen People were being encircled by the forces of Antichrist. Unless "the *Devil,* the *Pope,* and the *French King*" were defeated, the millennium would be delayed indefinitely. The future of the entire world, from this perspective, depended on what happened in North America. Victory in the

French and Indian War was an essential prerequisite for the establishment of Christ's Kingdom on earth.[27]

And when victory came, the entire psychology of the colonial
situation changed. Previously, the American colonists had been
dependent on Britain for protection against their Catholic enemies. Now, with the French out of the picture, the ties with the
mother country became much looser. In these conditions,
Britain's subsequent attempts to tighten its control of the
American colonies generated considerable resentment and resistance, which found expression in an increasingly radical language
of civil and religious liberty.

Within the growing list of colonial grievances, the Quebec Act
of 1774 figured prominently. By recognizing the Catholic Church
in Quebec, and extending the boundaries of the newly conquered
colony into the American west, Britain appeared to be aligning
itself with Antichrist and projecting papist power into the heart of
the continent. In response, radical colonists fused secular arguments of liberty with religious millenarianism as they pushed for
their own independent Empire of Liberty that would eventually
tower over the world.

Central to this process was a radical reinterpretation of the
Book of Revelation, which was now seen to have foretold the
American Revolution. We move here into the familiar territory of
the retrospective prophecy. The key passage concerned the mysterious "woman clothed with the sun" who had been persecuted by
a "great red dragon" and who "fled into the wilderness, where she
hath a place prepared of God." "And to the woman were given
two wings of a great eagle," the passage continued, "that she
might fly into the wilderness." The dragon, in contrast, was
associated with a beast with "the mouth of a lion."[28] Suddenly,
everything made sense: the dragon represented Britain, whose
emblem was a lion; the woman was the true church; and the
wilderness could only be America, the land of the eagle.

Among the many variations on this theme, one of the most striking was a sermon delivered by Samuel Sherwood in New York in January 1776 – the same time that Thomas Paine's *Common Sense* hit the bookstores. Connecting British policy with biblical prophecy, Sherwood spoke of "the flood of the dragon that has been poured forth to the northward, in the Quebec bill, for the establishment of popery, and other engines and instruments that have been set to work, to bring the savages down upon us, to our utter destruction." Antichrist, as slippery as ever, was now working through Britain and its Native American allies to crush the true church. Against him, though, stood America's patriotic politicians and soldiers, "whom God in his providence," declared Sherwood, "has raised up to be his glorious instruments, to fulfil scripture-prophecies, in favour of his church, and American liberty, to the confusion of all her enemies."[29]

If the American Revolution was fulfilling the prophecies, there could be no doubt about its outcome. Despite the fact that thirteen loosely knit colonies were taking on the mightiest empire in the world, the patriots must win in the end. Almost imperceptibly the retrospective prophecy, with its emphasis on explaining and justifying American resistance, slid into the revolutionary-generated prophecy, with its essentially morale-boosting function. "The time is coming and hastening on, when Babylon the great shall fall to rise no more," Sherwood insisted; "when all wicked tyrants and oppressors shall be destroyed for ever. These violent attacks upon the woman in the wilderness, may possibly be some of the last efforts, and dying struggles of the man of sin. These commotions and convulsions in the British empire, may be leading to the fulfilment of such prophecies as relate to his downfall and overthrow, and to the future glory and prosperity of Christ's church."[30] This argument takes us into Ebenezer Baldwin's world: the American Revolution was preparing the way for the millennium and therefore could not fail.

Because millenarianism was in the mainstream, and because the American Revolution was driven more by opposition to Britain than by internal social tensions, we do not find the emergence of ultra-radical sects analogous to the Ranters or the Fifth Monarchists. Instead, those Americans who were motivated by millenarianism were diffused throughout the resistance and revolutionary movements. They ranged from the Philadelphia Presbyterians who in 1765 called for "No King but King Jesus" to a radical Quaker like Christopher Marshall, who associated Britain with the "prince of the power of darkness" and believed it would not be long before "the kingdoms of this world are become the kingdoms of our Lord, and of his Christ."[31]

Most Americans who thought in these terms believed that Christ would return only after the true church had achieved earthly perfection. This belief implied an optimistic vision of progress, in which the Second Coming would cap the achievements of the American people themselves. But others, such as the religious revivalists of the New Light Stir that swept through rural New England during the War of Independence, took a very different position. In their view, the whole notion of earthly perfection was illusory. Only after the Second Coming would it be possible to establish a truly virtuous, just, and peaceful society on Earth.

In contrast to ministers like Baldwin and Sherwood, who projected the Second Coming into the moderately distant future, the revivalists believed that it was imminent. The War of Independence portended the end of the world, they believed: their own revival was proof of that. And then, on May 19, 1780, came the most ominous sign of all. New York and New England were suddenly plunged into darkness, amid reports of distant thunder and of a ball of fire hurtling over the water. At the best of times, such phenomena would have produced considerable anxiety; in the context of the war, the revival, and heightened millenarian expectations, the Dark Day of 1780 occasioned something close to panic. The Day of Judgment was at hand. There had been nothing like it since the "miraculous eclipse" during the crucifixion of Christ, and people prepared to meet their Maker. As the subsequent days passed quietly, the sense of apocalyptic expectation gradually faded. Nevertheless, it remained a powerful latent force in American society, one that could easily be reactivated under circumstances of stress.[32]

With the victory of the United States over Britain it seemed that the prophecies were indeed being fulfilled – that the woman had overcome the dragon. The sense that these were no ordinary times was intensified by the French Revolution, which ignited an explosion of millenarian literature in America. Earlier prophetic tracts, such as the *Prophecies of the Rev. Christopher Love,* were republished and revised to meet the new mood. Attributed to an English Presbyterian minister who had been executed by Cromwell, the first American edition of Love's prophecies had appeared in 1759 and predicted the beginning of the millennium in 1762. Now, in 1794, the chronology was updated: the prophecies remained the same, but the dates were changed. Thus the original American edition had predicted "a great Earthquake over all the World, in 1762. God will be universally known in all in general, and a Reformation and Peace forever, when People shall learn War no more. Happy is the Man that liveth to see this Day." The 1794 edition had almost identical wording, but simply changed the date of the "great Earthquake" to 1805.[33]

During the 1790s American ministers watched events in France with a mixture of fascination and horror. From one perspective, the French Revolution could be seen as the victory of civil and religious liberty over the tyranny of monarchical and papal power, and the anti-Catholic character of the revolution deeply impressed American Protestants who were anticipating the imminent fall of the Roman Antichrist. Yet the revolution was also characterized by infidelity and terror, neither of which could be condoned by American ministers. From this perspective, the French Republic could be associated with the "man of sin" or the "little horn" in Daniel that symbolized the destructive power of evil. By the end of the decade, this was the view that prevailed.[34]

But on one thing, most Americans could agree: whatever the nature of events in France, there could be no doubt that God had marked out the United States for his special purpose. The French Revolution, wrote David Austin, may have been God's instrument for "sapping the foundation of this antichristian structure" of European Catholicism, but hardly constituted a model for others to follow. On the contrary, it led straight to "the millennium of Hell!" America, in contrast, was God's true "millennial temple," the "national edifice from which is yet to beam forth, the light and glory of the world."[35] The central question, in fact, was not whether but when America would receive the Second Coming; the answers ranged from 1805 to 2000.

This view of America was particularly appealing to many of the radical immigrants who crossed the Atlantic to escape the tyranny of church and state at home. One such figure was Thomas Ledlie Birch, a democratic republican Irish Presbyterian minister who was exiled to the United States in 1798. Five years earlier, writing against the background of the French revolutionary war, Birch maintained that the Battle of Armageddon was already in progress and that the millennium would begin in 1848.[36]

Shortly after Birch arrived in the United States, his millenarianism became thoroughly Americanized. The gospel of liberty had been travelling progressively westwards, he wrote, towards the pristine purity of the American wilderness. It would find its final home, Birch was convinced, in the town of Washington, Pennsylvania. And why not? The town lay beyond the "worldly refinement and pride" of the seaboard cities, was named after the *"illustrious founder* (under God) of American liberty," and belonged to the state that was "most exemplary for its brother-hood." For the rest of their lives, and in the teeth of much mock-ery, Birch and his Irish followers insisted that this apparently obscure western town was destined to become the site of the Second Coming in 1848.

The belief that America was moving inexorably towards the millennium was paralleled by secular notions of progress. With their essentially anti-historical outlook, American Republicans embraced the "principle of hope" and looked forward to a future in which economic and territorial expansion would enable the "free and independent man" to flourish. The very act of imagin-ing the future in this way undermined reverential attitudes to the past. Rather than becoming mired in the manuscript-assumed authority of the dead, American Republicans would focus on universal rights, the present, and the future. "The boisterous and precipitate revolutions of Greece and Rome," said one radical, "vanish into nothing when compared to the revolution of America." Just as religious figures believed that America would usher in the millennium, secular politicians believed that America would guide the world into a democratic republican utopia. Whether construed in religious or secular terms, the American Republic was a "City upon a Hill," and its inhabitants would lead the world to the Promised Land.[37]

Still, more pessimistic cyclical views of the future had not been entirely banished from the political consciousness and continued to exert a powerful pull over many minds. As long as such views were projected back across the Atlantic to Britain, this negativity did not matter very much. In fact, the prospect of eventual British decline could appear quite satisfactory. In a short essay published in 1769, two Americans arrived in Britain in the year 1944. After their voyage of forty days, they made their way by horseback through "bad roads and miserable villages" to London. When they arrived, they could hardly believe what they saw. The streets

were largely deserted, the few remaining people were impoverished, and all its formerly famous buildings were in ruins. Where
the Houses of Parliament had once stood there was now a turnip
patch; Westminster Abbey had become a stable; the South Sea
House functioned as a public urinal. Not that there were many
people around to relieve themselves: most of the useful citizens,
such as artisans and mechanics, had left for the "American
empire." Commercial speculation had produced corruption, and
corruption had depraved the government. "These, with many
other acts of dissipation," remarked one of the Americans,
"intemperance, injustice, violence, ignorance, and despotism, all
introduced by a baneful favourite, are the true cause of your
present forlorn and wretched condition." Meanwhile, the
America of 1944 was enjoying independence, "imperial
grandeur," sobriety, justice, peace, knowledge, and liberty.[38]

So far, so good. America embraced unlimited linear progress,
while Britain became trapped in the Old World cycle of empire
and had "fallen to a similar decay and ruin with Balbec,
Persepolis, Palmira, Athens, and Rome."[39] But the United States
was not immune to such a critique itself: what was sauce for the
goose could be sauce for the gander. Thus, in 1793, one British
writer concluded that the American republican experiment was
doomed to failure: "As soon as America shall become a manufacturing country, and a land of cities," he wrote, "one of two events
must follow: either that the states must separate, and exhibit the
vices, and experience the miseries, of republics in such circumstances, or they must resort to a mixed government, in which a
monarchy, and a nobility, may consolidate and balance the political system."[40] The same attitudes were being voiced in Canada,
where Loyalist exiles consoled themselves with the prospect that
the United States must eventually self-destruct or return to the
imperial fold.

More surprising, perhaps, is the fact that some Americans

themselves retained nagging doubts about the future of their republic. Westward expansion could not last forever, and it was feared that once all the land had been occupied, the population would start crowding into cities. Commercial growth and large-scale manufacturing would undermine civic virtue and intensify class divisions. Under these circumstances, the ideal of a relatively egalitarian, harmonious, prosperous, and free society would become impossible to sustain. At the end of the day, the New World would replicate all the problems that were now besetting the Old. Having run out of space, the United States would eventually run out of time. Among the people who were occasionally haunted by this pessimistic long-term scenario was the fourth president of the United States, James Madison. In 1829 he predicted that the republic would have to grapple with these issues in "a century or a little more" – which put him right on track for the Wall Street Crash of 1929 and the Great Depression of the 1930s.[41]

As it turned out, the United States in the twentieth century fulfilled both the optimistic and the pessimistic predictions. The dominant ideology continued to emphasize progress, political liberty, equality of opportunity, faith in technology, and America's mission to enlighten and liberate the world. But the social realities of industrialization, urban unrest, and widening class divisions all bear a distinct resemblance to the fears expressed by Madison and others. The result has been a fundamental contradiction between the ideal and the real at the heart of the American polity.

• • •

Meanwhile, in late eighteenth-century Britain, the momentous events of the Age of Revolution reactivated millenarian traditions that had been sleeping since the Civil War. The air was full of apocalyptic expectations: the French Revolution, it was widely believed, heralded a decisive stage in the struggle against Antichrist. As Joseph Priestley observed, people were living through "great calamities, such as the world has never yet experienced," and desperately needed to make sense of what was happening.[42] "A serious application to the study of the prophecies, and an attentive observation of the signs of the times," wrote James Bicheno in 1793, "have produced in my mind the strongest persuasion, that the utter downfal [sic] of the papacy, the final overthrow of despotism, the restoration of the Jews, and the renovation of all things, are near at hand; and that every year will astonish us with new wonders." But without the guidance of prophecy, he concluded, "all seems confusion."[43]

In this atmosphere, the writings of earlier prophets were republished at popular prices and reinterpreted in the light of the French Revolution. Memories bubbled to the surface of Seth Darwin, the seventeenth-century Ranter who had once walked into a church "naked up to the waist" and disturbed the congregation with "alarming speeches," not to mention his alarming appearance. Among other things, he had predicted great turmoil in France "before the death of the next hundred years." Now, if somewhat belatedly, his prophecies appeared to be coming true.

A similar approach was taken to the sermons of Pierre Jurieu, the Huguenot minister who in 1685 had foretold the collapse of Catholicism in France. The awkward fact that he had expected this to happen around 1710 was happily left aside. Nostradamus was pressed into service, as were obscure figures such as "a Poor Man in Norfolk," who in 1775 had apparently predicted that "France will run with blood, and tens of thousands of her children will be slain." The French would turn against the priesthood, he had said, and would plan an unsuccessful invasion of England. The pope would flee from Rome, Islam would fall, and the road to the millennium would be clear in 1805.[44]

By far the most influential prophecy, though, was that of Robert Fleming, whose *Apocalyptical Key* of 1701 was widely republished and reproduced in radical newspapers. Fleming had argued that the entire history of the world was contained in the sixteenth chapter of Revelation, in which seven angels were commanded to "pour out the vials of the wrath of God upon the earth." Attempting to match historical events with the pouring of the vials, he concluded that the Fourth Vial would run out "about the year 1794." By this time, Fleming argued, "the *French Monarchy,* after it has *scorched others,* will itself consume by doing so; its fire, and that which is the fuel that maintains it, wasting insensibly; till it be exhausted at last towards the end of this century." He then predicted the weakening of the papacy between 1794 and 1848 and the beginning of the "*blessed Millennium of Christ's spiritual reign on earth*" around 2000.[45]

The effect was electric. When Louis XVI was executed in January 1793 it appeared that Fleming had indeed unlocked the future. And when, five years later, French armies engineered a coup in which the pope was imprisoned and Rome became a republic, it seemed that his next prediction was also coming true. Loyalists and radicals alike were struck by the force of Fleming's prophecies, but drew opposite conclusions from them. The "friends of order" attempted to harness Fleming to their own cause and maintained that he had predicted the destruction of the French nation. Against them, radicals such as Joseph Lomas Towers combined "interpretations of prophecy" with "some political truths" to demonstrate that the French Revolution would shatter superstition, overthrow monarchies throughout Europe, spread true Christianity, and bring the millennium into motion.

Among other things, Towers wanted to divert popular beliefs about fortune-telling and reading the future into revolutionary political and religious channels. The government, it seems, was sufficiently concerned to take strong counter-measures. Written on the fly-leaf of one of the few remaining copies is the message: "This work is said to have been rigidly suppressed thro' the influence of W. Pitt," the prime minister.[46]

Like their American counterparts, many British democrats found it difficult to reconcile their support for the principles of the French Revolution with the practice. "Some however object," commented Bicheno, "that the progress of the French revolution has been marked with too much outrage and blood; and that the persons engaged in it are of a character too bad to admit it to be from God." One way of dealing with this problem was to shift all the blame for revolutionary violence onto the shoulders of the royalists. Had they not opposed liberty, the argument ran, there would have been no bloodshed at all. Another was to point out that God had often employed "unworthy characters" to further his plans. Henry VIII, for example, had hardly been a model of virtue, but it was thanks to him that Britain had become a Protestant nation. According to Priestley, the "prevalence of infidelity" in France had been a reaction to the country's "antichristian establishments." Now, he wrote, Catholic tyranny and revolutionary infidelity were cancelling each other out, leaving the way open for "true Christianity" and the Second Coming.

Priestley believed that the millennium was imminent; Bicheno reckoned that Antichrist would be defeated by 1819 and that Christ would return in 1864; others calculated that the Second Coming would occur in 2060. But whatever the specific dates, the preoccupation with the millennium prompted people to consider its character. In the process, they articulated a form of religious utopianism that not only revealed their hopes for the future but also threw a reverse light on the problems and injustices of their own era.

This optimism is particularly apparent in the millenarian speculations of Joseph Lomas Towers. He looked forward to a world in which medicine would cure the sick, animals would be friendly, people would feel secure in their own homes, and travellers would be safe from highwaymen and pirates. During the millennium, Towers believed, there would be no more capital punishment, no more duelling, and no more suicide. Sorrow and pain would pass away, and men would study war no more: "no longer," he wrote, "will thousands of the human race be collected together to slaughter each other, upon the field of battle, or upon the bosom of the deep."

With the overthrow of "Bad Government and False Religion," all aspects of life would be transformed: "not only war, discord, and pestilence will, in a great degree, be banished from the world," predicted Towers, "but also those other evils which naturally flow from the same sources, sloth and ignorance, hypocrisy and persecution, superstition and infidelity, excessive poverty and intemperate labour." This image of the future fused perfectly with the aspirations of popular radicals on both sides of the Atlantic. Towers had made the millennium synonymous with the utopian dreams of democratic republicanism.[48]

If the renewed interest in the predictions of people like Fleming and Jurieu was part of the "retrospective prophecy" syndrome, the millenarian expectations of Bicheno, Priestley, and Towers belonged to the new, revolutionary-generated view of the future. Meanwhile, apocalyptic sects clustered around charismatic self-proclaimed saviours such as Richard Brothers and Joanna Southcott.

Originally from Newfoundland, Brothers had been born in 1757 on Christmas Day – a date that he took as a sign of his divine destiny. "I am the prophet that will be revealed to the Jews," he declared in 1794, "to order their departure from all nations, to go to the land of Israel, their own country, in a similar manner to Moses, but with additional power." The Battle of Armageddon had begun when revolutionary France went to war with conservative Britain. George III was one of the "four great beasts" in the Book of Daniel, and Brothers himself had been appointed by God to preside over the millennium.[49]

Brothers not only conversed with God but exerted considerable influence over Him. He explained it all in his *Revealed Knowledge of the Prophecies and Times*, one of the best-selling

James Gillroy takes on the soft target of Richard Brothers.
©The British Museum

books of the 1790s. God had been furious with the sinfulness of London, Brothers told his readers, and was about to "burn her immediately with fire from heaven." The thunderclap that had shaken the city in January 1791, Brothers wrote, had actually been the opening salvo in the destruction of London. But he, Richard Brothers, had personally intervened with God and begged him to give the city another chance. At first God was "highly displeased" by this request to reverse Divine Judgment, but after a few days He decided to relent. "I pardon London and all the people in it, for your sake," Brothers quoted God as telling him; "there is no other man on earth that could stand before me to ask for so great a thing."[50]

The same thing happened in August 1793, when God was once again on the brink of destroying the world for its sins. This time Brothers managed to cut a deal with God, ensuring that he and his friends would be spared from the holocaust. As he assured his followers:

> The fulfilling of the judgments of God, however destructively they may prove to the governments and nations which they are directed against, are not allowed to affect my personal safety, or operate in the least to my prejudice: for the certainty of my elevation, to the greatest *principality* that ever will be in the world, cannot be prevented by the rise or fall of any human power on earth; because it is the repeated covenant of God to my forefathers, and his sacred promise now by revelation to myself.

After more negotiations, Brothers managed to win a further extension of God's deadline: the people of London would be given one more opportunity to mend their wicked ways.[51]

But the wicked ways continued, God was running out of patience, and this time He would not change his mind. London,

Brothers announced, was going to be obliterated by an earthquake on the king's birthday, June 4, 1795. That evening a young Irish revolutionary living in London, John Binns, was walking to a political club when one of the most violent thunderstorms London had ever experienced broke out. He took shelter in a barroom, where he found fifty to sixty people huddled together, some on their knees in prayer, terrified that Brothers' prophecy was coming true. Earlier that day there had been a major exodus from the city: all the roads were clogged with thousands upon thousands of people who were trying to escape God's wrath.[52]

By this time, Brothers had been arrested on suspicion of treason. He had preached against Britain's war with France, supported revolutionary democrats, and promised to replace George III – all at a time when the government feared a French invasion, political radicalism was on the rise, and high bread prices were triggering widespread discontent. Not only that, but his writings had "caused much sensation throughout England" and his following was growing larger. It even reached into the House of Commons, where a prominent member of parliament took up his cause. The government wanted him out of the way and, shortly after his arrest, he was declared legally insane and kept in an asylum until 1806.[53]

Fascinated by these events, John Binns decided to visit Brothers in prison. "He assured me, with all solemnity and placidity of manner," Binns wrote, "that the earthquake had, at his earnest and oft-repeated intercession, been by the Almighty, postponed, and the destruction of London averted." Brothers, recalled Binns, was a tall, soft-spoken, and inoffensive man who genuinely believed that God was communicating with him. Over the next few months, Binns "sat with him for hours, listening to him with deep interest, regarding him as insane on the one subject, sane on all others, and intelligent on many." From Binns' perspective, we can be sure, the "sane" component of Brothers' thought was his support for the French Revolution and democratic republican principles. The "insane" part was Brothers' millennial belief that he was God's appointed "Prince and Prophet" who would single-handedly save the world.[54]

Tapping into the same millenarian mood of the French revolutionary era was Joanna Southcott, a domestic servant and "wise woman" from Devonshire who came to believe that she was the "woman clothed with the sun" in Revelation and who attracted many of the same people who had followed Brothers.[55] She herself did not take kindly to her prophetic rival, whom she denounced as an agent of Satan. Nor was she a woman to be taken lightly. One Anglican minister who was too kind to tell her what he really thought of her prophecies, and who did not explicitly discourage her, became an early object of her obsession. She followed him around everywhere, praised him as a kindred spirit, and then denounced him as a Judas when he tried to extricate himself from his increasingly awkward situation.

Southcott began prophesying in 1792, when she was "strangely visited, by day and night, concerning what was coming upon the whole earth" and was "ordered to set it down in writing." Among other things, she predicted the war between Britain and France, the bad harvests of the mid-1790s, and the naval mutinies of 1797 – all of which gave her an extremely impressive track record. When she got things wrong, she did not miss by much: there would be an Irish rebellion in 1795, she said; in fact, it occurred three years later, in 1798. When she published her prophecies in 1801, after they had already been fulfilled, she quickly assumed the status of a national cult figure.

Like many of the prophetesses who preceded her, Southcott turned traditional class and gender roles upside down. Here was a domestic servant who commanded the attention of those who were regarded as her social superiors; here was a woman who preached to congregations that hung on her every word. Central to her message was the feminization of religion. Unconsciously

Thomas Rowlandson ridicules Joanna Southcott.
©The British Muscum

echoing the early fourteenth-century arguments of Prous Boneta, Southcott believed that God had chosen a woman to save the world, to compensate for Eve's original temptation of Adam. Her followers expressed this view in a hymn:

> A woman Satan chose at first, to bring on man the fall;
> A woman God has chose at last, for to restore us all.
> As by a woman death did come, so life must come the same,
> And they that eat the fruit she gives, may bless God's holy name.

The woman, of course, was Southcott herself. Her destiny was to defeat Satan, deliver humankind from evil, and free women from the guilt of Eve. In 1814, when she was sixty-four years old and still a virgin, God told her exactly how she was going to do it. She would conceive a child by the Holy Ghost, become the world's second Virgin Mother, and bring forth the man-child from the Book of Revelation who would "rule all nations with a rod of iron."

And then something remarkable happened: Joanna Southcott began to show all the signs of pregnancy. No fewer than twenty-one doctors examined her, including some of London's leading surgeons, and seventeen of them concluded she was indeed with child. Her followers began planning for the birth: they bought an expensive cradle, procured an elaborately designed copy of the Bible, made a quilt, and knitted clothes for the coming Messiah. Southcott herself could barely believe it was happening; she kept the names of everyone who offered presents, so their gifts could be returned if it turned out she was wrong.

The doubts began to grow as first the days and then the weeks stretched out past the expected delivery date: not only was there no baby, but the signs of pregnancy began to disappear. She became weaker and weaker, until she eventually died two days after the Christmas of 1814. According to one of her doctors, she said that "it all appears delusion" just before her death. But many of her followers refused to give up hope, even then. They wrapped her body in flannels, covered it with hot-water bottles, and waited for her to rise again after the third day. When she did not, an autopsy was performed. The doctors dissected her on a table, while her followers watched and waited for the promised child to be delivered. The final medical verdict was unequivocal: there had been no pregnancy and there was no baby. Joanna Southcott's vision of the future had turned out to be as wrong as that of Richard Brothers. All the gifts were returned.

• • •

There is a certain poignancy, indeed tragedy, in all these stories. The revolutionizing of the revolution, the linear view of history, the sense of unlimited progress, and the dreams of the millennium were not only different manifestations of the search for meaning during confusing and cataclysmic times but also reflections of the deepest human aspirations for a better world. It is hard to read Towers' image of the millennium, in which there would be medical advances, personal safety, peace, justice, and prosperity, without feeling that such things are worth striving for. But whether revolution and revelation are the best routes to that destination is another matter altogether.

On the contrary, there is much to be feared in approaches to the future that contrast the real with the ideal, and that envisage a revolutionary or apocalyptic leap from one state to the other. The result, all too often, is particularly conducive to shudders: life under the Fifth Monarchists would have been literally no laughing matter, just as life under the French revolutionary democrats was anything but a human paradise. There are other problems as well. The American sense of destiny could become insufferably smug and self-righteous, and prophets such as Abiezer Coppe, Eleanor Davis, Richard Brothers, and Joanna Southcott were indeed insane, however much their historians may shy away from the word. Beyond these particulars, the search for meaning is littered with prophetic failures. Virtually every optimistic prediction that came out of the Age of Revolution failed to come true.

With these reservations in mind, I would like to conclude with the one person who called correctly the future course of the French Revolution – the Irish liberal conservative Edmund Burke. In contrast to his democratic republican contemporaries, Burke had a much deeper sense of historical complexity, the fragility of the social order, the power of human passion, the relationship between ends and means, and the potential consequences of attempting to restructure society according to abstract first principles. All these characteristics lay behind his *Reflections on the Revolution in France* (1790), which detected hidden totalitarian tendencies within the revolution at a time when almost everyone within the British political nation was applauding events in France.

Before the radicalization of the revolution, before the proclamation of a French Republic, before the outbreak of revolutionary war, before the Terror, and before anyone had ever heard of Napoleon, Burke predicted both the pattern of change and its eventual outcome:

> In the weakness of one kind of authority, and in the fluctuation of all, the officers of an army will remain for some time mutinous and full of faction, until some popular general, who understands the art of conciliating the soldiery, and who possesses the true spirit of command, shall draw the eyes of all men upon himself. Armies will obey him on his personal account. There is no other way of securing military obedience in this state of things. But the moment in which that event shall happen, the person who really commands the army is your master; the master (that is little)

of your king, the master of your assembly, the master of your whole republic.[56]

Ironically, none of the anti-historical democratic republicans had envisaged this outcome, nor had the millenarians whose writings had been so charged with hope during the early 1790s. In the end, it was the person with the deepest historical consciousness of all, and who dismissed prophecies and predictions as being entirely chimerical, who saw most clearly into the future.

·5·

UTOPIA

ULTIMATELY, UTOPIA EXISTS ONLY AS a state of mind. The word and the concept originated in 1516 with Thomas More, who defined utopia as a good place that was no place. In his hands, and in those of his successors, it represented an imaginary ideal against which society could be measured, and towards which people should be encouraged to strive. Originally, it was not connected to the future. Instead, it was part of a more general attempt to judge contemporary behaviour in the light of external standards. Rather than looking forwards to find these standards, most social reformers before the late eighteenth century located them in the past, in newly discovered lands, or in remote islands of the imagination.

Those who contrasted an idealized past with an imperfect present invoked memories of a mythical golden age, which varied from culture to culture. In eighteenth-century England, for example, popular democrats spoke of returning to the pristine purity of Anglo-Saxon liberty and praised the "People's Alfred" as the model of a true king. Seeking a historical "warrant" for their radicalism, they walked backwards into their future. In contrast, the Welsh golden age existed before thugs like Alfred came in and spoiled everything, while Irish nationalists equated Anglo-Saxon culture with barbarism and asserted the sophistication and beauty of ancient Celtic splendour against the present misery and degradation of English rule. Some Irish radicals even argued that Gaelic had been spoken in the Garden of Eden; others put in a modest claim for the Hibernian basis of Western civilization.

The runaway success of Thomas Cahill's *How the Irish Saved Civilization* indicates that such views continue to hit the resonant frequency. More generally, images of a golden age remain a familiar part of our own cultural landscape. They cut right across the political spectrum, from radical Afrocentric views that Socrates was black and that Greek philosophy was stolen from Egypt, to conservative Republican nostalgia for the culture of respect, discipline, and traditional family values that supposedly existed before the Beatles arrived in America and women entered the workforce. This way of thinking has always been with us and probably always will be.[1]

As well as looking backwards through time, social critics during the seventeenth and eighteenth centuries also looked outwards through space and employed the indigenous cultures of the so-called New World as a yardstick against which European civilization could be measured. This outlook found its clearest expression in the cult of the Noble Savage: the natives, who had been "savage" before they were conquered, became safely "noble" after they were no longer a threat to European expansion. Travellers to remote and "uncivilized" places such as North America and the west of Ireland frequently returned with stories that contrasted the virtues of "primitivism" with the vices of modern European society.

Such views revealed much about tensions within European society, but little or nothing about indigenous cultures, which were mythologized into an indistinguishable block. Consider, for example, this commentary on European hygiene, as recorded by a Jesuit in seventeenth-century New France: "Politeness and propriety have taught us to carry handkerchiefs. In this matter the Savages charge us with filthiness – because, they say, we place what is unclean in a fine white piece of linen, and put it away in our pockets as something very precious, while they throw it upon the ground." Now turn to this eighteenth-century account of the appearance of Granuaille, the Celtic pirate queen, at the court of Elizabeth I. When the proper use of a handkerchief was explained to her, she said "that in her country they were much cleaner than to pocket what comes from their nostrils." Native Americans or Celts, it did not matter much, really: they existed primarily to entertain and instruct the people of the metropolis. Nor has the notion of the Noble Savage entirely disappeared from contemporary culture, as the recent popularity of films such as *Dances with Wolves* and *Braveheart* attests.[2]

And then there were the imaginary islands, which provided the setting for the original Utopia and became inextricably associated with the genre from the sixteenth to the eighteenth centuries. Although they were located in space rather than in time, the very fact that such islands contained supposedly advanced civilizations meant that they could function as ideal models for the future. One of the best examples was Francis Bacon's "New Atlantis," published in 1627. His mythical island of Bensalem combined traditional corporate political ideals of peace and harmony with revolutionary speculations about the transformative power of science and technology.

In describing New Atlantis, Bacon managed to anticipate many features of our modern world. There are seedless plants and special diets that produce a healthier population; the people have "some degrees of flying in the air," as well as "ships and boats for going under water," and they have discovered "the means to convey sounds in trunks and pipes, in strange lines and distances." Among their more remarkable inventions were the "perspective-houses," which appear strikingly similar to cinema and television:

"We represent also all multiplications of light, which we carry to great distance, and make so sharp as to discern small points and lines; also all colorations of light, all delusions and deceits of the sight in figures, magnitudes, motions, colours, all demonstrations of shadows."[3]

Bacon's islanders were able to foretell the future through the application of scientific logic to natural phenomena: "And we do also declare natural divinations of diseases, plagues, swarms of hurtful creatures, scarcity, tempests, earthquakes, great inundations, comets, temperature of the year, and divers other things; and we give counsel thereupon what the people shall do for the prevention and remedy of them."[4] Not the least of Bacon's accomplishments was to predict the predictions industry and the scientific futurologists of the scientific future.

While Bacon's island was characterized by scientific and technological innovations, others functioned as models for revolutionary social arrangements. Among these was John Lithgow's *Equality – A Political Romance* (1802), America's first socialist utopia, which was located on the imaginary island of Lithconia. Again, the boundary between space and time is blurred: "If there be not such an island," wrote the book's publishers, "it is possible that there will be, some time or other." The Lithconians had come to realize that money "was the root of all evil" and that the "system of private property" had produced a society in which "nine-tenths of mankind groan'd under the most oppressive tyranny." Radical intellectuals had taught the people that human misery originated "in the folly of human institutions; and, that the remedy was within the powers of human reason." After a "stormy and factious period," the "equal right men" had overcome the "separate property-men" and established a society based on the principles of Reason.[5]

There was no money in Lithconia, lands were held in common, and the people worked four hours a day. Everything was regulated, right down to sexual relations:

> It was decreed, that all the young women of each district, who
> had arrived at a certain age, should, on the first day of the year
> after, inscribe the name of her lover in the matrimonial regis-
> ter of the district. – Next day, all the young men, unengaged,
> go to examine this register, and as many as are satisfied with
> the girls who have chosen them, signify their assent to the
> recorder. After which it would be regarded as a high misde-
> meanour, if either of the parties should be found to admit, or
> give encouragement to another lover.

Married couples continued to live in separate apartments "and
never sleep together only every seventh night" – suggesting that
Lithgow perhaps had a low libido. The children that issued from
these arrangements were all "the property of the state, educated
and brought up at the public expense."[6]

In this way, Lithconia existed as an imaginary embodiment of
the radical Enlightenment. For Lithgow the future meant a return
to the past: "the Lithconians," he wrote, "are not a people that are
progressing from a state of nature, to what is vulgarly called, civilization; on the contrary, they are progressing from civil society
to a state of nature." The time when "the reign of equality shall be
universally established all over the world" was also the time when
"the age of innocence" would be renewed. Lithconia was more
than an island: it was the point of convergence for a mythic
geography, a mythic past, and a mythic future – all of which
represented a rejection of and escape from the here and now.[7]

The projection of our hopes and fears onto islands recurs
throughout history, albeit in very different ways at very different
times. In ancient Celtic mythology, islands represented abstract
essences, such as laughter, joy, and sorrow. The Island of Women,
for example, was the quintessence of erotic pleasure. If we fast-for-

ward into the late twentieth century, we find that the islands have been relocated to Outer Space and renamed as planets. By the time we reach the 1970s the Island of Women was more likely to be a lesbian separatist utopia from which no man leaves alive.

No matter how the island is portrayed, however, space generally prevails over time. Refracted through a mythic geography, the imaginary future is presented in oblique forms, so that it is not confronted directly and immediately. During the eighteenth century this state of affairs remained very much the norm. Of the seventy-five British utopian and anti-utopian texts published between 1700 and 1802, all but three were set on islands or in unexplored territory.[8] Nevertheless, things were beginning to change: gradually, hesitantly, a conceptual revolution was occurring in which utopia was explicitly projected onto the future. By the late eighteenth century time was beginning to challenge space. Central to this process was the secular concept of progress. History, it seemed, was leading people out of chaos into order, out of tyranny into freedom, and out of poverty into prosperity.

• • •

The first book to be set in the future came from an unlikely source – an obscure Irish Protestant minister named Samuel Madden, who in 1733 wrote his *Memoirs of the Twentieth Century*. A satire on early eighteenth-century political life rather than a blueprint for utopia, Madden's work nevertheless marked the beginning of a new literary genre, as he himself was aware. His narrator described himself as "the first among Historians" who "dar'd to enter by the help of an infallible Guide, into the dark Caverns of Futurity, and discover the Secrets of Ages yet to come." The "infallible Guide" was a "Genius," who possessed the correspondence of the narrator's great great great great great grandson, the prime minister under King George VI in 1997.[9]

For the most part, the book failed miserably. A central theme was Britain's struggle against an international Jesuit conspiracy to take over the world – a conspiracy that was the direct result of the government's failure to take strong measures against Catholicism back in the 1730s. But it is not always clear whether Madden was satirizing or sanctioning anti-Catholic attitudes, and in any case the entire effort soon sank under the weight of its own verbosity.

Madden's other targets are more readily identifiable. He ridiculed those who elevated private interests above the public good and poked fun at the "projectors" whom his friend Jonathan Swift had mocked in *Gulliver's Travels*. But although *Memoirs of the Twentieth Century* contains flashes of satirical brilliance, its author manifestly lacked Swift's subtlety and skill. Madden seems to have known as much: according to one report he wound up destroying almost the entire print run of 1000 copies.[10]

One of the most interesting features of Madden's book is its essentially static view of the future. There is no sense of scientific progress or technological change, politics remains the preserve of the aristocracy, and Britannia continues to rule the waves. The same general outlook characterizes the only other eighteenth-century English book that is set in the future, *The Reign of George VI, 1900–1925*. In the hands of its anonymous author, King George VI emerges as a patriot king who single-handedly repulses a Russian invasion of England, invades France, and constructs an English equivalent of the Palace of Versailles – all while halving the national debt. By 1920 the battling British boys have conquered just about everything in sight, from Spanish America to Europe. The population of North America has skyrocketed to eleven million loyal colonists, who had "never made the least attempt to shake off the authority of Great Britain." Equally grateful were the French, who now enjoyed British liberty rather than suffering under Catholic despotism: "Happy for France," rejoiced the author, "that it was conquered by such a patriot King!"[11]

Although it was set in the early twentieth century, the *Reign of George VI* was not really about the future at all. Instead, it attempted to demonstrate to Britons the kind of benefits that they could expect if they rejected the scheming and back-stabbing of parliamentary politics and embraced instead a leader who was "resolute, wise and magnanimous at home, vigilant, intrepid, and fortunate abroad, successful against domestic factions, and victorious over foreign enemies, a promoter of arts and sciences, an encourager of religion and virtue, and in short ... a very great King, and a truly good man." As such, it is a model of eighteenth-century British Tory chauvinism.[12]

• • •

By the middle of the eighteenth century, then, we have a long-established tradition of utopias located on islands and an emerging genre of stories set in the future. In 1771 the two strands finally came together in the hands of a French Grub Street writer, a radical intellectual who was described by a government spy as a "fierce, bizarre man" and who wound up as a member of the revolutionary French National Convention in 1793. His name was Louis-Sebastian Mercier and his book, *L'An 2440*, was the first futuristic utopia ever written.[13]

Mercier had been born in 1740; he arrived at the year 2440 simply by adding seven hundred years to his date of birth. As befits someone who became a revolutionary republican, Mercier was motivated by a deep sense of anger towards injustice and oppression in *ancien régime* France. He attacked "that vile herd of kings, who have been, in every sense, the tormentors of mankind" and condemned the combination of "extreme opulence and excessive misery" in Paris. "Stupidity now reigns," he wrote; "the tranquillity of my country resembles that of the grave. I see nought around me but coloured carcasses, who move and talk, but in whom the active principle of life has never produced the least emotion." For Mercier, the Paris of 1771 was a bleak place, characterized by urban alienation, peopled by human zombies, and wracked by poverty, pollution, crime, cruel indifference, and endemic disorder. It was, in short, a nightmarish world, bereft of Reason.[14]

The Paris of 2440, in contrast, had become a model of rationality and civility. It was the dreamworld of the future, which the narrator entered after falling into a deep sleep. In some respects there had been little change: people still worked as tradesmen, artisans, and shopkeepers and travelled around on foot or by horse and carriage in a recognizably pre-industrial setting. But as far as social, political, religious, and cultural matters were concerned, everything had been totally transformed. And the central characteristic of twenty-fifth-century France was order: in place of the confusing, contradictory, overlapping institutions of the *ancien régime,* society had been reorganized along the mathematical principles of logic and consistency.

As the narrator took his first steps in the Paris of the future, he was immediately struck by the "strait lines" of the streets and the orderly disposition of the inhabitants. Although people still travelled by traditional methods, they were now directed by guards who stood in every street, making sure that the traffic flowed smoothly. Urban planning had replaced urban chaos and there were impressive public squares where the citizenry could assemble. Conspicuous by its absence was the Bastille, symbol of arbitrary power. It had been "totally demolished" by a just prince and replaced with a Temple of Clemency.

Not only the Bastille but the whole social and political edifice of hereditary power had collapsed in the France of the future. There was still a king, but he was a constitutional monarch who rubbed shoulders with the people. He "frequently goes on foot amongst us," the narrator was told, "rests himself in the shop of some artisan," and "loves to observe that natural equality which ought to reign among men; he meets in our eyes with nothing but love and gratitude." The parasitic aristocracy that used to crawl about the throne had long since disappeared. France was now a meritocracy, in which distinctions arose from virtue, talent, and industry rather than the accident of birth. Everyone was equal under the law, which was the "voice of the general will of the people."[15]

This vision was deeply influenced by the writings of Jean-Jacques Rousseau, the Genevan political theorist whose book *The Social Contract* – written nine years before Mercier's – became a kind of political bible for the men who would make the French Revolution. In contrasting the "ought" with the "is," Rousseau had developed the concept of the General Will, which supposedly expressed the general good of society as a whole and transcended narrow personal and class interests. Freedom, in Rousseau's view, consisted in the voluntary submission to laws that people had themselves created. In fact, he believed, the General Will incorporated the will of everyone in the society who established it. From this position, he argued that those people who in some way contradicted the General Will could and should be forced to be free.

In Mercier's 2440, this philosophical abstraction had become a living reality. This was a society in which the self-regulating and productive citizen had come into his own. Because there were no idle priests, monks, and nobles, taxes were minimal: people paid one-fiftieth of their annual income to the state, and did so with pleasure. "We give with a free will; our tribute is not by compulsion, but founded on reason and equity," the narrator learns. "There is scarce a man among us who does not esteem it a point of honour to discharge the most sacred and most legitimate of all debts."[16]

And because the people of 2440 regarded luxury and dissipation with horror, they worked only to meet their own modest needs. Employment was healthy, the hours were short, and external compulsion was unnecessary: "Labour has no longer an ugly and forbidding aspect, as it no longer resembles slavery; a gentle voice invites them to their duty, and all becomes easy, and even agreeable." Public granaries ensured that people paid a fixed and fair price for bread, while public hospitals provided free health care in humane conditions. In this way, a social safety net protected people from hunger and the worst effects of illness.[17]

The inhabitants of this future society had long since rejected traditional forms of religion and embraced a transcendent form of deism. It was enough to know that there was a Supreme Being, who had given us the ability to tell right from wrong, and whose divinity was revealed through nature. "It is with religion as with laws," said one of the citizens; "the most simple are the best. Adore God, love thy neighbour; hearken to that conscience, that judge which continually attends thee; never stifle that secret and celestial voice; all the rest is imposture, fraud, falsehood."[18]

Anyone who doubted the existence of a Creator had only to gaze into the heavens. As part of the passage to full adulthood, the citizens of 2440 were allowed to look through a telescope, so they could see for themselves the beauty and harmony of God's universe. The telescope had made redundant all the old theological disputations. It was the "moral cannon that has lain in ruins all those superstitions and phantoms that tormented the human race. It seems as if our reason has been enlarged in proportion to the immeasurable space that has been discovered and traversed by the sight."[19]

Not surprisingly, given this approach, science occupied a central role in the educational system. Rather than wasting their time studying dead languages such as Latin and Greek, students were taught "useful" subjects such as algebra and physics to improve their powers of reasoning and turn them into enlightened citizens. "That science," it was said of physics, "properly investigated, delivers us from an infinity of errors, and the unformed mass of prejudices give place to that pure light which it spreads over all objects." All that you needed was your God-given conscience, your mathematical powers of reason, and your scientific understanding of the universe. Everything else was extraneous and even dangerous.[20]

This focus meant, among other things, that the study of history was almost entirely abolished in this world of the future. What was history but the record of crimes, follies, rapine, and ambition, which raised kings to the status of gods and glorified war and oppression? Who in their right mind would want to remind their children of such things? And so, as part of the effort to "rebuild the entire structure of human knowledge," all books that were deemed to be "frivolous, or useless, or dangerous" had been publicly burned: "We have therefore done from an enlightened zeal, what the barbarians once did from one that was blind."

Only those books that accorded to the "true principles of morality," such as the works of Rousseau, had been spared from the flames. And history had been rewritten to block out anything that might taint or corrupt the public mind: "We have omitted those reigns where there were nothing to be seen but wars and cruelties. They ought to be concealed; for nothing should be presented that will not do honour to humanity." In this way, the invention of the future entailed the reinvention of the past – a concept that would undoubtedly delight those deracinated postmodernists who inhabit the halls of contemporary academia.[21]

Mercier's view of history also explains why he located his utopia in the future. If the past was little more than the story of oppression, how could it be used as a criterion from which to judge the present? Within radical Enlightenment thought in general, there was a strong sense that veneration for the past and respect for tradition were little more than smokescreens for oppression. The point was to throw off the dead weight of history and to reconstruct society along rational first principles, rather than staying stuck in the past. With Mercier, we find the anti-historical tendencies of the radical Enlightenment pushed to their ultimate conclusion – the obliteration of knowledge in the name of Reason.

A crucial aspect of this future world was the way in which people had internalized the values of reason and morality. The voice of conscience was more important than the force of external authority in establishing social order and harmony. People had freely and willingly chosen to pay taxes, to work, and to renounce the temptations of luxury. They drank no coffee, tea, or alcohol, smoked no tobacco, did not gamble, played chess and "useful" mathematical games rather than cards, watched politically correct plays about republican heroes such as Oliver Cromwell, and aspired towards vegetarianism. Free from superstition, tyranny, and history, they had voluntarily become model citizens.

Strange to say, there were some people who deviated from these wholesome norms and who liked a cup of coffee or a glass of wine, did not like paying taxes, or dared to question such perfect social arrangements. Shortly after he arrived in the future, the narrator encountered a man with a mask, a writer who had published "dangerous principles, such as are inconsistent with sound morality." "By way of reparation, he wears a mask, in order to hide his shame, till he has effaced it by writing something more rational and beneficial to society," we learn. "He is daily visited by two worthy citizens, who combat his erroneous opinions with the arms of eloquence and complacency, hear his objections, confute them, and will engage him to retract when he shall be convinced. Then he will be re-established."[22]

Shame and reason, it is clear, were the central mechanisms of social control. Criminals, including those guilty of holding dangerous views, were held up to public contempt, forced to do useful work, and re-educated until they genuinely embraced and internalized the principles of reason and morality. The most vivid illustration comes when the narrator witnesses the public execution of a man who committed murder in a fit of jealous passion. Such events were rare, we are told, and always produced sorrow rather than feelings of vengeance or rejoicing.

What was particularly revealing was the attitude of the condemned man himself. He was full of remorse and "judged himself deserving of death," which he felt was infinitely preferable to living with the shame and ignominy of knowing that he had deprived a fellow human being of life. And so, like a true Enlightenment man, he went willingly to the scaffold. The narrator was deeply impressed: "With a heart full of tenderness and commiseration, I said, O, how is humanity respected among you! The death of a citizen is the cause of universal mourning to his country."[23] Meanwhile, the corpse twisted in the wind.

Not only men but also the women of 2440 had internalized the values of reason and the principles of nature. As the "weak and delicate sex," they no longer lugged heavy loads around the marketplace while men looked on lazily. Neither did they "daub their faces with paint ... or sing licentious songs, or practice the least indecency with men." Instead, they "attended to those duties only, which the Creator has enjoined them," which consisted solely in "pleasing their husbands, and educating their children."[24]

As a result, everyone was always happy: "Every man is bound to provide for his wife; and she, depending entirely upon her husband, is the better disposed to fidelity and obedience." Because their duties coincided with their desires, the women of the future were "delighted with domestic pleasures," such as shopping and cooking, cleaning, sewing and darning, decorating and gardening, and changing diapers. Besides, when you got right down to it, all women were pretty much the same anyway: "Nature has defined women to domestic employments, and to cares every where of the same kind. They have much less variety in their characters than have men; almost all women resemble each other; they have but one end, and which they manifest in every country by similar effects."[25] And as joyful baby-producing machines, mothers had a special role in transmitting the values of this utopia to the next generation. They formed young minds in the principles of virtue, truth, and humanity and inculcated into their children a love of nature and the Supreme Being.

Nor should we forget that if some women were odd enough to question this state of affairs, they would have to wear masks of shame and undergo a prolonged course of re-education until they became happily reconciled to their role. And if any of them should be driven into a homicidal rage by their domestic duties, they would eventually come to realize that they deserved the death penalty and go gladly to the gallows.

It was always possible, of course, that such deviant women might be banished from the country. But since, in 2440, the entire world now followed the same principles of reason, there would be no escape. There were different nations, it was true, but they all lived in peace and harmony. Within Europe, natural-frontier doctrines had prevailed. In the wider world, colonies had become independent and slaves were now free.

Across the Atlantic, the federated empires of North and South America were "united under one spirit of legislation." Pennsylvania, in particular, was a Quaker paradise on Earth, where "humanity, faith, liberty, concord, and equality" have reigned for hundreds of years. The English celebrated the memory of Cromwell rather than their kings, and their neighbours wanted to join them: "The Scotch and Irish have presented a petition to parliament, that the names of Scotland and Ireland may be abolished, and that they make but one body, spirit, and name, with the English, as they are one by that patriotic spirit with which they are animated."[26] One suspects that Gerry Adams might have found that one rather hard to take.

In this way, Mercier constructed a future that inverted the present. Where there had been chaos, there was now order; where there had been external compulsion, there were now internal controls; where there had been tyranny, superstition, corruption, and luxury, there was now liberty, rationality, virtue, and simplicity, where there had been dynastic wars, there was now international peace. The key words in this future society were reason, nature, conscience, and science: people had learned to regulate themselves in the same way that Newtonian principles apparently regulated the universe. That is why the telescope was the central symbol of twenty-fifth century Paris; that is why women, supposedly designed by Nature to please their husbands and nurture their children, lived happily at home. And just as Newtonian science offered a model of an unchanging, predictable, and orderly cosmos, Mercier's ideal society was quintessentially static. It had banished history and foreclosed its own future.

As a guide to the actual year of 2440, Mercier's book now appears completely useless. But as a map of the revolutionary mind in late eighteenth-century France, it is highly revealing. In the guise of futuristic speculation, Mercier produced one of the most subversive books of the *ancien régime*. Nor was it simply a "theoretical" work: during the Terror of 1793–94 the French revolutionaries pursued policies that matched Mercier's prescriptions point by point.

By this time, the Bastille had already been demolished – not by a "patriot prince," as Mercier had envisaged, but by a Parisian crowd under revolutionary middle-class leadership. The king had been executed as well, rendering Mercier's image of a "people's monarch" redundant. But, in other respects, it seemed that Mercier's future was actually occurring, 647 years ahead of schedule. Like the men of Mercier's 2440, the revolutionary democrats of 1793 and 1794 worshipped the Supreme Being rather than the Christian God, restructured the educational system to create model republican citizens, revolutionized public architecture and urban planning, embraced commerce while fixing the price of bread, adopted the principles of meritocracy, attempted to eradicate corruption and luxury, and worked for a Republic of Virtue.

They did not, however, use public shame and humiliation to punish their enemies. Instead, they used the guillotine – a recent invention that had itself been welcomed as the progressive death machine of the future. It applied modern technology to ensure that capital punishment was quicker and less inhumane than the old practices of hanging or execution by the axe. The revolution, declared one of its leaders, could succeed "only by ploughing its way boldly through a Red Sea of blood."[27] By July 1794 blood had streamed from more than ten thousand throats in the effort to create the Republic of Virtue.

The Terror, of course, cannot be reduced to a single cause and has to be placed in the context of international war, economic crisis, and internal instability. But running through it all was an ideological imperative to transform society along the lines that Mercier and Rousseau had imagined some twenty years earlier. The revolutionary democrats were attempting to implement the future of 2440 in 1793. And the result was anything but utopia.

• • •

If the French Revolution was partly influenced by radical futuristic fantasies, it generated new visions of political and moral progress that gripped the popular imagination. One of the most influential books of the late eighteenth century was the Comte de Volney's *Ruins of Empires,* published in 1791, which projected the democratic and deist dreams of the French Revolution into the future. Like Mercier, Volney began with a grim picture of the contemporary world: the so-called civilized countries of Europe were controlled by wealthy elites who reduced their own population to "the level of cattle" and ruthlessly exploited the people of China, India, and Africa. "Ignorance, tyranny, and wretchedness have every where struck the nations with stupor," he wrote; "and vicious habits, depraving the natural senses, have destroyed the very instinct of happiness and truth." Humanity, it seemed, was doomed to perpetual misery.[28]

But at this point the narrator is comforted by a "Genius" – the same conduit to the future that Madden had employed earlier in the century. "Let us revive the hope of this man," the Genius says; "for if he who loves his fellow creatures be suffered to despair, what is to become of nations? The past is perhaps but too much calculated to deject him. Let us then anticipate futurity; let us unveil the astonishing age that is about to arise, that virtue, seeing the end of its wishes, animated with new vigour, may redouble its efforts to hasten the accomplishment of it." The dream of a better future would revive hope, hope would lead to action, and action would make the dream come true.[29]

And so the Genius reveals the path to future liberty. The population, he explains, will become polarized between the productive members of society, consisting of "labourers, artisans, tradesmen, and every profession useful to society," and a parasitic elite of priests and aristocrats. Aware of their power, and exasperated by injustice, the "people" challenge the presumptions of the "privileged." Some of the privileged decide to join the people, realizing that "they are men like ourselves"; others, however, say that to "mix with the herd would be degrading and vile; they are born to serve us, who are men of a superior race."

The civil authorities demand submission in the name of the law. The people, their mouths full of Rousseau, reply that the law is the general will. The military authorities order the troops to put down the people, but the soldiers lay down their arms and proclaim that they, too, "are part of the people." The religious authorities tell the people that God has appointed kings and priests to rule over them, but the people demand proof, and the priests can only offer faith rather than reason. "It is over with us," the privileged exclaim; "the multitude are enlightened. And the people replied: You shall not be hurt; we are enlightened, and we will commit no violence. We desire nothing but our rights: resentment we cannot but feel, but we consent to pass it by: we were slaves, we might command; but we ask only to be free, and free we are."[30]

In presenting this confrontation between the "people" and the "privileged," Volney was providing his readers with a stylized and sanitized version of events in France during the revolutionary year of 1789. The French Revolution, in Volney's "ideal" form, became the model for the future; its example would ultimately enlighten and liberate the rest of the world. In this respect, the contrast between Volney's *Ruins of Empires* and Mercier's *L'An 2440* is illuminating. Mercier had only dreamt of the fall of the Bastille; Volney had actually experienced it. Mercier had spoken vaguely of a "philosophic prince" who singlehandedly transformed France into a free country; Volney could offer a route to the future based on the actions of the National Assembly and the Parisian crowd. Mercier had simply juxtaposed an ideal future with an imperfect present; Volney had been able to extrapolate the "astonishing age that is about to arise" from events that had already happened. And this method of extrapolation marked a dramatic and far-reaching conceptual shift in secular futuristic writing.

The new approach found its classic formulation in the writings of the Marquis de Condorcet, the revolutionary philosopher and mathematician who in 1789 fitted into Volney's category of the "privileged" who decided to join the "people." Condorcet believed that if the laws of calculus were applied to the process of historical change, the result would be nothing less than "a science to foresee the progression of the human species." He practised what he preached: during his youth he apparently studied calculus for ten hours a day – enough to skew anyone's sense of reality.[31]

Condorcet was far from being the first person to view mathematics as the key to the future. During the late sixteenth century, for example, John Napier had invented logarithms as part of his effort to identify the Beast of the Book of Revelation. Napier's complex mathematical calculations revealed that the pope was Antichrist (no surprise here, for a good Scottish Presbyterian), that Rome would fall in 1639, and that the world would end in 1688 – not the best of track records. What made Condorcet unique, though, was his attempt to turn mathematics into a secular science of the future, in which it could be demonstrated that human improvement would progress to infinity. His results, as things turned out, would not be much better than those of Napier.[32]

"Nature," Condorcet wrote, "has fixed no limit to our hopes." The advances that had already occurred in science, civilization, and human understanding, along with the enlightened principles of the French Revolution, were bringing humanity into a new historical era. Throughout Europe, political privilege and religious superstition were collapsing. It was only a matter of time until the benefits of reason and commerce broke the old colonial system apart and spread liberty throughout the world.

Once "the people" were in power, Condorcet believed, they would be "too enlightened as to their own rights to sport with the rights of others." Benevolent Europeans would enlighten countries they had previously enslaved: "Settlements of robbers will then become colonies of citizens, by whom will be planted in Africa and Asia the principles of the freedom, reason, and illumination of Europe." This colonization would pave the way for a new international order in which war would become obsolete: "As the people of different countries will at last be drawn into closer intimacy, by the principles of politics and morality ... all the causes which produce, envenom and perpetuate national animosities, will one by one disappear, and will no more furnish to warlike insanity either fuel or pretext."

To match this new reality, a "universal language" would soon emerge – a kind of Esperanto of Liberty, based on rational mathematical principles. This language in turn would transform the nature of human thought, by removing everything that was vague and ambiguous. "It might be shown that this language," he wrote, "improving every day, acquiring incessantly greater extent, would be the means of giving to every object that comes within the reach of human intelligence, a rigour, and precision, that would facilitate the knowledge of truth, and render error almost impossible. Then would the march of every science be as infallible as that of the mathematics, and the propositions of every system acquire, as far as nature will admit, geometrical demonstration and certainty." Before long, erroneous opinions would become literally unthinkable.

In this new international order, equality of opportunity and freedom of commerce would reduce the enormous gap that had opened up between the privileged few and the impoverished many. At the same time, a social security system would protect old people, widows, and orphans. The principles of actuarial science would come into their own, and young men starting out in life would be given a small amount of startup capital, based on "the application of mathematics to the probabilities of life and the interest of money." A system of comprehensive education would increase equality and liberty by giving people the resources to improve themselves and society, and by insulating everyone from "popular errors," "superstitious fears," and "chimerical hopes." As the population became more educated, it would become more equal; as it became more equal, it would become more educated.

The result, Condorcet believed, would be the collective unlocking of creative talent and a corresponding leap forward in science and technology. Agricultural and industrial productivity would increase, liberating people from excessive labour and giving them more time for intellectual and moral pursuits. All remaining prejudices would disappear. In particular, women would no longer be regarded as inferior beings and would henceforth enjoy equal rights – although Condorcet, in the standard eighteenth-century fashion, still associated women primarily with the domestic sphere of life.

These developments would produce an enormous improvement in the overall quality of life. As social inequalities were reduced, the general level of health would increase; at the same time, advances in medical science would eliminate all infectious diseases. "Would it even be absurd," Condorcet asked, "to suppose ... that a period must one day arrive when death will be nothing more than the effect of extraordinary accidents, or of the slow and gradual decay of the vital powers; and that the duration of the middle space, of the interval between the birth of man and this decay, will itself have no assignable limit?" Through their own efforts, it seemed, men and women might eventually be able to bring about their own immortality; heaven threatened to become superfluous.

There was, indeed, a certain mathematical logic to this view of the future. Once you accepted the premises, all the pieces fitted together so that progress would increase exponentially. The principles of reason would produce a new international political order characterized by equality of opportunity, commercial growth, social security, and enlightened education. It would result in increased productivity, which would, in turn, enable moral goodness and creative talents to flourish in an ever-expanding spiral of improvement. From this perspective, Condorcet's conclusion appeared incontrovertible: "The perfectibility of man," he wrote, "is indefinite."

And yet, underlying this theory was an enormous irony. At the very time that Condorcet penned his thoughts about the "Future Progress of Mankind," he was in hiding from the revolutionary government, trying to escape the Terror that was being perpetrated in the name of Liberty. Because he had voted against the king's execution and was aligned with a rival faction, Condorcet was regarded by the government as a traitor to the Republic of France – and there was only one fate that traitors could expect. Condorcet's optimistic vision of unlimited human progress was created under the shadow of the guillotine. The gap between his intellectually driven view of the future and the political realities of the present could hardly have been greater.

Condorcet was acutely aware of the discrepancy; indeed, it could hardly have been otherwise. But he treated the Terror as a monstrous aberration, as if someone had put the wrong number in a mathematical equation. Condorcet made all his extrapolations from the principles of the French Revolution rather than from its practices. The possibility that the principles were organically connected to the practices, that the attempt to create a perfect future was producing a totalitarian present, completely eluded him. In Condorcet's mind there were really two revolutions going on: the "true" one, which existed in the abstract realm of political calculus, and the "false" one, which just happened to exist in the streets of Paris.

As the net closed around him, Condorcet increasingly found solace in his belief that perfection must inevitably triumph. In the process, he came to sound very like those earlier religious millenarians for whom the future became a compensatory myth. The prospect of future emancipation, he wrote, was admirably calculated "to console the philosopher lamenting the errors, the flagrant acts of injustice, the crimes with which the earth is still polluted." He himself had done all he could to promote reason and liberty, he wrote, referring to himself in the third person:

This sentiment is the asylum into which he retires, and to which the memory of his persecutors cannot follow him: he unites himself in imagination with man restored to his rights, delivered from oppression, and proceeding with rapid strides in the path of happiness: he forgets his own misfortunes while his thoughts are thus employed; he lives no longer to adversity, calumny and malice, but becomes the associate of these wiser and more fortunate beings whose enviable condition he so earnestly contributed to produce.

Shortly after writing these words, Condorcet was caught trying to get out of Paris. He was thrown into prison, where he died within days; there were rumours that he committed suicide. It seemed an unlikely end for an apostle of human perfectibility. In fact, it was not quite as unlikely as it appeared, for the personal tragedy also possessed a wider symbolic resonance. There was a collective sense in which the utopian quest for social and political perfection, the ruthless pursuit of an unattainable ideal, destroyed the living in the name of the future. And that was something that Condorcet's calculus could not comprehend.[33]

• • •

The futuristic writings of Mercier, Volney, and Condorcet formed the template for all subsequent utopian literature. All the central characteristics of the futuristic utopia had been established before 1800: an optimistic faith in political, scientific, and technological progress; the assumption that human nature was infinitely malleable and could therefore be programmed for perfection; the belief in order, reason, and equality; the anticipation of a peaceful and harmonious international order; and the conviction that the "laws" of historical change could be plotted with mathematical certainty.

But there were also significant differences of emphasis and approach between eighteenth-century utopias and their nineteenth-century counterparts. Mercier's image of a technologically static society quickly became discarded, while Condorcet's vision of infinitely expanding productivity appeared much more relevant to the new world of the Industrial Revolution. And later in the

nineteenth century, futuristic utopias began to incorporate changing views about the place of women in society, the relationship
between industrial change and political organization, and the role
of biological engineering in the creation of a perfect society.

One way into these shifts in emphasis is through the writings
of three important utopian writers in the nineteenth- and early
twentieth-century English-speaking world: Mary Griffith,
Edward Bellamy, and H.G. Wells. Of the three, Griffith is the
least known. Yet her *Camperdown: Or, News from our
Neighbourhood* (1836) stands as one of the first futuristic utopias
written in the United States and is also a significant landmark in
the history of women's attitudes to the future. As has been seen,
the earliest futuristic utopias had been written by men and cheer-
fully consigned women to a subordinate role within the domestic
sphere of life. Griffith, it must be said, did not completely emancipate herself from such notions, but she did not entirely accept
them either.

Her book tells the story of Edgar Hastings, who fell into a
trance after an avalanche buried his house in 1835 and was eventually thawed out three centuries later. He found himself in a
world where a new form of power enabled people to travel "in
locomotive cars, without either gas or steam." Cities and towns
were connected by a vast network of railways, and air travel had
been made possible by balloons. Steamboats had become obsolete
around 1950, and people had stopped going around on horseback
since the early twenty-first century.[34]

Although the actual nature of the new technology remained
suitably vague, its impact on society was abundantly clear. Not
only transportation but also agriculture had been revolutionized:
"The fields were no longer cultivated by the horse or the ox, nor
by small steam engines, as was projected in the nineteenth century, but by a self-moving plough, having the same machinery to
propel it as that of the travelling cars ... The same power mowed

the grass, raked it up, spread it out, gathered it, and brought it to the barn – the same power scattered seeds, ploughed, hoed, harrowed, cut, gathered, threshed, stored and ground the grain – and the same power distributed it to the merchants and small consumers." "The machines," Hastings learns, "have done every thing – they fill up gullies, dig out the roots of the trees, plough down hills, turn water courses – in short, they have entirely superseded the use of cattle of any kind." As a result, agricultural productivity had quadrupled, while the demand for physical human labour had virtually disappeared.[35]

This revolutionary technological power, Griffith wrote, had been invented by a woman. By the twenty-second century women had achieved "an equality in money matters," resulting in equality of status, respect, and recognition.[36] Their accomplishments in the fields of science, medicine, literature, and education revealed that women had broken out of the domestic sphere. In this sense, Griffith's view of gender relations is strikingly modern. But in other respects, her position was more conventional and traditional. She assumed that the clergy and university professors would continue to be male, and she gave no indication that the women of 2135 could vote.

More generally, her book reflects the early nineteenth-century American concept of women as "Republican Mothers" and "Republican Wives." According to this view, women were naturally inclined to be nurturers. Through socializing their children and humanizing their husbands, it was believed, women were uniquely equipped to soften the barbaric behaviour of men. It was an ideology that cut both ways: on the one hand, it implied that women should stay in the home; on the other, it suggested that women were not simply equal but actually superior to men, and that they could exert enormous indirect political influence through their dominant position within the family.

For Griffith, the key was economic emancipation. Once

women were no longer financially dependent on their husbands, they could use their influence to create a new moral order. Rather than trying to follow "men's pursuits and occupations," the women of the future weaned their children from "savage propensities," and taught them to abhor war and revere religion. As good "Republican Wives," they also stopped their husbands from fighting and drinking. In 1901, Griffith wrote, a law had been passed "granting a divorce to any woman whose husband was proved to be a drunkard." Realizing that they would perish without their wives, the drunkards quickly sobered up. Meanwhile, a law prohibiting all "spirituous liquors" removed any temptation to start again. "It is a very rare thing," Hastings was told, "to see a drunkard now."[37]

The world of 2135, then, was mechanized, feminized, peaceful, religious, sober, and upright. There was no more tobacco, no more spitting in the streets, and no more exploding boilers on steamboats – something that emerged as a minor obsession of the author. There were no books that might offend public morals. The works of Shakespeare had been edited to remove all the naughty bits, and the same thing had been done to the writings of Sir Walter Scott – although it is difficult to imagine anything in Scott that might remotely be considered naughty. And there were no dogs. "Yes, every dog – pointers, setters, hounds – all were exterminated." Dogs, after all, were associated with biting, barking, and rabies, and served no practical function. Besides, dogs were dirty. Griffith's world was clean – very, very clean.[38]

In combining technological progress with the economic and social emancipation of women, Griffith anticipated the futuristic writings of late nineteenth-century women utopians in Britain and America. The common ground lay in the assumption that once the machine liberated humanity from physical labour, the intellectual and moral qualities of women would flourish. There were, however, two crucial differences. First, Griffith's successors,

writing against the background of the campaign for women's suf-
frage, moved far beyond images of the "Republican Wife" and
"Republican Mother" and envisaged a future in which women
participated directly in the previously male world of public politics. Second, where Griffith set her story "three hundred years
hence," late nineteenth-century feminists generally located their
utopias in the immediate future: rapid change appeared to be just
around the corner. Thus Lady Florence Dixie wrote in 1890 about
the "revolution of 1900," in which women would deliver themselves from domesticity through disciplined and energetic political action. The future of 1900, in this sense, marked a significant
advance over the future of 2135.[39]

• • •

Whatever the time frame, though, there appeared no doubt that
the future would be better than the present. Among the many
books that took this view, none was more influential than Edward
Bellamy's *Looking Backward, 2000–1887*, published in Boston in
1887. Intended as "a forecast, in accordance with the principles of
evolution, of the next stage in the industrial and social development of humanity," it became an instant bestseller and brought
the future into the popular imagination in a way no previous
writer had accomplished. So great was its influence that a new
political party, the Nationalist Party of America, built itself on the
book's foundations. The future, in late nineteenth-century
America, was seen largely in terms of the affirmation, qualifica-
tion, or rejection of Bellamy's vision of the year 2000.

Bellamy was writing against the background of severe social
unrest in the United States. The gap between the rich and the
poor was growing, and a series of industrial strikes threatened to
tear the country apart. This reality was hard to reconcile with
notions of linear progress. Not surprisingly, cyclical theories of
human history began to make a comeback, and a number of com-

mentators began to fear that America was moving into a phase of terminal decline.

Looking Backward certainly reflected the sense that the United States was wracked with problems. The Boston of 1887, Bellamy wrote, was a "festering mass of human wretchedness," characterized by poverty, pollution, and profligacy. He compared American capitalism to a "prodigious coach which the masses of humanity were harnessed to and dragged toilsomely along a very hilly and sandy road." The coach was driven by hunger and its passengers comprised a wealthy elite, who "could enjoy the scenery at their leisure, or critically discuss the merits of the straining team." From time to time, though, some of the passengers were jolted out of their seats and onto the road, with the result that there was "a constant cloud upon the happiness of those who rode." The poor endured unremitting toil and misery, while everyone experienced insecurity.[40]

But Bellamy did not subscribe to cyclical theories of history and did not succumb to pessimism about the future. Offering reassurance where there was uncertainty and anxiety, *Looking Backward* maintained that the forces of progress were at work beneath the veneer of chaos. Compared with the late nineteenth century, Bellamy argued, the United States of the year 2000 would be a social paradise.

The journey to the future was undertaken by the twenty-year-old Julian West, who had been mesmerized in 1887 and came out of his trance, mind and body fully intact, one hundred and thirteen years later. He awoke to a Boston that was prosperous, orderly, and clean: the first thing that struck him was the absence of chimneys and smoke. Shortly afterwards, he discovered there were no stores, no banks, and – the classic characteristic of all self-respecting utopias – no lawyers. Everyone looked healthy and happy, walking along streets in which public advertisements no longer polluted the landscape and living in houses that were equipped with all the latest inventions – including "musical tele-phones," or loudspeakers, through which classical concerts could be heard simply by the turn of a screw.

As he inquired how this state of affairs came about, West learned that the concentration of monopoly capital in nineteenth-century America had become so great that eventually the state, embodying the wishes of the people, had taken over all economic activity. This transition had been effected by a new "national party," which had reorganized the production and distribution of goods along rational lines. The state was now "the sole employer, the final monopoly in which all previous and lesser monopolies were swallowed up, a monopoly in the profits and economies of which all citizens shared." All citizens were now employees of the state and, because they had a common interest in the common good, they gladly contributed their "industrial or intellectual serv-ices to the maintenance of the nation." As in Mercier's earlier utopia, an internal sense of duty had replaced external compul-sion in motivating people to work.[41]

Everyone between the ages of twenty-one and forty-five was part of a vast industrial army, in which people chose their occupations according to their aptitudes and interests. Workers were divided into different grades, which correspond-ed to their levels of ability. Within this system, there were plenty of opportunities for talented individuals to rise through the ranks. There was a separate grade for the mentally and phys-ically handicapped: "All our sick in mind and body, all our deaf and dumb, and lame and blind and crippled," West was informed, "belong to this invalid corps, and bear its insignia."[42] The burden of work was distributed evenly, so that those people with the hardest jobs worked the shortest hours. And, reflecting the moral assumption that each person would do his or her best, all workers received an equal share of the gross national product.

This sharing naturally raised the question of incentives. West

argued that people would produce more only if they were rewarded for their efforts. His host, Dr. Leete, agreed, but pointed out
that the concept of "reward" could not be reduced to narrow
monetary considerations. There were also the "higher motives" of
honour, prestige, and patriotism. "Diligence in the national service," West learned, "is the sole and certain way to public repute,
social distinction, and official power. The value of a man's services to society fixes his rank in it."

There were, it was true, a few people who refused to work.
They were treated as social outcasts and sentenced to solitary
imprisonment. But although there may have been imprisonment,
there were no actual prisons in the Boston of 2000: "We have no
jails nowadays," Dr. Leete says. "All cases of atavism are treated in
the hospitals." To reject the system was to become a parasite; to
become a parasite was to exhibit a form of mental illness; solitary
confinement and a diet of bread and water would cure such anti-
social tendencies.[43]

Everything in this society was geared to the common good
rather than to individual self-seeking. Buying and selling were
regarded as anti-social activities. All workers received credit cards
at the beginning of the year and obtained their goods directly
from national storehouses. Order forms travelled through a network of tubes until they reached the central warehouse, and the
goods themselves were delivered through larger tubes to individual houses. All in all, there were more tubes in Edward Bellamy's
Boston than there were in Terry Gilliam's *Brazil*. People ate in
public dining halls and did their washing at public laundries.
Housework was a thing of the past, and women were liberated
from the drudgery of domesticity.

In Bellamy's future the notion that women belonged to the
domestic sphere had long since been jettisoned. They formed a
separate but equal part of the industrial army, with its own female
officers and commander-in-chief. Women were given lighter work,

shorter hours, and longer vacations on the grounds that they were physically weaker than men, and they could take as much maternity leave as they required. Marriage and children actually advanced rather than impeded their careers. "The higher positions in the feminine army," West was told, "are intrusted only to women who have been both wives and mothers, as they alone fully represent their sex."

All women, regardless of their situation, were paid exactly the same as men – something West found particularly hard to believe. As a result, the women of 2000 enjoyed personal independence, liberty, health, and happiness – a marked contrast to their nineteenth-century predecessors, with "their ennuied, undeveloped lives, stunted at marriage," and "their narrow horizon, bounded so often, physically, by the four walls of home, and morally by a petty circle of personal interests."[44]

There was another side to this change as well. West noted that people in the year 2000 married for love rather than money or power. His host told him that this development was even more significant than he realized: "It means for the first time in human history the principle of sexual selection, with its tendency to preserve and transmit the better types of the race, and let the inferior types drop out, has unhindered operation." This selection occurred because "wealth and rank no longer divert attention from personal qualities." "The gifts of person, mind, and disposition; beauty, wit, eloquence, kindness, generosity, geniality, courage, are sure of transmission to posterity," Dr. Leete informed West. "Every generation is sifted through a little finer mesh than the last."[45]

The reference to preserving and transmitting "the better types of the race" strikes a new note in the history of the future – the ghost of Charles Darwin haunted the Boston of 2000. "We can so far take a prophetic glance into futurity as to foretell that it will be the common and widely spread species ... which will ultimately prevail," Darwin had written a few years before Bellamy began his book. "Hence we may look with some confidence to a secure future of great length. And as natural selection works solely by and for the good of each being, all corporeal and mental endowments will tend to progress towards perfection."[46]

In Bellamy's view, a just social, economic, and political order would automatically promote this process and improve the species. Other writers – such as Francis Galton, Darwin's cousin – pushed the argument still further and concluded that the state should make a conscious and deliberate attempt to improve the population through controlled selective breeding. Here, we move into the deeply disturbing territory of eugenics.

• • •

From our vantage point, eugenics is usually associated with fascist theories of racial purity and the horrors of the holocaust. It comes as something of a surprise, then, to learn that it was a progressive, democratic socialist intellectual who did more than anyone else in the English-speaking world to inject eugenics into the utopia of the future – none other than H.G. Wells. In Wells' utopian writings we encounter human beings who have become dehumanized in the name of humanity.

Consider, for example, his *Modern Utopia,* published in 1905. Here Wells bracketed together the world's "congenital invalids, its idiots and madmen, its drunkards and men of vicious mind, its cruel and furtive souls, its stupid people," and asserted that "the species must be engaged in eliminating them." Infants who were deformed or diseased presented no problem: they would all be killed at birth. That would not in itself solve the problem, however: "There remain idiots and lunatics, there remain perverse and incompetent persons, there are people of weak character who become drunkards, drug takers, and the like. Then there are persons tainted with foul and transmissible diseases. All these people spoil the world for others." It would be cruel to kill such people, said Wells. Instead, they should be isolated on remote islands, where they would be free to do anything except have children. They would be prevented from polluting the gene pool and from generally "spoiling" things for people as enlightened, compassionate, kind, and intelligent as Wells himself.[47]

This distinction was only the beginning. As well as eliminating the "base," Wells wanted to breed out those whom he defined as the "dull." "The Dull," he explained, "are persons of altogether inadequate imagination, the people who never seem to learn thoroughly, or hear distinctly, or think clearly ... They are the stupid people, the incompetent people, the formal, imitative people, the people who, in any properly organised State, should, as a class, gravitate towards and below the minimum wage that qualifies for marriage." To discourage them from procreating, the state must insist that only people who met basic standards of responsibility, health, and solvency should be allowed to have children. If they broke the rules, the parents would be fined or imprisoned and their children reared by the state.[48]

Through such methods, Wells believed, the people of the future would achieve mental and physical perfection. Eventually, everyone would rise to the level of the enlightened elite who had presided over the eugenics of utopia. In his appropriately titled *Men Like Gods,* Wells imagined the outcome: "There are few dull and no really defective people in Utopia; the idle strains, the people of lethargic dispositions or weak imaginations, have mostly died out; the melancholy type has taken its dismissal and gone; spiteful and malignant characters are disappearing."[49]

Along with eugenics, there would be broader environmental engineering. The Utopians had accomplished the "systematic extermination of tiresome and mischievous species," including almost all insect life. As in Mary Griffith's world of 2135, there would be no dogs; neither, for that matter, would there be any cats. Perfect humans now exercised perfect control over nature. What Griffith had achieved through the moralizing influence of emancipated women, Wells had accomplished through the rigorous intellect of rational scientists.[50]

All this was quite fine, unless of course you happened to be a handicapped child, or have a weak character, a tendency towards either anger or depression, an addiction to drink or drugs, a hereditary illness, a learning disability, or a fondness for dogs or cats. Then you were one of the "stupid people," one of the "defective people," who dragged society down and ruined things for everyone else. And even though you might not be intelligent enough to realize it, the measures taken to prevent you from procreating were really for the best. You could at least take some comfort from the scientifically proven fact that your "underlying racial taint" was slowly being bred out of existence for the benefit of the clever, the capable, the honest, and the creative members of society.[51]

• • •

There is more to Wells than eugenics, of course, and we will turn to other aspects of his thought in chapter 6. We will also encounter many of the central characteristics of the futuristic utopia, only to find them cast in a much darker light. The very changes that apparently presaged perfection during the late eighteenth and nineteenth centuries increasingly became reconceptualized as harbingers of doom. The dream of reason began to produce nightmares.

As it developed between the time of Louis-Sebastian Mercier and H.G. Wells, the ideal future society was an orderly, rational place, where individual citizens freely and voluntarily contributed to the common good. There was a mathematical logic to social organization, and the combined voice of reason and conscience prompted people to behave in a civil and virtuous manner. International relations were characterized by peace and harmony, and nations were united by commerce, reason, and friendship. There were no more colonies, there was no more slavery, and Ireland and Scotland were trying to become part of England. For most of the nineteenth century, there was little talk of a future world government, but that would soon change – again largely through the influence of H.G. Wells.

Operating on the assumption that human beings were blank slates whose personality was determined by environment and education, utopian writers believed in the malleability of human nature. Once the environment and the education system were controlled by enlightened leaders, all things would become possible. A new mathematically based language would make error unthinkable; dangerous books would be burned; anything that might undermine morality would be edited out of plays and novels; social delinquency would be cured by rigorous programs of re-education; and criminals would repent their sins before demanding their own execution. By the end of the nineteenth century, eugenics pushed this thinking onto a different plane: selective breeding would weed out weakness and create a superior, god-like race of men and women.

Personal liberty was inseparable from public order and there were no extremes of wealth and poverty. The definition of equality fluctuated: it could mean equality of opportunity or equality of condition. Either way, meritocratic principles prevailed, and creative talent would be rewarded by money or by social esteem. At the same time, the poor and the sick would be cared for, although, in Wells' world, they would not be allowed to have children. There would be universal medical care, first-rate hospitals, and social programs for those who could not help themselves. And because people were now rational and virtuous, there would be no alcohol, no tobacco, and no gambling in utopia. Everybody would be happy and healthy; longevity would increase, and it was not impossible that people would eventually live forever.

Meanwhile, technology would emancipate humanity from the drudgery of heavy physical labour, enable people to live in comfort, and provide them with enough leisure to improve their rational and moral faculties. Machines would improve agricultural and industrial productivity; the air would be full of balloons taking people from city to city; railways would criss-cross the land; and new forms of power would create vehicles that generated their own motion rather than being led by horses. It would also be possible for sound to travel over long distances, and the quality of life would be enhanced by classical music concerts that could be heard in every room of the house.

Within this future world of order, liberty, equality, and sophisticated technology, there was a common belief that women would no longer be exploited or oppressed. Precisely what this meant, though, varied over time. During the late eighteenth century the women of the future would become liberated through living in harmony with nature. Since nature had designed women to be mothers and wives, the argument ran, they would find true happiness in the domestic sphere of life.

By the middle of the nineteenth century, the domestic role of women assumed a wider social, moral, and political significance. As good republican wives and mothers, the future women of America would stop men from drinking, fighting, and generally being obnoxious and aggressive. At the same time, there were glimpses of a future in which women contributed to the general good through their own scientific creativity. Towards the end of the century, traditional notions that confined women to their "natural" domestic started to fade, husbands and children began to drop out of sight, and the women of the future were increasingly portrayed as participants in public politics.

This, then, was the kind of composite future that emerged from the utopian writings of the eighteenth and nineteenth centuries. It was associated with optimism and progress, and cyclical theories about the rise and fall of civilizations had been replaced by linear concepts of unlimited improvement. It was as close as you could get to heaven on earth, and its desirability appeared beyond debate.

And yet, from the viewpoint of the actual 2000, rather than nineteenth-century imaginings of the year, there is something unsettling about such a future. It seems more likely to suffocate than to set free the human spirit. The futuristic utopia has many positive features and is a fascinating place to visit. But who would actually want to live there?

·6·

SERPENTS IN THE GARDEN

"IF YOU WANT A PICTURE OF THE FUTURE, imagine a boot stamping on a human face – for ever."[1] These are the words of O'Brien, the interrogator and torturer in George Orwell's *Nineteen Eighty-Four*. They are the distilled essence of twentieth-century experiences of total war, total revolution, mass destruction, death, and devastation. The "war to end all wars" between 1914 and 1918 wiped out or maimed millions of men; the Soviet Revolution of 1917 culminated in a totalitarian dictatorship that killed even more Russians than would die in the Second World War; the rise of fascism resulted in oppression, the attempted "extermination" of the Jewish people, and a war that was unparalleled in the breadth of its brutality; and the atomic bomb signalled the possibility of the self-destruction of humankind. Simply to sketch out this picture can convey no idea of the individual stories of horror, fear, terror, grief, and loss that lie beneath the figures. As Joseph Stalin said, in his typically cynical fashion, when one person dies, it is a tragedy; when a million people die, it is a statistic.

No wonder, then, that the future became a darker place, and that notions of unlimited progress became harder and harder to sustain. In the late eighteenth and nineteenth centuries technology had generally been associated with the diffusion of prosperity and the emancipation of humanity from unremitting physical toil. During the twentieth century it was inseparable from the machine gun, the tank, air war, and the atomic bomb.

Utopian writers had imagined that the combined effects of education and the environment would recast human nature in the mould of perfection. During the twentieth century the malevolent aspects of mind control became terrifyingly apparent, as totalitarian regimes attempted to manipulate public opinion through the techniques of mass propaganda. The utopians had implicitly assumed the benevolence of those in power, but Hitler and Stalin suggested otherwise. As it became clear that power could be ruthlessly exercised either for its own sake or in the name of ideological purity, the utopian dream of an orderly society was transformed into a dystopian vision of authoritarianism and regimentation.

Where utopian writers wrote enthusiastically about enlightened citizens who freely contributed to the common good, their dystopian counterparts saw a brainwashed population who had become accomplices in their own oppression. Similarly, the abstract utopian ideal of reason now turned into a rationale for totalitarianism. It is no coincidence that all the defenders of dictatorship in twentieth-century dystopian literature were highly intelligent, articulate, and persuasive people.

The utopian future, in short, was one of the many casualties of the sequence of events triggered by the outbreak of hostilities in August 1914. The gap between the imagined and the actual twentieth century could not have been greater. The Great War of 1914–18 was not supposed to happen. Even when it did, it was not expected to last long: the boys, it was believed, would all be home by Christmas. Ten million lives and four years later, nothing would ever be the same again.

Nevertheless, the contrast between nineteenth-century optimism and twentieth-century pessimism is not as straightforward and clear cut as it may appear. On the one hand, positive images of the technological future proved remarkably durable, particularly in North America, and utopian literature eventually began to make a comeback in the 1970s – as we shall see. On the other, there were signs of scepticism, nagging fears about the future, which can be detected in the subordinate clauses of nineteenth-century literature.

Sometimes these doubts and forebodings emanate from the least-expected sources. The name of Jules Verne, for example, is normally and properly associated with science fiction adventure stories – with exciting journeys to the centre of the Earth, the depths of the sea, or (courtesy of a giant cannon) the surface of the Moon. Less known about Verne is the fact that one of his earliest novels took a much more critical approach to the social implications of technological change. Nor is it generally realized that his very last story, written a few weeks before his death in 1905, implicitly challenged the dominant notion of unlimited, linear progress. These aspects of Verne's literary career require further investigation.

• • •

The year is 1960. Paris is now 105 kilometres in diameter and is ringed by a series of smokeless, noiseless elevated railways, built back in 1913. On the streets, with their brightly lit luxury shops, horses have given way to "gas cabs," automobiles that are powered by gas combustion engines. Everyone is in a hurry, driven onwards by the "demon of wealth." Through the construction of canals linking Paris to the sea, the city has become "something like a Liverpool in the heart of France," with enormous warehouses and steamships from all over the world. Towering above them all is a 152-metre Electric Lighthouse, the "highest monument in the world," which can be seen forty leagues away as it penetrates the cloud of pollution that hangs over the city: "by means of ten thousand factory chimneys, the manufacture of certain chemical products – of artificial fertilizers, of coal smoke, of deleterious gases, and industrial miasmas – we have made ourselves an air which is quite the equal of the United Kingdom's."[2]

We are in the future that Jules Verne imagined almost a century earlier, when he wrote *Paris in the Twentieth Century* in 1863. The story begins on August 13, 1960, Prize Day at the Academic Credit Union. Private corporations and the national government have taken over the educational system, which has become entirely functional: subjects such as mathematics, civil engineering, commerce, finance, applied sciences, and the living languages have almost completely obliterated literature, classics, and history. The central character is Michel Dufrenoy, a sensitive, long-haired student who studies the obsolescent subject of Latin verse and wins first prize. "He must have been the only competitor!" remarks one observer, amid a general atmosphere of derision. Michel's guardian uncle is conspicuously absent from the ceremony. He is ashamed and embarrassed by his nephew's prize and wants the boy to do something useful and profitable with his life.[3]

The uncle himself is a paragon of practicality: "This man, raised in mechanics, accounted for life by gears and transmissions; he moved quite regularly, with the least possible friction, like a piston in a perfectly reamed cylinder; he transmitted his uniform movements to his wife, to his son, to his employees and his servants, all veritable tool machines, from which he, the motor force, derived the maximum possible profit." He owned a banking house, in which there were calculating machines the size of grand pianos, electric telegraphs that facilitated instantaneous communication throughout the world, and a form of "photographic telegraphy" that "permitted transmission of the facsimile of any form of writing or illustration, whether manuscript or print." In the real world of 1960, as opposed to Verne's imagined version, "photographic telegraphy" did not exist; thirty years later, though, along came fax machines.[4]

The uncle insisted that Michel must work in the banking house and become as functional as the rest of the family. Although there were fax machines in Verne's 1960, there were no typewriters or keyboards (in fact, they would be invented only four years after Verne wrote the novel), and people still wrote with quill pens. After proving himself "monumentally inept" on the calculating machines, Michel was transferred to the ledger department, where he was expected to keep meticulous records of all commercial transactions.

But he had no heart for the job. In desperation he decided to buy as many works of literature and poetry as possible, so he could be consoled in the evenings for the drudgery of the days. The only trouble was that all great works of French literature had long since been forgotten. Technical manuals were now the bestsellers, and such poetry that did exist merely sang the praises of science, chemistry, and mechanics. Nor was much relief to be found in modern music, which was sharply divided between popular jingles and esoteric jangling clashes of sound. "Either we endure the nauseating *melody of the virgin forest*, insipid, confused, indeterminate," says one of Michel's friends, "or else various harmony rackets are produced, of which you have given us such a touching example by sitting on the piano." To appeal to contemporary tastes, it was necessary to compose pieces without harmony, melody, or rhythm, and to give them titles such as "After Thilorier – a Grand Fantasy on the Liquefaction of Carbonic Acid."[5]

Within this utilitarian wasteland, Michel encounters a few kindred spirits. One of them is his other uncle – the one nobody talks about – who works in the neglected nineteenth-century literature section of the Imperial Library. Another is his fellow-worker in the ledger department, a young man called Quinsonnas. At

Quinsonnas' apartment, Michel joins a circle of alienated intellectuals who spend all their spare time discussing art and life. "Art is no longer possible unless it produces a tour de force," argues Quinsonnas. "These days, Hugo would have to recite his *Orientales* straddling two circus horses, and Lamartine would perform his *Harmonies* upside down from a trapeze!" "This world is nothing more than a market," agrees one of his friends, "an immense fairground, and you must entertain your clients with the talents of a mountebank."[6]

Michel learns the truth of this opinion shortly after he is fired from the bank and tries his hand as a writer with the state-run Great Dramatic Warehouse. Plays were regarded as instruments of public utility, scripts were composed by teams of writers who followed formulaic principles, and applause experts were trained to monitor audience responses. Michel was placed in the Comedy Division, where writers were taught the art of plagiarizing the plays of earlier centuries. Suitable adjustments were made in the interests of topicality, or to avoid offending particular groups of people, such as lawyers' wives. Having failed miserably in this work, he was demoted to the Division of Drama, where narratives were developed through the same kind of conveyor-belt system associated with factory production.

But he couldn't handle that, either, and was moved further down the scale to the Vaudeville Division. Here there was a clerk in charge of rhyming couplets, and another who specialized in punch lines. There was a "section of naughty situations," a "Department of Puns," a "central office of jokes, witty repartee, and preposterous phrases," and a team of people who collected and categorized all possible plays on words in the French language. This was bad enough, but the last straw came when Michel was assigned to a play entitled *Button Up Your Trousers!*. "I shall not stay another minute in this charnel house!" he declared. "I'd rather starve to death!"[7]

And starve he did, during the bitter winter of 1961–62, the coldest in two centuries. At the end of the book, Michel is wandering through the snow-covered streets of Paris, deranged with despair. He finally falls unconscious in the city cemetery, near the neglected graves of all the forgotten poets.

Although the ending is dark, the general tone of *Paris in the Twentieth Century* is humorous and satirical, with an edge of anger. By describing a world in which technological, bureaucratic, and functional values had become totally triumphant, Verne asserted the importance of the creative, artistic imagination and took a stand against narrow-minded technocracy and market-driven entertainment. In this sense, the future was a means to an end, for his primary concern was with the present. Nevertheless, when it came to the actual future, Verne turned out to be much more prescient than most.

He got some things very wrong, of course. Apart from the quill pens, Verne thought that war would become obsolete in the future world of commerce and calculations. Instead, we got the twentieth century. Even here, though, Verne was not entirely off the mark. He believed that the countries with the greatest wealth would gradually dominate the others, and that the power of money would succeed where the power of arms had failed.

In other respects, Verne repeatedly got it right. Near the site where he had imagined the Electric Lighthouse, 152 metres tall, the Eiffel Tower, 300 metres tall, was actually built in 1889. His vision of an educational system dominated by corporate interests and neglecting the liberal arts strikes a contemporary chord, as does his description of pollution in the modern industrial city. The Great Dramatic Warehouse is not a million miles away from the contemporary world of cinema and television, right down to the teams of writers and the "applause experts." There are times when one suspects that *Paris in the Twentieth Century* is actually a modern forgery, a great hoax falling within the "retrospective prophecy" syndrome. But it is not.

And consider the theme itself. The book describes an alienated, long-haired poet in the 1960s who is rebelling against a materialistic world of fax machines, automobiles, and lowest-common-denominator entertainment. Michel's reaction to the prospect of working in the banking house is about the same as Benjamin's reaction to "plastics" in the movie *The Graduate*. But *Paris in the Twentieth Century* never actually saw the light of day in Verne's lifetime. In 1863 it was rejected for publication. The reason? "No one today will believe your prophecy," Verne was told. It was simply too far-fetched to be taken seriously.[8]

Here, then, Verne had entered his protest against a society in which quantity threatened to destroy quality, and where the pursuit of wealth turned people into automatons. In contrast to those writers who associated utilitarianism with utopia, Verne found little to admire and much to fear in a purely functionalist future. The Paris of 1960 was a much more constricting and conformist place than the Paris of 1863, and such an outlook implicitly rejected the pieties of progress. For the most part, this attitude remained beneath the surface of Verne's subsequent writings. Towards the end of his life, however, it found full expression in a story that he set forty thousand years in the future, entitled "Eternal Adam."

At first, the story is very puzzling: the geography does not make any sense, and it is unclear where and when we are. Apart from one obscure islet, the only land on the globe is the continent of Hars-Iten-Schu. After a long history of strife and warfare, bloodshed and butchery, everyone has been drawn into a single empire. With peace and stability, science begins to flourish: the art of writing and printing have been discovered, coal is being mined as a source of energy, and the potential of electricity is about to be tapped. But the origins of humanity remain unknown: although popular myths speak of Hedom and Hiva as the first man and woman, educated people are becoming aware of the principles of evolution.

In the course of their investigations into the origin of species, scientists such as the "learned Doctor Sofr" are exploring the seabed. Much to their surprise, they find human remains and signs of a civilization much older and more sophisticated than their own. Among the discoveries is an ancient metal-cased manuscript in an unknown language, which Doctor Sofr spends many years trying to decipher. And when he does, he is brought face to face with what we call the twentieth century.

The manuscript has been written by a Frenchman who lived in Mexico around 1905 and who regularly debated Darwinism and the Bible with a small circle of friends. Despite their differences about Adam and Eve, they are united in "admiring the high culture attained by humanity, whatever had been its origin." They drink toasts to progress – to railways and steamships and aeroplanes, to the "innumerable machines, increasingly ingenious, that could perform the work of hundreds of men," and above all to electricity, "the agent that was so versatile and controllable ... that, dispensing with wires, we could use it to run all kinds of machines, navigate any vessel, marine, submarine, or aerial, and write, see, or speak – and all at whatever distance we pleased."

But suddenly, in the midst of this conversation, something strange and terrifying happens. The ground begins to tremble and sink into the sea. Everywhere, buildings are collapsing and the earth is vanishing. They rush into a car and drive into the mountains, with the sea enveloping the land immediately behind them. Eventually, they reach a mountain top, only to realize that they are surrounded by the sea. They have become stranded on an obscure islet. After several days of starvation, they are rescued by a British ship. Shortly afterwards, a ferocious gale blows up, which lasts over a month and drives them to where China should have been. No land is anywhere to be seen. As they continue on their travels, the horrible realization dawns on them that the entire known world, with all its people and all its progress, has been drowned out of existence.

Out in the Atlantic, though, they come across a land mass that has arisen from the sea – the former Atlantis and the future Hars-Iten-Schu. Here they struggle for survival, scrape out a living, and begin to produce children. Their prospects, though, remain bleak. "Alas!" wrote the author of the manuscript, "it is only too certain that humanity, of which we are the sole representatives, is on the road to rapid regression leading to brutehood." "I seem to see them," he continued, "those men of the future, ignorant of articulate language, intelligence extinguished, bodies covered with coarse hair, wandering in this dreary desert."

And so Doctor Sofr is left to ponder the fragility of civilization. "What had been needed to abolish forever all the science of so mighty a people – and to erase even the memory of their existence?" he asks himself. "Less than nothing: simply an imperceptible shudder that ran through the crust of the globe." All his own assumptions about progress and the meaning of life have been shattered. To recognize what has happened in the past is "to gainsay the *future*, to cry out that *our* effort is in vain! That all human change is as aimless and as little secure as a bubble in the froth of the waves!"

The only thing that has been carried over from the one civilization to the other is the myth of origin: Hedom is a corruption of Adam, as Hiva is of Eve. Everything else in the past has been lost; everything in Doctor Sofr's present will meet the same fate. The notion of unlimited progress is utterly illusory. "The Truth, when found," Doctor Sofr concludes, "would prove to be the endless ordeal of regeneration."[9]

Verne's stories, then, were framed by warnings. There were no guarantees that the future would be a better place. The very forces that led to material improvement threatened to imprison the imagination, and it was entirely possible that everything would eventually collapse. The common theme is a protest against the hubris of progress – the comfortable assumption that technology could solve all problems, produce happiness, and control nature. Against the arrogance of technocracy, Verne insisted on the need for a sense of wonder and a sense of humility. As it turned out, humility would be in short supply during the first half of the twentieth century.

· · ·

Whatever else you could say about H.G. Wells, you could hardly describe him as humble. He had no doubt about the requirements of utopia, such as world government, rational scientific planning, technological progress, biological engineering, and the challenges of change. But he also issued a series of warnings about the kind of world that would result if these conditions were not met: there would be extreme class differences, technological unemployment, mass destruction, and a general drift towards social decay. In this sense, Wells' utopianism was designed as an antidote to the dystopian tendencies he perceived around him – even though his utopian prescription appears at least as bad as the disease. His writings contained elements of hope and fear, both of which were intended to stimulate social and political activism. Without such activism, he believed, the future would be a bleak place.

Certainly, anyone expecting to find a bright view of the future in *The Time Machine* (1895) would be deeply disappointed. The first thing to note about this book is so obvious that its significance can easily be overlooked – the title. Before Wells, people had encountered the future in their dreams, through the revelations of a "Genius," or after a prolonged period of suspended animation. This was the first time that someone had travelled into the future by machine. In the past the future had been about sophisticated technology; now it was sophisticated technology that got you there in the first place.

Wells' Time Traveller moved forward from 1895 to the year 802,701 – far in advance of most other imaginative futures, which were usually pitched anywhere between ten and seven hundred years ahead. The traveller had expected to find the people of the future "incredibly in front of us in knowledge, art, everything"; instead, he encountered ruined buildings, dilapidated palaces, and a fragile, childlike people called the Eloi. He was even more surprised to discover that another group of people, the sinister and ape-like Morlocks, inhabited the world beneath the ground.

Gradually, the Time Traveller put the pieces together. The capitalists had evolved into a leisure class that triumphed over nature and became totally secure. Meanwhile, the labourers increasingly worked underground, where they eventually adapted to their subterranean conditions. But the Eloi became victims of their own success: "The too-perfect security of the Upper-worlders had led them to a slow movement of degeneration, to a general dwindling in size, strength and intelligence."

While the Eloi had lost their intelligence and initiative, the Morlocks had lost their compassion and warmth: to survive in their underground dwellings, they had become resourceful and ruthless. When the Morlocks ran out of food, they began to capture, kill, and eat the Eloi. In effect, the Eloi had become the upper-world cattle who sustained the creatures of the underworld. "I grieved to think how brief the dream of the human intellect had been," said the Time Traveller. "It had committed suicide. It had set itself steadfastly towards comfort and ease, a balanced society with security and permanency as its watchword, it had attained its hopes – to come to this at last."[10]

There are two crucial points of contact between Wells' imaginative future and his actual present. First, the division between the Eloi and the Morlocks was based on tendencies that Wells detected in his own society. Class differences were not only becoming deeper, he believed, but were also reflected in the changing social organization of space. The "less ornamental purposes of civilization" were being pushed out of sight and beneath the surface: London's new underground railway system, the first in the world, was only the most dramatic symptom of a more general trend. The late nineteenth-century working class, Wells argued, already lived in artificial conditions that separated them from "the natural surface of the earth."

At the same time, the richer people were attempting to insulate themselves from "the rude violence of the poor" and were establishing their own enclaves in the countryside: "About London, for instance, perhaps half the prettier country is shut in against intrusion." The nightmarish world of 802,701, from this perspective, was simply the logical culmination of a process that was already under way. Similar assumptions lay behind Fritz Lang's futuristic film *Metropolis,* in which an exploited working class, enslaved to the machine and existing in vast underground industrial complexes, was contrasted with the comfortable and complacent bourgeoisie who lived on the surface.[11]

The second link between 1895 and 802,701 can be found in Darwinianism, which continued to exert a profound influence on Wells' outlook. Both the Eloi and the Morlocks had been shaped by the requirements of their respective environments, to the point at which they were turning into different species. There was an important lesson to be learnt here, Wells believed: without the stimuli of struggle, all utopias would eventually self-destruct. "It is a law of nature we overlook," he wrote, "that intellectual versatility is the compensation for change, danger, and trouble ... There is no intelligence where there is no change and no need of change. Only those animals partake of intelligence that have to meet a huge variety of needs and dangers."

Wells also registered a sense of ultimate cosmic decay. Pushing into the furthest reaches of the future and the outer rim of the imagination, the Time Traveller journeyed through millions of years into what had become a wilderness. The Moon had vanished, the Sun was a gigantic red star, the sky was dark, and menacing giant crabs crawled over the land where London once had been. "I cannot convey the sense of abominable desolation that hung over the world," the traveller reports. Moving still further through time, he reached a world of darkness and silence on the edge of oblivion. In the very long run, all human endeavours would sink without trace and eventually the world itself would disappear.[12]

But this projection should not stop us from trying to improve the quality of human life, Wells believed. The fate of the Eloi and the Morlocks could and should be avoided. The key was to apply the standards of scientific rationalism to the historical process. A central task facing humankind was to establish a world state that would combine the need for security and order with the demand for initiative and individuality.

Such a state would be led by an enlightened elite, a kind of futuristic samurai, who recognized that human progress hinged on "experiment, experience, and change." The state would provide for food, clothing, order, and health, but would also encourage the entrepreneurial spirit. Economic incentives would reward people who contributed to the quality of life, and wage differences would be retained as an "inducement to effort." The aim, Wells wrote, was to change the nature of incentives, "to make life not less energetic, but less panic-stricken and violent and base, to shift the incidence of the struggle for existence from our lower to our higher emotions."[13]

Under this system of rational control, technological advances would produce the "effectual abolition of a labouring and a servile class." Women would also become as free as men, Wells argued, despite their obvious inferiority. The fact of the matter was – and he was big on "facts" – that women were characterized by "weaker initiative," "inferior invention and resourcefulness," and a "relative incapacity for organisation and combination." They were, however, good at being mothers, and should be paid for their work by the state. Such recompense would also release them from economic dependence on their husbands.

In line with his theory of eugenics, Wells believed that women's wages should increase according to the number of healthy children they produced. As a consequence, "a capable woman who has borne, bred, and begun the education of eight or nine well-built, intelligent, and successful sons and daughters would be an extremely prosperous woman." The state would encourage the institution of marriage, always recognizing that "the one unavoidable condition will be the chastity of the wife." "Her infidelity being demonstrated," Wells wrote, "she must at once terminate the marriage and release both her husband and the State from any liability for the support of her illegitimate offspring." This restriction applied only to women: Wells said nothing whatsoever about the chastity of the husband. Perhaps this is not surprising, coming from someone who had several affairs outside his own marriages.[14]

All in all, when considering his passion for eugenics, his sexual double standards, and his own assumptions of superiority, it is hard to read H.G. Wells without wanting to vomit.

It was one thing to write about the need for "rational" control and world government, and quite another to figure out how this state of affairs could actually be accomplished. Here, again, the dialectic between dystopia and utopia came into play: only when people were brought face to face with the potentially disastrous consequences of their existing behaviour patterns, Wells believed, could the work of construction begin.

While earlier utopians had viewed technology in positive terms, Wells was acutely aware of its capacity for destruction. It was crucial, then, to bring technology under control. This need was all the more urgent given the rapid advances that were occurring in atomic physics. Shortly before the First World War, Wells tackled these developments in *The World Set Free,* the first futuristic novel to envisage and examine the impact of nuclear power on society, war, and politics.

The story began in 1933, when atomic energy was finally harnessed by humankind. The scientist responsible realized that he had opened up "worlds of limitless power," but also recognized the danger of his discovery: "Felt like an imbecile who has presented a box full of loaded revolvers to a Creche," he noted in his diary. Within twenty years, nuclear power produced electricity and fuelled cars, trains, and planes. On the one hand, there was a vast increase in production; on the other, traditional industries such as oil, coal, and steel were becoming outmoded. The result was social and economic catastrophe: unemployment, suicide, and violent crime all skyrocketed and "it seemed as though human society was to be smashed by its own magnificent gains."[15]

Such developments all stemmed from the widening contradiction between technological progress and political stagnation. Men were using science to create unprecedented wealth, but were stuck fast in traditions of government that were becoming increasingly obsolete. "These traditions come from the dark ages when there was really not enough for everyone," comments one of Wells's characters, "when life was a fierce struggle that might be masked but could not be escaped." And by far the most dangerous of these outworn traditions, in the new age of atomic power and aerial warfare, was the continued existence of separate, competing, and chauvinistic nation states.[16]

Some two and a half centuries earlier, a Jesuit named Francesco de Lana-Terzi had speculated about the possibility of flying boats that could deal death and destruction from the air. His conclusion was both profoundly humanistic and tragically naive:

God would not suffer such an invention to take effect, by reason of the disturbance it would cause to the civil government of men. For who sees not that no city can be secure against attack, since our Ship may at any time be placed directly over it, and descending down may discharge Souldiers; that the same would happen to private Houses and Ships on the Sea: for our Ship descending out of the Air ... may over-set them, kill their men, burn their ships by artificial fireworks and Fireballs. And this it may do not only to Ships but to great Buildings, Castles, Cities, with such security that they which cast these things down from a height out of Gun-shot, cannot on the other side be offended by those from below.[17]

Fifty years after *The World Set Free,* in the aftermath of the Cuban missile crisis, Bob Dylan wrote an anti-war song, "With God on Our Side," that unconsciously echoed de Lana-Terzi's argument: "If God's on our side," ran the last line, "he'll stop the next war."

Wells was much more steely eyed about such things. Aeroplanes and atomic power plus nationalism and imperialism equalled mass destruction, God or no God. *The World Set Free* mapped out the most likely scenario. A crisis in the Balkans drew in France and England on the one side, Germany and the central European powers on the other; during the 1950s Europe and then the entire world became engulfed in war. At first, the war was conducted along conventional lines, with infantry columns marching against each other. Then the Germans dropped a new kind of bomb – an atomic bomb – on the War Control Centre in Paris. There was a deafening, never-ending sound and a great ball of unquenchable crimson-purple fire that burrowed into the earth "like a maddened living thing" and destroyed all before it. In that moment, everything in the world changed.[18]

With the War Control Centre obliterated, all communications broke down. In these circumstances, local leaders took the initiative and planned for retaliation. You have to imagine Wells' scene, with its strange combination of the old and the new. Pilots and bomb-throwers set out on bi-planes and are intercepted over Berlin by German pilots, who try to warn them off with megaphones and shoot at them with rifles. The bomb-thrower lifts up the atomic bomb, "a black sphere two feet in diameter," bites off its celluloid stud, and throws it over the side. From our perspective, such images of the bombing mission may seem darkly comical, but there was nothing remotely funny about its effect. Where Berlin had once stood, there was something that looked like the crater of a continuously erupting volcano.[19]

This was a totally new kind of war, even worse than the kind that had haunted the seventeenth-century imagination of de Lana-Terzi. The power to destroy had reached unparalleled magnitude, while the ability to defend had disappeared. In a futile attempt to save themselves, governments throughout the world attempted to get their retaliation in first: "Power after power about the armed globe sought to anticipate attack by aggression. They went to war in a delirium of panic, in order to use their bombs first."

Thousands of planes battled for supremacy in the air. The central European airforce dropped atomic bombs on the dykes of Holland, flooding the country and drowning almost the entire population. China and Japan bombed Russia, the United States bombed Japan, India experienced nuclear civil war, and the Balkans blazed with atomic weapons. The "whole world was flaring ... into a monstrous phase of destruction." All the major cities were obliterated, all economic activity was shattered, and the world hovered on the brink of mass starvation. "One's sense was of a destruction so far-reaching and of a world so altered," recalled one survivor, "that it seemed foolish to go in any direction and expect to find things as they had been before the war began."[20]

As it became clear that nuclear war made nonsense of all traditional military and political objectives and produced nothing but universal devastation, a conference of governments met at Brissago in Italy to salvage the situation. Here we move into classic Wells territory – the formation of an enlightened elite who would end the war and oversee the task of reconstruction. There were ninety-three "leaders of thought and learned investigators" at Brissago. Together they proclaimed the unity of the world, recognizing through bitter necessity that the continued existence of nation-states would only perpetuate a conflict that would bring everyone down in its wake. The one holdout was the king of the Slavs and his chief minister Doctor Pestovich, who attempted to lull the new leaders into a false sense of security, nuke the lot of them, and take over the world. But they were hunted down and shot, leaving the Assembly of Brissago free to establish a new world order.

Under international direction, there were coordinated efforts to demobilize troops and to feed, house, and employ the "drifting millions of homeless people." Atomic power was now harnessed for exclusively peaceful purposes, scientific laboratories increased agricultural productivity, and economic activities were reorganized along the lines of democratic guild systems. There was a universal language (English, of course), education system, calendar, and currency.

The new freedom from insecurity and fear unlocked the immense creative potential that existed within humanity and the "long smothered passion to make things" now broke out into action. Human nature had adapted itself to the new realities: "It is not as if old things were going out of life and new things coming in," Wells wrote; "it is rather that the altered circumstances of men are making an appeal to elements in his nature that have hitherto been suppressed, and checking tendencies that have hitherto been over-stimulated and under-developed."[21] Paradoxically, then, nuclear war had created the conditions in which humankind had liberated itself, in the world set free. "The catas-trophe of the atomic bombs which shook men out of cities and businesses and economic relations," commented Wells, "shook them also out of their old established habits of thought, and out of the lightly held beliefs and prejudices that came down to them from the past."

In taking this position, Wells unconsciously placed himself in a long-standing apocalyptic tradition. His secular notion that dystopia engendered utopia echoed the religious view that the world would be destroyed before the thousand-year reign of love, peace, and joy could begin. Where Wells had predicted nuclear war, the seventeenth-century catastrophist Thomas Burdet had prophesied Armageddon: "The cities of the earth are in one uni-versal blaze. Innumerable millions of either sex and of every rank sink under the agonies of death, in its most frightful forms." And where Wells had imagined utopia, Burdet had looked forward to a millennium in which "war, discord, and pestilence" would be "banished for ever." The scientific rationalism of Wells and the apocalyptic fantasies of Burdet had more in common than at first appeared.[22]

The notion of universal peace flowing from universal war took a viciously ironic twist shortly after the publication of *The World Set Free*. Wells had imagined a nuclear conflict, originating in the Balkans, which would become the war to end all wars. What the world actually got between 1914 and 1918 was trench warfare, originating in the Balkans, in which the slaughter of millions was rationalized by the very concept of the "war to end all wars." And at the end of it all, the prospects for world government appeared as remote as ever. Wells himself dismissed the new League of Nations as "a melancholy and self-satisfied futility."

It seemed that the human condition was more conducive to despair than to hope. Significantly, Wells began his postwar utopi-an novel, *Men Like Gods,* with the same kind of apparent pessimism that could be found in the opening pages of Mercier and Volney: "Everywhere there was conflict, everywhere unreason; seven-eighths of the world seemed to be sinking down towards chronic disorder and social dissolution."

And yet, like Mercier and Volney before him, Wells insisted on the possibility, indeed the inevitability, of utopia. *Men Like Gods* was the last kick of the Enlightenment, in combination with modern theories of eugenics. It was also an acerbic attack on the values of nationalism, imperialism, and militarism. One of the characters, a thinly disguised version of Winston Churchill, plots to take over utopia and establish an Anglo-American-French empire that would exclude the Russians, Germans, and all non-white people. But his plans are defeated and revealed for what they are — the products of a primitive and violent era, best described as the Age of Confusion.

The road from the Age of Confusion to utopia would be long and hard, Wells argued. The struggle against "greedy, passionate, prejudiced and self-seeking men" would continue for at least five centuries, but eventually the ideas of enlightened writers, teachers, and scientists would prevail. Free and fair discussion would gradually expose the lies and shams that poisoned the political atmosphere; education would provide people with the knowledge to set them free; and physiological and psychological science would create a new kind of human being for a new kind of world.

The message, then, was one of hope: the apparently futile efforts of liberal intellectuals were actually preparing the way for a better future. Before his trip to utopia, the central character, Mr. Barnstaple, "had been in a mood of depression." Afterwards, he could "see plainly enough how steadily men on earth were feeling their way now, failure after failure, towards the opening drive of the final revolution."[23]

In this way, Wells maintained his faith that humankind would come through the hell of war, in whatever form it took, and would ultimately establish a form of heaven on earth. Out of suffering, he believed, would come redemption. There would still be changes and challenges, and there would still be clashes of values, for, without them, humankind would stagnate into something like the Eloi. But the world would be run by scientists, intellectuals, and psychologists who would establish an efficient and rational order. Through the methods of these latter-day samurai, human beings would finally conquer nature. Indeed, through eugenics they would finally conquer human nature itself. How could there possibly be any serpents in this garden?

• • •

Perhaps not surprisingly, it was Soviet Russia, the first putatively proletarian state in the world, that produced the first major published anti-utopian novel. Utopia was all very well in theory and at a safe distance; in practice and up close it took on a very different aspect. If the idea of utopia was a good place that was no place, the reality was a bad place that was right in your face.

Already, long before Stalin came to power, the Russian Revolution of 1917 was developing along totalitarian lines. At Kronstadt, the working class had been destroyed in the name of the Working Class. Wherever their power reached, the Bolsheviks employed the means of intimidation, censorship, and terror for the end of safeguarding a revolution that was supposed to usher in the final stage in human history. Individual freedom was being suppressed in the name of collective happiness. Against this background, but not wholly in response to it, a disenchanted revolutionary named Yevgeny Zamyatin projected this tendency one thousand years into the future, in a work appropriately entitled *We.*

In many respects Zamyatin's *We,* the first dystopian novel, is remarkably similar to Mercier's *L'An 2440,* the first futuristic utopia. Mercier imagined a future in which reason, order, science, and logic produced perfection: his Time Traveller had been impressed by the "strait lines" and rational organization of twenty-fifth-century Paris. Zamyatin imagined a future in which reason, order, science, and logic produced a living hell. The futuristic One State of *We* set out to "unbend the wild, primitive curve and straighten it to a tangent," worshipped the "great, divine, exact, wise straight line – the wisest of all lines," and applied mathematical logic to the problem of human happiness. Such linear rationalism had been quite at home during the Enlightenment, but in Zamyatin's hands it plunges the world into darkness. What Zamyatin did, in effect, was to take radical eighteenth-century attitudes to reason and mathematics, push them to their illogical conclusion, and stand them on their head.[24]

All aspects of life in the One State were regulated, to ensure the greatest happiness of the greatest number. Indeed, people themselves had become numbers, with designations such as D-503 and I-330 instead of individual names. They all wore identical uniforms, lived in identical houses, and marched together along identical streets.

As in Mercier's utopia, none of them smoked or drank. Again, mathematical models set the standard, in a calculus of morality that would have delighted someone like Condorcet. "Everyone who poisons himself with nicotine, and especially alcohol," we learn, "is ruthlessly destroyed by the One State." Mathematical logic demonstrated that the quick destruction of the few was better than the slow death of the many. To kill one individual was to diminish the total sum of human lives by fifty years, but to allow "the partial killing of millions" through substance abuse was to diminish the total sum by around fifty million years. Any ten year old, the narrator informs us, could solve such an obvious mathematical moral problem in half a minute.[25]

Sexual activities were also carefully controlled, just as they had been in earlier utopian works. We have already seen that John Lithgow's *Equality: A Political Romance* imagined a world where women registered for their lovers, where men and women lived in separate apartments, and where they could have sex only once a week. In Zamyatin's One State each person, or number, filled in a pink coupon to register for a sexual partner, and the couple would then be allotted a fixed time for intercourse. "Each number has a right to any other number, as to a sexual commodity," ran one of the rules of the One State.

Sex was fine, but love was out of the question. Love led to jealousy, jealousy led to unhappiness, and unhappiness was anathema; consequently, love had been "organized and reduced to mathematical order." "And so," we are told, "what to the ancients was the source of innumerable stupid tragedies has been reduced to a harmonious, pleasant, and useful function of the organism, a function like sleep, physical labor, the consumption of food, defecation, and so on."[26]

Along with the mathematical monitoring of morality, the One State established an equally mathematical efficiency through a Table of Hours that determined virtually every detail of daily life. Here, Zamyatin was satirizing the new techniques associated with Frederick Taylor, the American exponent of scientific management, who was regarded in the One State as "the greatest genius of the ancients." Taylorite principles had been pushed to their limit, so that all the numbers became cogs in the social machine: "Every morning, with six-wheeled precision, at the same hour and the same moment, we – millions of us – get up as one. At the same hour, in million-headed unison, we start work; and in million-headed unison we end it. And, fused into a single million-handed body, at the same second, designated by the Table, we lift our spoons to our mouths." Even the act of eating was controlled: there were exactly "fifty prescribed chewing movements for each bite." And, at work, the "Taylor system" ensured that everyone moved in "regular, rapid rhythm," like "humanized machines, perfect men."[27]

In Mercier's *L'An 2440* the future was deeply influenced by Rousseau's notion of forcing men to be free; in Zamyatin's One State they were forced to be happy. "If they fail to understand that we bring them mathematically infallible happiness," declared the *One State Gazette,* "it will be our duty to compel them to be happy." Such compulsion took a number of forms. The One State was ruled by the Benefactor, who presided over public executions in which dissidents were theatrically and literally liquidated – turned into water in front of a vast and admiring audience. The Benefactor was assisted by the Guardians, who responded to the first hint of aberrant behaviour by bringing out their electronic whips and who tortured people in a Gas Bell to extract information about any subversives who may have existed. All the houses were made out of transparent glass, to ensure that all numbers were visible at all times, though they were allowed to lower the shades when they were having sex. The streets were lined with "gracefully camouflaged" listening devices, "recording all conversations for the Office of the Guardians."[28]

These methods of control were designed to promote the maximum degree of happiness and to protect people from the destructive consequences of their own passions. Liberty, in the One State, was incompatible with happiness, and happiness was the ultimate goal of human life. It all made mathematical sense, according to the narrator: "Freedom and crime are linked as indivisibly as ... well, as the motion of the aero and its speed: when its speed equals zero, it does not move; when man's freedom equals zero, he commits no crimes. That is clear. The only means of ridding man of crime is ridding him of freedom."[29]

The story of the One State is told through the diary of D-503, the builder of the *Integral,* a space ship that is intended to spread the benefits of reason throughout the galaxy. At first D-503 fully endorsed the "mathematically perfect life of the One State," embraced its values, and could only express himself in the language of arithmetic. Everything in life was "clear" and rational for D-503 until he encountered a mysterious woman known as I-330. At their very first meeting she drew attention to his hairy hands, which he viewed as a "relic of a savage epoch." There was a "constant, irritating x" beneath her smile: she affected him "as unpleasantly as an irresolvable irrational member that has slipped into an equation."[30]

I-330 registered for D-503 and set out to seduce him from allegiance to the One State. She kissed him when her mouth was full of alcohol – possession of which was a capital offence – and let it flow into him. Even before this happened, D-503 had been experiencing strange new feelings about I-330 and had been having disturbing dreams. In the One State, dreams were by definition disturbing. They were "a serious psychic disease" because of their chaotic, irrational, and unpredictable character.

After the alcohol kiss, D-503 was completely unhinged. His personality split in two: there was the number, and there was the person beneath the number. Previously repressed primitive emotions were unleashed and all the old certainties came crashing down. That night he was unable to sleep – another crime against the One State. Nor could he distinguish between dreams and reality. Confusion replaced clarity, as D-503 was plunged into the world of irrational numbers. "Now I no longer live in our clear, rational world," he wrote; "I live in the ancient nightmare world, the world of square roots of minus one."[31]

There is an obvious parallel here with the story of Adam and Eve. Just as Eve gave Adam the apple, I-330 gave D-503 a "mouthful of fiery poison" (cider, one assumes), out of which came knowledge and the terrifying possibility of individual freedom. As a result, D-503 experienced a profound identity crisis. At one moment he saw himself as a passionate human being; at the next he desperately tried to reassert reason over his "delirium." His friend, the poet R-13, made the biblical connection explicit:

> That ancient legend about paradise ... Why, it's about us,
> about today. Yes! Just think. Those two, in paradise, were
> given a choice: happiness without freedom, or freedom with-
> out happiness. There was no third alternative. Those idiots
> chose freedom, and what came of it? Of course, for ages after-
> ward they longed for the chains. The chains – you under-
> stand? That's what world sorrow was about. For ages! And
> only we have found the way of restoring happiness ... We have
> helped God ultimately to conquer the devil – for it was he
> who had tempted men to break the ban and get a taste of
> ruinous freedom, he, the evil serpent. And we, we've brought
> down our boot over his little head, and – cr-runch! Now
> everything is fine – we have paradise again.

But, to compound the irony, we later learn that R-13's defence
of the system was utterly insincere. In fact, the poet was part of a
secret resistance movement and had simply been spouting the
official line. Other supposedly compliant numbers were also
secret subversives, including the doctor who solemnly diagnosed
D-503 as suffering from an incurable disease. "You're in a bad
way!" the doctor said. "Apparently, you have developed a soul." In
this way Zamyatin was highlighting one of the central characteristics of the emerging Soviet regime in Russia – the enormous gap
between what people said and what they actually thought. Lying,
hypocrisy, and insincerity were all embedded in utopia – indeed,
they were necessary prerequisites for survival.[32]

Within the One State, emotions and passions kept breaking
through the cracks of reason, like grass through concrete. And
beyond its borders there lay a wild, primitive, and savage world,
shut out by an apparently impenetrable Green Wall. This notion
of the "wilderness without" became a recurring feature of dystopi-

an literature and provided an emotional counterpoint to the city of logic. The metropolis associates itself with reason, order, and prosperity, and defines itself against a periphery that is connected with passion, chaos, and poverty. In the case of *We*, the dissidents within the One State find a way into the world beyond the Green Wall and plot revolution. The internal revolt against reason links up with the externalized projection of passion.

Because D-503 was the builder of the *Integral* space ship, the rebels needed to win him over so they could use the ship in the impending struggle against the One State. I-330 succeeded in her task, and D-503, who had fallen completely in love with her, agreed to join the revolution. Meanwhile, the One State had just announced a medical breakthrough that would destroy the last remaining barricade to total happiness – a Great Operation that would excise the imagination from the human brain and make the Taylorite revolution complete.

While the population was being cajoled and coerced into having the Great Operation, the plot to seize the space ship began. But the Guardians had been tipped off and prevented the ship from falling into rebel hands. Shortly afterwards, D-503 himself had the operation and told the Benefactor all about the "enemies of happiness." I-330 was brought to the Benefactor and tortured in the Gas Bell, and D-503 watched her agony without compassion: "Her face became very white, and since her eyes are dark and large, it was very pretty."

But the revolution had not been completely crushed. The Green Wall had been blown up and the tightly defined world of the One State was falling apart. "In the western parts of the city," noted the post-operation D-503, "there is still chaos, roaring, corpses, beasts, and – unfortunately – a considerable group of numbers who have betrayed Reason." He reassured himself, though, with the conviction that the One State would conquer its enemies – "Because Reason must prevail."[33]

The fundamental flaw with utopias based on reason, happiness, and the collectivity, in Zamyatin's view, was that they obliterated emotion, freedom, and individuality, all of which were essential to the full development of humankind. Although he wrote in the immediate aftermath of the Russian Revolution, it would be facile to view *We* simply as a reaction to an emerging Soviet totalitarianism. That was part of it, but it was not the whole story.

In fact, Zamyatin was satirizing not only a false antithesis between freedom and happiness but also the tendency of the radical Enlightenment to turn reason, mathematics, and utilitarianism into moral absolutes. Nor is it a coincidence that Frederick Taylor was singled out for special treatment. The dehumanizing nature of work in the early twentieth-century capitalist economy was one of Zamyatin's central targets. Anyone who wanted to turn Zamyatin's *We* into an attack solely on Soviet communism would have to omit a lot of awkward material.

That did not, however, stop some people from trying. Almost two decades after Zamyatin wrote *We,* Ayn Rand wrote a highly derivative futuristic story, *Anthem,* in which the same concepts were employed to attack communism and glorify the absolute power of the individual ego. Like Zamyatin, Rand wrote of a collective society where people were conditioned to think of themselves as part of the "great WE." Like Zamyatin, she imagined a world where the characters had numbers rather than names. Where Zamyatin had the great wilderness beyond the Green Wall, Rand had the "Uncharted Forest" beyond the so-called civilized world of the collectivity.

Some people might suspect that Rand was involved in plagiarism here – a highly ironic charge when applied to the Apostle of Individualism. Such a suggestion, however, underplays her own original variations on Zamyatin's theme. For one thing, her collective state is much cruder than Zamyatin's: anyone who uses the first person singular, in Rand's story, has his or her tongue cut out and is then publicly burned alive. For another, Zamyatin's general criticisms of totalitarianism, the radical Enlightenment, and industrial capitalism are narrowed into a sustained attack on the Soviet-style command economy alone. There is a third difference as well. Zamyatin had satirized a society in which the collective obliterated the individual. Rand, in contrast, praised a world in which the individual obliterated the collective. Through a form of simplistic, bipolar thinking, Rand replaced an oppressive "We" with a megalomaniac 'I'."

The hero of her story is Equality 7-2521, who combines utter contempt for the weak with a staggering sense of his own superiority. Rising above the ignorant and enslaved masses, he renames himself "The Unconquered" and escapes into the Uncharted Forest. Shortly afterwards he is joined by Liberty 5-3000, a woman whom he has named "The Golden One." Together, they find freedom, discover the "I" word, and spend a considerable amount of time glorifying themselves: "I wished to know the meaning of things. I am the meaning. I wished to find a warrant for being. I need no warrant for being, and no word of sanction upon my being. I am the warrant and the sanction."[34] The new, liberated man must think and will for himself; he must pursue his own happiness as an end in itself; he must worship "this god, this one word: 'I'." In fact, Equality 7-2521 and Liberty 5-3000 become even greater than gods: he now calls himself "Prometheus," the man who stole fire from the gods, and renames her "Gaea," the mother of the Earth and of all the gods.

When they were not singing their own praises, Prometheus and Gaea (as we must now call them) did what any self-respecting freedom-loving couple would do: they built an electric security fence around their house to keep out intruders. This was essential because, as Prometheus put it: "There is nothing to take a man's freedom away from him, save other men. To be free, a man must be free of his brothers. That is freedom. This and nothing else."

Others might find it ironic that true freedom consists in building a fortress to protect the strong and mighty against the weak and foolish. Not Ayn Rand, though. Nor did she perceive any irony in the fact that women occupied a subordinate role in this world of individualism. It was, after all, Prometheus who named Gaea and who believed that freedom would be transmitted through the male line: "Gaea is pregnant with my child. Our son will be raised as a man. He will be taught to say `I' and to bear the pride of it." One can only hope that Gaea did not let him down by producing a daughter.[35]

Prometheus expected that his fortress would become a magnet for all men who wanted freedom and that he would emancipate the world from the tyranny of "we." "I shall break all the chains of the earth," he declared, and raze all the cities of the enslaved, and my hope will become the capital of a world where each man will be free to exist for his own sake." Unfortunately Prometheus, who was not quite as intelligent as he thought, could only accomplish this end with the help of his fellow men. This meant that the fight for freedom would have to be a collective one in which the "we" acted in the name of "I" – a contradiction which completely escapes the author. The now taboo "we" word even creeps into the final declaration of the book: "And here, over the portals of my fort, I shall cut in the stone the word which is to be my beacon and my banner. The word which will not die, should we all perish in battle. The word which can never die on this earth, for it is the heart of it and the meaning and the glory. The sacred word: EGO."[36]

This glorification of the self, projected into the future, bears a remarkable similarity to a phenomenon that we have already encountered in the past – the cult of the Free Spirit, with its narcissistic delusions, pathological egomania, false dreams, and fake messiahs. The Free Spirits believed they had become one with

God, but Rand's characters believed that they had become even greater than God. And their Creator was not a million miles from those Christs and Marys who dotted the landscape of the Dark Ages over a thousand years before she put pen to paper.

• • •

One of the central aspects of the late nineteenth-century futuristic utopia was the use of eugenics to ensure the improvement and ultimate perfection of the human stock. One of the central aspects of its late eighteenth-century prototype was the emergence of a "model citizen" who would internalize and act upon the values of reason and morality. Both these themes, in the form of sophisticated techniques of selective breeding and social conditioning, were at the heart of Aldous Huxley's *Brave New World* (1932) – a book that has become one of the classic dystopian texts, despite or possibly because of the author's deep ambivalence about the future he described.

Huxley's original intention in writing the book was to satirize the eugenically engineered utopia that had been embraced with such enthusiasm by H.G. Wells. As we have seen, Wells envisaged a period of conflict and chaos out of which would emerge a scientifically planned state of genetically improved human beings. In his *Modern Utopia,* Wells had divided humankind into the Poietic (those with brilliant minds), the Kinetic (the clever and capable), the Dull, and the Base. Although he wanted to discourage the Dull and prevent the Base from breeding, he did not think it would be possible actually to "develop any class by special breeding." The "intricate interplay of hereditary," he believed, was "untraceable and incalculable."[37]

Like the people of Wells' future, the inhabitants of Huxley's twenty-sixth-century world had passed through the crucible of war and constructed a rational social order on the ashes of the past. But Huxley's biologists and psychologists had succeeded in unravelling the "intricate interplay of hereditary" and were indeed able to develop new classes of people. His book takes us into the Central London Hatchery and Conditioning Centre, where babies are manufactured like standardized products on the assembly line. Revolutionary new procedures enable one egg to produce up to ninety-six identical embryos. Through genetic engineering, the babies are categorized into five broad classes, corresponding roughly to Wells' typology.

At the top are the highly intelligent Alpha-Plus group. From here we move down the ladder until we reach the Epsilon-Minus Semi-Morons, who do the most menial and mindless jobs in the economy. The breeding techniques are reinforced by intensive and extensive conditioning programs. Drawing on "neo-Pavlovian" techniques, electric shock treatment, and hypnopaedia, or sleep teaching, scientists are now able to instill the "appropriate" moral values into each category of infants. Children would grow up not only accepting but loving their place in the social order. As Huxley put it, the "really revolutionary revolution is to be achieved, not in the external world, but in the souls and flesh of human beings ... The love of servitude cannot be established except as the result of a deep, personal revolution in human minds and bodies."[38]

While selective breeding paralleled Wellsian eugenics, social conditioning paralleled Enlightenment notions of *tabula rasa,* which maintained that the personality was determined by the imprint of environment and education. For eighteenth-century utopians, this development was entirely positive. Once you controlled the environment and instructed children in the principles of reason and morality, you were home and dry. The minds of children were entirely malleable, it was believed: through the "hope of reward" and the "fear of chastisement," they could be moulded into model citizens. The logic of *Brave New World* was the same, but the results were anything but appealing: reason destroyed emotion, morality destroyed freedom, and the model citizen became a self-regulating robot.

The more Huxley developed his picture of the future, the further his parody of Wells began to spin out of control. New satirical targets arose, including an American popular culture that certainly seemed like the wave of the future. The people of Huxley's future listened to jazz groups such as Calvin Stopes and his Sixteen Sexophonists, had sex-hormone chewing gum, took happiness-inducing drugs like *soma* (a twenty-sixth-century "anticipation" of Prozac), and entertained themselves at the "feelies," an advanced form of the movies. This was the culture of Instant Gratification, in a social order that aimed to reduce as far as possible the gap between a desire and its fulfilment.

Central to this society was the principle of sexual promiscuity, which had an important political as well as personal function. In this respect, Huxley's dystopia had something in common with the Marquis de Sade's prescription for the future. Back in 1795 de Sade had argued that there was a direct connection between sexual licence and political stability. The repression of sexual desires, he believed, would make men vent their frustrations on the government. If you allowed a man to do whatever he wanted, though, "he will issue forth satisfied and with no desire to disturb a government that secures so willingly for him every object of his lusts." For de Sade, this freedom meant the legitimization of rape and a total disregard for the rights of women, who were merely the "objects of public lust."[39]

Huxley's dystopia did not go that far, contenting itself with conditioning children in compulsory erotic play and viewing monogamy as a species of social deviance. The operating principle, however, was the same. "As political and economic freedom diminishes," Huxley wrote, "sexual freedom tends compensatingly to increase. And the dictator ... will do well to encourage that freedom. In conjunction with the freedom to daydream under the

influence of dope, the movies, and the radio, it will help to reconcile his subjects to the servitude which is their fate."[40]

Along with his satire on American popular culture, Huxley
mocked Keynesian economics, which maintained that the world
could break out of its economic depression through public works
and increased consumption. In Huxley's image of the future, public works became ends in themselves: the suburbs of London were
full of weird towers that were built to boost the economy.
Consumerism became part of the conditioning process:
hypnopaedic messages continually told children that "ending is
better than mending," "the more stitches, the less riches," "I love
new clothes," and so on. Any activity that detracted from consumption, such as reading or walking, was discouraged, and
under-consumption became a crime against society.[41]

Beyond the borders of this civilization, and fulfilling the same
functions as Zamyatin's world beyond the Green Wall and Rand's
Uncharted Forest, lay the Savage Reservation of New Mexico. In
Huxley's story, two of the central characters visited the reservation
and returned with John the Savage. Like the first "Indians" who
were brought from North American to Europe during the sixteenth century, John the Savage became an object of great curios-
ity in London. And just as the "savages" of the sixteenth century
were used either to affirm or to challenge the values of "civilization," John the Savage became the external yardstick against
which twenty-sixth- century London was measured.

Here, Huxley's book limps and stumbles. In the reservation,
the Savage had encountered the works of Shakespeare, which
formed the medium through which this latter-day Caliban
responded to the "brave new world." The sections in which the
Savage reacts to civilization, spouting Shakespeare all the while,
are contrived and embarrassing, as Huxley himself seems to have
realized. Still, the exchanges between John the Savage and
Mustapha Mond, the World Controller, were one of the most

gripping parts of the book. And they were made all the more interesting by the fact that Huxley gave Mond all the best lines, much as Milton had given Satan the best lines in *Paradise Lost.*

The Savage contended for art, liberty, and God; Mustapha Mond argued for utility, stability, and happiness. Art thrives on conflict, Mond explains. Where there was no conflict, the tragedies of a Shakespeare were redundant and incomprehensible. Besides, in the scheme of things, artistic creativity was a small price to pay for human happiness:

> The world's stable now. People are happy; they get what they want, and they never want what they can't get. They're well off; they're safe; they're never ill; they're not afraid of death; they're blissfully ignorant of passion and old age; they're plagued with no mothers or fathers; they've got no wives, or children, or lovers to feel strongly about; they're so condi-tioned that they practically can't help behaving as they ought to behave. And if anything should go wrong, there's *soma.* Which you go and chuck out of the window in the name of liberty, Mr Savage.[42]

Happiness may be less spectacular than liberty, Mond concedes, but it was infinitely preferable to the misery, loneliness, death, and destruction of earlier eras, such as the early twentieth century.

To clinch his case, the Controller told the Savage about the Nine Years' War, when scientific progress, in the form of anthrax bombs, almost wiped out the world. After that, people realized they had a choice – control or destruction. Not surprisingly, they opted for control – the Wellsian trajectory is unmistakable. But, unlike Wells, Huxley envisaged a future in which scientific knowl-edge would itself be carefully circumscribed. In this scientifically controlled world, the rulers recognized that the free pursuit of sci-entific knowledge constituted a threat to stability and could

reopen the doors to destruction. Hence the paradox: this scientifically planned state was profoundly anti-scientific.

Nor was there any need for God in a world where there was
"universal happiness" and where you could carry half your morality in a bottle of soma, or "Christianity without tears." When the
Savage objected that all this control and conditioning degraded
humanity, Mond countered with a nice piece of moral relativism:
"Degrade him from what position? As a happy, hard-working,
goods-consuming citizen he's perfect. Of course, if you choose
some other standard than ours, then perhaps you might say he
was degraded. But you've got to stick to one set of postulates."[43]
Taken on its own terms, accepting its own postulates, the world
of the Controller appeared logically unassailable.

Anyone who couldn't fit in, because of some accident or over-
sight on the infant assembly line, was simply taken out of society
and deposited on a remote island – just as the diseased, the drunkards, and the drug-takers were banished to islands in Wells'
Modern Utopia. This is what happened to two of the central characters in Huxley's book – Bernard, who had too much alcohol in
his blood-surrogate, and Hemholtz, who was "too much interested in beauty." Hemholtz could have gone to Samoa, but opted
instead for the more bracing climate of the Falkland Islands.[44]

The Savage, though, was a special case. Towards the end of his
conversation with the Controller, he took his stand against this
brave new world:

> "But I don't want comfort. I want God, I want poetry, I want
> real danger, I want freedom, I want goodness. I want sin."
>
> "In fact," said Mustapha Mond, "you're claiming the right
> to be unhappy."
>
> "All right, then," said the Savage defiantly, "I'm claiming
> the right to be unhappy."
>
> "Not to mention the right to grow old and ugly and impo-

tent; the right to have syphilis and cancer; the right to have too little to eat; the right to be lousy; the right to live in constant apprehension of what may happen tomorrow; the right to catch typhoid; the right to be tortured by unspeakable pains of every kind."

There was a long silence.

"I claim them all," said the Savage at last.

Mustapha Mond shrugged his shoulders. "You're welcome," he said.[45]

In the end, the Savage killed himself rather than live as a freak in this totally controlled society.

The moral seems obvious. Huxley is warning us about what is likely to happen if we make happiness, order, and scientific planning the central criteria of society. In comes eugenics, conditioning, and instant gratification in the form of sex, drugs, and consumerism; out goes creativity, freedom, and morality. For Huxley, freedom comes first. He tells us this himself in the foreword he wrote for the 1946 edition of the book, fourteen years and another world war after the original publication in 1932. The book, he wrote, was really a call "to decentralize and to use applied science, not as the end to which human beings are to be made the means, but as the means to producing a race of free individuals."[46] Huxley, it is clear, sided with the Savage.

Stop. Go back. Consider that "long silence" with which the Savage greeted the Controller's graphic description of the suffering associated with freedom. This was not an easy decision to make; beneath the silence lay a riot of conflicting emotions and arguments. Nor should we assume that Huxley unambiguously supported the Savage. In fact, there is considerable evidence to suggest that he was intellectually closer to the Controller, Mustapha Mond. As David Bradshaw has pointed out, Huxley wrote *Brave New World* against the background of the Wall Street

Crash of 1929, the Great Depression, and what seemed like a general collapse into chaos. And Huxley had a deep aversion to chaos. "It may be," he had written as early as 1927, "that circumstances will compel the humanist to resort to scientific propaganda, just as they may compel the liberal to resort to dictatorship. Any form of order is better than chaos." During the Depression, it seemed that these circumstances had now arrived.

Huxley's attraction to planning became abundantly apparent when he visited a modern industrial plant in northern England, just before he started writing his novel. He liked what he saw. The plant, he wrote, constituted "an ordered universe ... in the midst of a world of planless incoherence." The industrialist who was responsible was the controller of the newly formed Imperial Chemical Industries. His name was Mond.

Even more striking, it turns out that Huxley had actually been a proponent of eugenics. In 1932, the year that *Brave New World* was published, he argued on a BBC radio program that eugenics could prevent the "rapid deterioration ... of the whole West European stock." Like many other intellectuals, Huxley later abandoned such ideas when Hitler and the Holocaust pushed them to their horrifying conclusion. At the time of writing, though, they were less reprehensible to him than they later appeared.

In short, Huxley in 1932 was intellectually attracted and emotionally repelled by planning and eugenics. That is why he gave the Controller the best lines. That is why he made the Savage choose freedom. And that is why he wrote such a chilling book about the future.[47]

• • •

By far the best-known and most disturbing dystopian novel was George Orwell's *Nineteen Eighty-Four,* described by E.M. Forster as "that hateful apocalypse." Contrary to popular belief, *Nineteen Eighty-Four* the book had nothing to do with 1984 the year.

Orwell had originally intended to call it "The Last Man in Europe" and arrived at the actual title simply by inverting the last two years of the date of composition, 1948. This was entirely appropriate, since the book was really about totalitarianism in his own time. In the best "prophecy as warning" tradition, Orwell extrapolated a possible future from sinister tendencies that already existed in embryonic form. The point was not to predict the totalitarian future but to prevent it: the book was written for 1948, not 1984. And precisely because it was so closely attuned to the experiences of his own era and was written with such honesty and clarity, *Nineteen Eighty-Four* possessed an immediacy and pointedness that marked it out from everything else in its genre.[48]

Experience was central to Orwell's writing in general and *Nineteen-Eighty Four* in particular. He described himself as a man who "loved the surface of the earth," disliked grand intellectual theories, and developed his ideas from a first-hand knowledge of imperialism, revolution, totalitarianism, and propaganda – beginning with his own career during the 1920s in the Indian Imperial Police in Burma. Forced to suppress his private feelings and thoughts while performing his public duties, Orwell became acutely aware both of the dynamics and dangers of self-censorship and of the difference between outward obedience and inward rebellion – themes that would resurface in *Nineteen Eighty-Four.*

During his later service with the anarcho-syndicalists in the Spanish Civil War, Orwell encountered the full force of Communist Party oppression and the sheer power of its propaganda machine. He witnessed the communist reign of terror against the anarchists in Barcelona, read the lies that were being perpetrated in the left-wing press, and experienced what he called the death of history:

> In Spain, for the first time, I saw newspaper reports which did not bear any relation to the facts, not even the relationship

which is implied by an ordinary lie. I saw great battles reported where there had been no fighting, and complete silence
where hundreds of men had been killed. I saw troops who had
fought bravely denounced as cowards and traitors, and others
who had never seen a shot fired hailed as the heroes of imaginary victories; and I saw newspapers in London retailing these
lies and eager intellectuals building emotional superstructures
on events that had never happened. I saw, in fact, history
being written not in terms of what happened but of what
ought to have happened according to various `party lines.'[49]

Against those intellectuals who were naive enough to believe that
the left generally told the truth while the right always lied through
their teeth, Orwell recognized that, as far as their totalitarian
methods were concerned, there was actually little difference
between communists and fascists.

This awareness could only be heightened by the Hitler-Stalin
Pact of 1939, when apparent opposites converged. The Communist
Party of Great Britain, which had been about as anti-Nazi as you
could get, abruptly switched its position and supported the alliance.
A parody of the popular song "O My Darling Clementine," now
entitled "O My Darling Party Line," summed it up:

> Leon Trotsky was a Nazi
> Yes, I knew it for a fact.
> First I read it, then I said it,
> Till the Hitler-Stalin Pact.

And then, when Hitler began his attempted invasion of the Soviet
Union in 1941, Britain's Communist Party switched back equal-
ly abruptly to its former position and acted as if the Hitler-Stalin
Pact had never occurred. All this would be grist for the world of
Nineteen Eighty-Four, with its shifting alliances and wars among

Oceana, Eurasia, and Eastasia, its rewriting of history, and its capacity for "doublethink," or the ability to hold two conflicting opinions at the same time.

But it would be wrong to assume that Orwell equated totalitarianism only with European fascism and Soviet communism. In fact, he recognized both tendencies within British society, and in *The Road to Wigan Pier* had speculated about the possible emergence of fascism in his own country – "a slimy Anglicized form of Fascism, with cultured policemen instead of Nazi gorillas," as he put it. During the Second World War, Orwell worked for the BBC and became part of Britain's own wartime propaganda machine. It was not a happy experience. He described the BBC as "a mixture of whoreshop and lunatic asylum," and tried to console himself with the thought that he had "kept our propaganda slightly less disgusting than it might otherwise have been." Nevertheless, propaganda was propaganda, and its power in the future seemed both inescapable and terrifying. Indeed, so pervasive did it seem that Orwell began writing his own "War-time Diary" as proof against any subsequent reworking of the history through which he had actually lived – not unlike Winston Smith, the central character of *Nineteen Eighty-Four*.[50]

All these elements, along with Orwell's direct experiences of popular culture in Britain and his indirect knowledge of the torture techniques of Hitler's and Stalin's secret police, were incorporated into his portrait of dystopia. Even before he went to Spain, Orwell had rejected the concept of utopia as being impractical and undesirable. "The Socialist world," he wrote in *The Road to Wigan Pier,* "is to be above all things an *ordered* world, an *efficient* world. But it is precisely from that vision of the future as a sort of glittering Wells-world that sensitive minds recoil."[51] Besides, the utopians, with all their abstractions about an enlightened, disinterested elite, had been utterly naive about the question of power. As Orwell recognized, power had a strong addictive quality and could easily be exercised as an end in itself.

This point was made most forcefully by O'Brien as he was torturing the rebel Winston Smith, the "flaw in the pattern." The Party, explained O'Brien, "seeks power entirely for its own sake. We are not interested in the good of others; we are interested solely in power." Where the Nazis and the communists deluded themselves into believing that power was an essential prerequisite for the creation of paradise, the Party had transcended such illusions: "We know that no one ever seizes power with the intention of relinquishing it. Power is not a means, it is an end. One does not establish a dictatorship in order to safeguard a revolution; one makes the revolution in order to establish the dictatorship. The object of persecution is persecution. The object of torture is torture. The object of power is power. Now do you begin to understand me?"[52]

But power could not exist without the powerless, and the exercise of power was meaningless without inflicting pain and suffering on the weak. Obedience was not enough: people could pretend to accept the system while secretly despising it, just as Orwell himself had pretended during his years with the police in Burma. The point was to impose the will of the powerful on the minds of the powerless, through methods of torture. "Power," says O'Brien, "is in inflicting pain and humiliation. Power is in tearing human minds to pieces and putting them together again in new shapes of your own choosing. Do you begin to see, then, what kind of world we are creating? It is the exact opposite of the stupid hedonistic Utopias that the old reformers imagined."[53]

In a world where progress now meant "progress towards more pain," the Party had obliterated the private sphere and monitored every detail of its members' lives. In each apartment there were telescreens that "received and transmitted simultaneously": they picked up every noise above a whisper and could see virtually everything in the room. At the other end of the wires were the

Thought Police, ready to pounce on the slightest hint of heresy, from a look of indifference (or *facecrime,* as it was called) to the words mumbled in dreams. Nothing, not even sexual relations, was outside the control of the Party.[54]

Although the dystopias of Zamyatin and Huxley had encouraged sexual promiscuity, Orwell's *Nineteen Eighty-Four* was characterized by strict puritanism, in which young people were enlisted in organizations such as the Junior Anti-Sex League. "It was not merely that the sex instinct created a world of its own which was outside the Party's control and which therefore had to be destroyed if possible," Winston Smith noted. "What was more important was that sexual privation induced hysteria, which was desirable because it could be transformed into war-fever and leader-worship."[55]

In effect, de Sade's view that sexual repression produced rage was now being harnessed in the service of the Party. All the deep and dark emotions that had been bottled up were unleashed during the Party's "Two Minutes Hate" periods, in which "the face of Emmanuel Goldstein, the Enemy of the People," became the focus of fury: "A hideous ecstasy of fear and vindictiveness, a desire to kill, to torture, to smash faces with a sledgehammer, seemed to flow through the whole group of people like an electric current, turning one even against one's will into a grimacing, screaming lunatic." Then the powerful and reassuring figure of Big Brother would appear on the screen, amid slow rhythmical chants of relief and praise, and all the emotional intensity of a religious revival.[56]

Not only sexual instincts, but also family relations became perverted in the interests of the Party. Parents were encouraged to be fond of their children, but children were taught to spy on their parents and to report their "deviations" to the Thought Police. Intimacy had become politicized, fear was pandemic, and there were hardly any cracks and crevices for anything approaching independent thought.

But these methods of constant surveillance and psychological terror were only part of the Party's apparatus of power. "Reality is inside the skull," O'Brien tells Winston Smith — and here lay the central principle of the Party's *modus operandi*. Because reality was merely a matter of perception, the Party could change reality by changing perceptions. The past, after all, only existed in written records and human memories: the records could be altered and the memories could be reshaped. Thus a small army of employees at the Ministry of Truth (including Winston Smith) worked at falsifying the past to suit the Party line. Truth was whatever the Party said it was. And by controlling the past, the Party could also control the future.[57]

We have seen that Mercier, in his *L'An 2440,* believed that books should be burned, and the past forgotten, in the quest for utopia. The Party had extended, elaborated, and "improved" upon the logic in its quest for power. We have also seen that Condorcet, in his musings about utopia, anticipated a new mathematically infallible language that would expand to embrace all forms of thought and "render error almost impossible." In Orwell's *Nineteen Eighty-Four* the rulers also recognized the relationship between words and thought, but they sought to contract the language so that "error" as defined by the Party would become completely impossible.

To this end, the Party had invented "Newspeak," whose features were delineated by Symes, one of Winston Smith's colleagues at the Ministry of Truth:

Don't you see that the whole aim of Newspeak is to narrow the range of thought? In the end we shall make thoughtcrime literally impossible, because there will be no words in which to express it. Every concept that can ever be needed will be expressed by exactly *one* word, with its meaning rigidly

defined and all its subsidiary meanings rubbed out and forgotten ... Every year [there will be] fewer and fewer words, and
the range of consciousness always a little smaller ...
The Revolution will be complete when the language is perfect.

Condorcet had been turned upside down. And just as Condorcet
had been destroyed by a regime that aspired towards utopia, the
fictional Symes would be destroyed by the dystopia that he mis-
takenly associated with perfection. After listening to him,
Winston Smith thought to himself that Symes would be vaporized by the Party: "He is too intelligent. He sees too clearly and
speaks too plainly. The Party does not like such people. One day
he will disappear." And, sure enough, one day he does.[58]

This blinding, deafening, crushing apparatus of power pressed
down upon all members of the Party. But beyond the Party, and
comprising 85 per cent of the population, lay the "proles," the
"swarming disregarded masses." In some respects the world of the
proles was analogous to Zamyatin's world beyond the Green Wall,
Huxley's Savage Reservation, and even Rand's Uncharted Forest.
It was the "other" putatively primitive and supposedly subhuman
world that existed in sharp contrast with the regimented character of the "official" order. And it could also be a place of hope,
presenting a possible challenge to the tightly sealed culture of
control. "*If there is hope,*" Winston Smith wrote in his secret
diary, "*it lies in the proles.*"[59]

Yet it became increasingly apparent to him that the proles
lacked any kind of political consciousness, except for a kind of
"primitive patriotism" that served the interests of the state.
"Heavy physical work, the care of home and children, petty
quarrels with neighbours, films, football, beer, and, above all,
gambling filled up the horizon of their minds," Winston reflected. His one attempt to engage a prole in conversation about life
before the revolution ended in total failure and frustration.

Besides, the Thought Police moved through their ranks, identifying and eliminating "the few individuals who were judged capable of becoming dangerous." While Zamyatin's world beyond the Green Wall offered the possibility of change, the proles of *Nineteen Eighty-Four* would never threaten the system. The future was uniformly grim; the boot would stamp on the face forever.[60]

To make matters worse, the face would actually learn to love being stamped on, as the Party specialized in tearing minds apart and putting them together again to fit the prevailing orthodoxy. Winston had taken refuge in the comforting belief that the Party could never actually change his innermost thoughts. But O'Brien knew better:

> When finally you surrender to us, it must be of your own free will. We do not destroy the heretic because he resists us; so long as he resists us we never destroy him. We convert him, we capture his inner mind, we reshape him. We burn all evil and all illusion out of him; we bring him over to our side, not in appearance, but genuinely, heart and soul. We make him one of ourselves before we kill him.[61]

And O'Brien made good on his promise to squeeze Winston empty and "fill you with ourselves," through a process of torture and humiliation so graphic it is almost impossible to read twice. The Party reconstructed his memories and his mind so that he genuinely believed that two and two equalled five, truly loved Big Brother, and looked forward to being shot through the head while his thoughts were still pure.

We have come full circle from Mercier's utopia, where self-regulating citizens supported the state through their own free will, and where deviants publicly and sincerely proclaimed that they wished to be executed. The utopia of yesterday had become the dystopia of tomorrow.

· 7 ·

THE AMBIVALENT FUTURE

THROUGH ALL THE SHIFTING SHAPES OF THE FUTURE over the past thousand years, certain patterns seem to have emerged. In the Middle Ages and the early modern period, the future was generally seen through the prism of biblical prophecy or a set of folk beliefs clustered around pagan divinations, magic, witchcraft, and astrology. Gradually, between the sixteenth and the eighteenth centuries, the forces of secularization and scientific knowledge began to break through older assumptions about the nature and meaning of human history. During the Age of Revolution, traditional apocalyptic thought fused with secular notions of progress to propel North American and European societies in radically new directions.

In the process, secular views of the future eventually prevailed, even though millenarian expectations continued to exert a powerful influence over political and social movements. The first futuristic utopias, which appeared in the late eighteenth century, relegated religion to a relatively minor role and envisaged a world in which deism had replaced Christianity. Reason, order, technological progress, and liberty were the central characteristics of the ideal future society. The ways of the past, associated with irrationality, chaos, stagnation, and oppression, would be left far behind. God and Heaven appeared redundant; Man the Maker (and it was man) would create perfection on Earth, using such methods as education and, by the late nineteenth century, eugenics.

During the first half of the twentieth century, though, the new realities of total war, economic depression, ideologically inspired dictatorships, and the death camps all forced a radical reconceptualization of utopian thought. There were many ways to kill a man, ran a poem from the period, though the easiest was simply to put him in the twentieth century and leave him there. Reason had failed or had been twisted into the service of tyranny; order had become synonymous with suffocating collectivist control; technological progress had produced nerve gas and the atomic bomb; and liberty had become an empty word, squeezed dry of meaning. By the time Orwell wrote *Nineteen Eighty-Four*, the future had become a very dark place. Utopia, as a literary genre, appeared dead and buried.

Meanwhile, in all these futures, whether apocalyptic, utopian, or dystopian, women remained in a decidedly subordinate position. There were exceptions, such as the thirteenth-century "cult of Guglielma," with its vision of a new church run by Spiritualized Women, and the eighteenth-century followers of Joanna Southcott, who believed their leader would usher in the millennium. In the nineteenth century, Mary Griffith asserted the intellectual equality and moral superiority of women, while her suffragist successors looked forward to a future in which women had won political emancipation.

In the most widely read books about the future, though, men remained very much in control. Bellamy believed that women would receive equal pay and participate fully in the workforce, but he still assumed that they were the weaker sex and that the doctors would be male. Wells thought he had a progressive attitude to women's equality, but was actually one of the most offensive chauvinists around, even by the standards of his time. Zamyatin's Benefactor and Huxley's World Controller were both men; Ayn Rand was to feminism as Margaret Thatcher was to socialism; Orwell never imagined the possibility that the Party's torturer might have been a woman. The same male-dominated attitude permeated the world of science fiction, as Ursula Le Guin pointed out: "It was like this. `Oh, Professor Higgins,' cooed the slender, vivacious Laura, `but do tell me how does the antipastomatter denudifier work?' Then Professor Higgins, with a kindly absent-minded smile, explains how it works for about six pages, garble garble garble."[1] Similar assumptions lay behind the predictions of the supposedly scientific futurologists who came onto the scene during the 1950s and 1960s. They wrote rapturously about all the labour-saving devices that would transform the home, but never dreamed that women could be anything else other than housewives.

It seems, then, that we have a composite picture of the future, as it appeared around the middle of the twentieth century: the promise of technology had turned into a threat; the Book of Revelation was no longer taken seriously as a literal guide to the future; and women were going to remain happy homemakers, as they had supposedly been in the past. What is wrong with this picture?

•••

For a start, the notion of "technology as threat" cut against the grain of a deeply embedded belief that "useful science" was the panacea for all social, political, and even military problems. This was particularly the case in the United States, the country that originally regarded itself as the embodiment of scientific Enlightenment rationalism. Benjamin Franklin, after all, experimented with both electricity and electoral politics, and his contemporaries connected the conduction of lightning with the emancipation of humanity: "But what dareing [sic] mortals you are!" exclaimed the English pottery manufacturer Josiah Wedgwood, "to rob the Thunderer of his Bolts, – and for what? – no doubt to blast the oppressors of the poor and needy, or to execute some public piece of justice in the most tremendous and conspicuous manner, that shall make the great ones of the Earth tremble!"[2]

The same sentiments were expressed by Thomas Paine in 1775, only weeks after he arrived in America. "*The degree of improvement which America has already arrived at is unparalleled and astonishing,*" he wrote, "but 'tis miniature to what she will one day boast of." Asserting that America's "reigning character is love of science," he praised organizations that spread "useful knowledge" and began publishing articles on practical subjects that would promote the public good. When Alexis de Tocqueville visited the United States some sixty years later, he registered an equally optimistic mood: "Democratic nations," he observed, "care but little for what has been, but they are haunted by visions of what will be; in this direction, their unbounded imagination grows and dilates beyond all measure."[3]

Such attitudes were sufficiently resilient to withstand significant shocks, in a nation whose very traditions contradicted the notion of Tradition. Technological utopianism in the United States persisted through the Civil War, the First World War, the Great Depression, and the rise of communism and fascism. In 1939, on the edge of the abyss, the World's Fair in New York presented its theme of "Building the World of Tomorrow." Never mind Japan's invasion of China, Nazi racism and expansionism in Europe, and Stalin's ruthlessness in Russia: the "World of Tomorrow," as seen from New York, was a wonderful, exciting and hopeful place. The optimism was unlimited; the naivety was surreal.

Central to the World's Fair was the "Futurama" exhibit in the General Motors pavilion, which brought close to 30,000 people a day into the imagined world of 1960. And some world it was, with its smooth skyscrapers of steel and glass, well-planned sub-urbs, amusement parks and recreation areas, modern industrial districts, hydroelectric plants and dams, and orchards where trees grew beneath glass domes. Seven-lane expressways enabled the happy folks of the future to drive their General Motors automobiles with ease and comfort through this clean and orderly environment. "Unbelievable? Remember, this is the world of 1960!"[4]

It was as if H.G. Wells' scientists and intellectuals had joined forces with corporate America to produce a technological paradise. Only three years before the World's Fair, the Wells-inspired film *Things to Come* had presented an equally shiny view of the future, even though the world had to pass through the crucible of war and anarchy, and the audience had to endure a terrible script, to get there. The resulting "Everytown" of the year 2036 was a technocrat's dream, with amazing buildings, advanced communications, and glass elevators. This, then, was the pinnacle of human achievement: a future that looked just like the Eaton Centre.

This future was conditioned by consumer capitalism and reinforced by advertising. The key to future happiness supposedly lay in the purchase of more and more products, which were constantly being "improved." This year's detergent was always better than last year's; next year's would be better still. So it was with automobiles: "There's a Ford in Your Future," ran one advertising slogan in the 1930s. Even the slogans themselves were regularly renewed, to make change synonymous with excitement. Everywhere, variations on the same message rang in the ears: New equals Good; Old equals Bad.

No one did this better than General Motors, which followed up the "Futurama" of 1939 with an annual "Motorama" during the 1950s featuring the cars of the future. Here you could meet "Mr. and Mrs. Tomorrow" as they drove their gender-specific vehicles into a new dawn:

As nearly as cars can, they themselves had sex. The feminine car with its soft, sensuous shapes done in pastel colors was deftly guided into the driveway of the Frigidaire Home by provocative Mrs. Tomorrow, just returned from shopping. Alighting and stepping to the rear of the car, which looked most like the business end of a helicopter, she gracefully pulled out a drawer-like, grocery-laden trunk compartment that produced its own landing gear and was easily wheeled inside the house.

Mr. Tomorrow, for his part, had a car with "angular lines and bold brown coloring," from which he removed – in order – his golf bag, his brief case, and flowers for Mrs. Tomorrow.[5]

Nothing, it seemed, could upset the harmony of such touching domestic scenes. America appeared cocooned from the rest of the world, where, as in the news, horrible things always happened to other people. But if the United States was physically isolated from the battlefields of Europe and Asia, its global economic and strategic interests brought the country into both world wars, the Cold War, the Vietnam War, and attempts to undermine real or perceived hostile foreign governments, from Cuba to Chile. Throughout, technology played a central part in the military mindset: the United States has always preferred to rely more on sophisticated weapons systems than on the sheer weight of numbers. In this respect, the high-altitude bombing of Serbia in 1999 was not a new approach to warfare, but the logical culmination of long-standing strategic thinking.

This view was reflected in futuristic fantasies about American military supremacy. Scientific progress held out the promise of delivery from danger: the point was to get better technology than your enemies and then clobber them with it. Dreams and realities intermingled, technology became a new religion, and fantastic weapons were conjured up in the collective imagination. During the First World War, science fiction magazines were full of mind-boggling designs for war-winning death machines. To break the stalemate of trench warfare, these storytellers envisaged invincible mega-tanks the size of dreadnought battleships, which would destroy everything in their path. Behind them would come soldiers carrying death rays and machines that would spray electric currents on the enemy. In 1918 Hugo Gernsback took the logic still further and suggested that human soldiers should be replaced by electrically driven automatons, protected by shell-proof steel and equipped with lethal weapons.

It was all very adolescent and utterly impractical. The mega-tanks would have sunk into the Flanders mud, death rays and automatic soldiers belonged to the realm of make-believe, and the automatons could not have operated beyond the length of the cables connecting them to their generators. More interesting than the specific plans, though, is the cast of mind that called them into being. The archetypes of ancient folklore and mythology, with their warriors, giants, dragons, and magical swords, were being fused with modern dreams of technology, with their indestructible automatic soldiers, mega-tanks, fire-breathing machines, and death rays. Such images continue to grip and engage the popular imagination. Instead of automatic soldiers, we have Robocop; for mega-tanks, we have the mile-wide space ships of *Independence Day;* and no self-respecting science fiction film of the 1950s was complete without its super-hero, its death ray, and its fire-breathing monster.

Many of these films tapped into the growing apprehension about the possibilities of nuclear war. There were giant atomic cockroaches and squid-like creatures who rampaged through a terrified population, only to be nuked into oblivion by the Hero Who Saves the World. In the best melodramatic fashion, virtue triumphs over vice: good American technology prevails over bad mutant technology, which appears as a subconscious symbol of Soviet nuclear power. It was all very reassuring – especially when the squid-like creature was destroyed by an atomic bomb and the hero was able to protect himself simply by shading his eyes, at a distance of some fifty yards. The same kind of reassurance appeared in the civil defence films of the 1950s, in which children were enjoined to "Duck for Cover" under their desks to save themselves from the nuclear bomb about to hit their school.

As the number of nuclear weapons increased, their destructive capacity became greater, and the speed of their delivery became faster, such reassurance became harder and harder to provide. For the first time in its history, the United States was vulnerable to external attack, in a hair-trigger balance of terror. Nuclear deterrence was the obvious response, but was fraught with danger. Once Russian missiles had been launched, you could nuke Russia in return, but your own country was already doomed.

And so President Ronald Reagan launched his Strategic Defense Initiative during the 1980s, with its vision of satellites that would destroy nuclear missiles before they reached their target and provide the United States with much-needed protective covering. This strategy was the ultimate expression of technological hubris, which promised to release Americans from the intolerable anxiety of nuclear vulnerability and provide them with total safety and security. Technological fantasy had become public policy, as the science fiction world of death stars and laser beams was presented as the path to salvation. It was no coincidence that this scheme came from a man who had acted in those B-movies of the 1950s, appeared to have difficulty distinguishing between cinematic myth and day-to-day reality, and seemed to believe that all the world really was a stage. Appropriately enough, the scheme was called "Star Wars."

One of the most striking things about these developments was the way that images of technological progress coexisted with an essentially static conception of social relationships. Mr. Tomorrow would always drive his angular, masculine car with the golf clubs in the trunk, and provocative Mrs. Tomorrow would forever drive her pastel-coloured feminine car into the Frigidaire Home with the groceries, and generation after generation of Junior Tomorrows would scrub their teeth with constantly improving toothpaste. Reagan thought that life was a B-movie script (accurately enough, in his own case), dreamed of Death Stars, and set his face firmly against social change.

What seemed to be new was actually old, and technological utopianism actually reinforced social and political conservatism. If you can solve all your problems through technology, why bother with anything else? As Joseph Corn and Brian Horrigan argued: "By focusing on improving technology – rather than improving relations between classes, nations, or races, or changing the distribution of wealth or standard of living – the future becomes strictly a matter of *things,* their invention, improvement, and acquisition."[6] The American future, in the minds of many, would simply be a technologically enhanced version of the American present. But other, non-technological forms of change were more likely to be feared than welcomed. This fear of change would find its most powerful expression within the ranks of the religious right.

...

So much, then, for the first part of our composite picture. The twentieth-century "technology as threat" notion needs to be significantly qualified in the light of modern American attitudes towards progress: the eighteenth-century Enlightenment is alive and well and living in the United States.

But what of the second part of the picture, which assumes that biblical prophecy has become increasingly marginalized in the modern world? Well, this view also requires revision, when considered against the background of contemporary America. It is much too facile to say that apocalyptic images of the future withered away between the sixteenth and the eighteenth centuries. In fact, there are more people alive today who believe in the literal truth of the Book of Revelation than there have been at any time in history.

There are, of course, more people alive today generally, and the proportion of those who take biblical prophecies literally has almost certainly declined. Such beliefs are now outside the intellectual and political mainstream, despite sporadic attempts to prove otherwise. Nevertheless, powerful apocalyptic currents have continued to run through American popular culture, challenging notions of unlimited progress and carrying dark messages of moral decay.

From this perspective, the rot set in during the second half of the nineteenth century, when new-fangled theories threatened to undermine fundamental biblical truths. The chief culprit was Charles Darwin, whose theories of evolution made a mockery of the Book of Genesis. Echoes of the shock can still be felt today, and the Creationists are making a comeback in Kansas. Hard on the heels of Darwin came those namby-pamby do-gooder liberal theologians, who began to cast doubt on the literal truth of the Bible and arrogantly dismissed the prophecies of Daniel and Revelation as "primitive fantasies." And there were those pesky social gospel types, who peddled the false dream of a better world here below, instead of focusing on the glory of the Kingdom of Heaven above.

To hell with all of that, came the fundamentalist cry: if this was the way of the future, God was going to get really angry. And once God got angry, you'd better duck for cover. The millenarian counter-thrust was carried to a receptive audience by itinerant preachers, discussed at prophecy conferences, and spread by books and magazines. During the 1930s the radio opened up new opportunities, and the air-waves were full of fast-talking evangelists who predicted the imminent Second Coming. Technology and God were working together. And why not? This was America, after all.

Even the advent of television was initially seen as part of God's Divine Plan. Had it not been prophesied that Christ's return would be witnessed by the whole world? "In the past," commented the evangelist F.W. Pitt as early as 1936, "we have had to fall back on the explanation that it does not necessarily mean that all should see the Lord coming in the clouds of heaven at the same time, but now we know that by Television, that beatific sight can be seen the world over at one and the same moment."[7] It would be the ultimate prime time event: the End of the World, brought to you by simulcast, starring Jesus Christ, sponsored by soap companies that would scrub your soul clean, starting tonight at 9:00, and 9:30 in Newfoundland.

If the communications revolution in general, and television in particular, could pave the way for the Second Coming, other, more terrifying developments pointed in the same direction. Central to this scenario was the Great Fear associated with nuclear weapons. In sharp contrast to those who hoped that deterrence or some kind of nuclear shield might protect America, many fundamentalists believed that Armageddon was at hand and that apocalyptic biblical prophecies were about to be realized. "No shelter ... can protect us from the bombs being perfected today," declared one prophecy writer in 1962. "The only way *out* is *up*."[8]

There was no shortage of gory passages in the Bible that could be wheeled out as proof. "But the day of the Lord will come as a thief in the night," the apostle Peter had written; "in the which the heavens shall pass away with a great noise, and the elements shall melt with fervent heat, the earth also and the works that are therein shall be burned up." "And this shall be the plague wherewith the LORD will smite all the people that have fought against Jerusalem," said the prophet Zechariah; "their flesh shall consume away while they stand upon their feet, and their eyes shall consume away in their holes, and their tongue shall consume away in their mouth." "And men were scorched with great heat," ran the Visions of Judgment in Revelation, amid a general description of fire, brimstone, and plagues.[9]

Liberal theologians had argued that such passages were allegorical, but after Hiroshima and Nagasaki the case for their literal truth was much more convincing. The Second Coming was inseparable from nuclear war. Best-selling writers like Hal Lindsey took great delight in connecting biblical prophecies with thermonuclear blasts and the effects of radiation, in a kind of religious pornography of violence. There seemed to be a lot of hatred in the religion of love: "God so loved the world," remarked one sardonic observer, "that he sent it World War III."[10] Francesco de Lana-Terzi, the seventeenth-century Jesuit who had argued that God would never allow such mass destruction, had been stood on his head.

Because nuclear war had been prophesied, nuclear war was inevitable. No matter what they said or did, humans could not alter the Divine Plan. But true Christians could take great comfort from the fact that they would be spared from the holocaust. As one evangelist put it, they would "get a view of the Battle of Armageddon from the grandstand seats of the heavens."[11] For those who liked violence in sports, this was Heaven indeed. Even the National Hockey League pales in comparison to the cosmic World Wrestling Federation clash between God and Satan. Armageddon was the ultimate in Extreme Sport.

You got yourself a grandstand seat by accepting Jesus Christ as your personal Saviour. Society as a whole might be damned, but individuals could be saved. There was no point in working for social reform or nuclear disarmament, but there was every reason to rescue your fellow creatures from catastrophe by bringing them to the Lord. In its belief that there were individual solutions to collective problems, this outlook was quintessentially American. In effect, it was the religious equivalent of the self-help book.

Once the nuclear-apocalyptic framework had been established, it was relatively easy to fit other pieces into the picture. The Book of Ezekiel had written of Gog and Magog, the malevolent forces from the north that would be defeated at Armageddon. Could there be any doubt that they referred to Russia? President Reagan certainly thought so: the Soviet Union, he believed, "fits the description of Gog perfectly." More tangible proof was offered when Gorbachev came to power. For many fundamentalists, the very fact that he seemed relatively benign was all the more reason to fear him. Antichrist's job description, after all, was to appear as a false prophet and deceive multitudes. But the secret signs were there, ready to be decoded. One ingenious evangelist calculated that the numerical equivalent of "Mikhail S. Gorbachev" in Russian was 1332; divide by two, and you come up with the dreaded 666, the Number of the Beast. Besides, you had to be blind not to notice that he displayed the Mark of the Beast on his forehead.[12]

And then there was the fact that the state of Israel had been restored in 1948. For centuries the conversion of the Jews and their subsequent return to the Holy Land had been regarded as fundamental prerequisites for the Second Coming. True, the Jews were supposed to have been converted *before* their restoration, but this seemingly insuperable logical difficulty was swiftly skated over in silence. The key point was that the Jews had returned to their ancient homeland, just as the Bible had prophesied, and, therefore, the End of the World must soon follow. Precisely because the new state of Israel represented the fulfilment of ancient prophecy, evangelical American Protestants counted themselves among its strongest supporters.

Nuclear weapons, the appearance of Antichrist in the form of the Soviet Union, and the restoration of Israel – all this added up to Armageddon. But there was equally compelling evidence within American society itself that the end times were near. All you had to do was compare the contemporary world with Paul's description of the "last days":

> For men shall be lovers of their own selves, covetous, boasters, proud, blasphemers, disobedient to parents, unthankful, unholy, without natural affection, trucebreakers, false accusers, incontinent, fierce, despisers of those that are good, traitors, heady, high-minded, lovers of pleasures more than lovers of God ... For of this sort are they which creep into houses, and lead captive silly women laden with sins, led away with divers lusts, ever learning, and never able to come to the knowledge of the truth ... But evil men and seducers shall wax worse and worse, deceiving, and being deceived.[13]

Sometime in the late 1950s the fundamentalists saw Elvis Presley and began to shudder. In the 1960s they looked at Mick Jagger and began to worry. In the 1970s they encountered Kiss, Alice Cooper, and David Bowie, and they blew a gasket. Instead of progress, there was moral turpitude; instead of religious brotherhood, there was licensed selfishness; instead of religious piety, there were thrusting pelvises.

Social conservatism, fear of change, and apocalyptic expectations became part of a mutually reinforcing closed-loop belief system. Where a left-wing critic like Christopher Lasch criticized the "culture of narcissism," right-wing evangelists found striking confirmation of Paul's prophecy that men would become "lovers of their own selves." For "covetousness," you had materialism and greed, fed by consumer capitalism. For blasphemy and the "despisers of those that are good," you had secular self-seekers and their intellectual defenders, who ridiculed cherished religious beliefs and mocked ordinary decent Christians. And for the "fierce," you had violent criminals stalking the streets of an urban wilderness.

All these trends were related to the breakdown of the family, just as Paul had prophesied. Men who were "lovers of pleasure more than lovers of God," and women who were "led away with divers lusts," had put instant sexual gratification above all the ties of "natural affection." By the 1980s the bitter harvest was being reaped in the form of AIDs, which was itself connected to the plagues that would usher in the apocalypse. Not only that, but gay men and women were parading in the streets, when God had specifically told Moses that the penalty for such "abominations" was nothing less than death.[14]

Ladies were no longer ladies: they were calling themselves women, using Ms instead of Miss or Mrs., burning their bras, demanding equality, and putting their own selfish career interests above the care and nurture of their children and husbands. Children were becoming increasingly disobedient to their parents, and the kids just got worse and worse with every passing year – a parental complaint that has been expressed by just about every generation in history. There could be no doubt about it: sex, drugs, and rock-and-roll would be the ruin of us all.

In a familiar historical pattern, complex social issues were reduced to the level of caricature, a simplistic black-and-white model was imposed on complex realities, and collective anxieties were projected onto the forces of Antichrist. Paranoid religious fantasies fed the heart, in a general revolt against modernism. The targets included the United Nations, the mass media, consumerism, and computers. The fear of change was broadened to include modern technology itself, and there were dark fears that Antichrist was embedded in the microchip. Pat Robertson speculated that Satanic electronic implants were being put in babies' heads, and enterprising evangelists found the Number of the Beast, 666, everywhere they looked. It was hidden in shopping bar codes, credit cards, and advertisements. (I myself should record here, without comment, that when I punched in "future" on the University of Toronto's electronic library catalogue, exactly 666 items came up on the list.) And, for those who were into the New Math, you could find it in the very word "Computer." If you assume that Antichrist works in sixes, so that A equals 6, B equals 12, C equals 18, and so on, then this is what you get: C = 18, O = 90, M = 78, P = 96, U = 126, T = 120, E = 30, R = 108, for a total of 666. Using this system, "New York City" also comes to 666 – no surprise there – as does "Mark of Beast," as opposed to "Mark of the Beast."[15]

As with end-of-the-world prophesies, the use of such bizarre numerological keys to identify Antichrist has a long pedigree. In 1793, for example, James Bicheno proved that Louis XIV was Antichrist by translating Louis' name into Latin and adding the Roman numerals that corresponded to each letter: L = 50, U = 5, D = 500, O = 0, V = 5, I = 1, C = 100, U = 5, S = 0, for a total of 666. Not to be outdone, one of the characters in Leo Tolstoy's *War and Peace* used the French alphabet to show that Napoleon was Antichrist. This is how he did it:

a (1), b (2), c (3), d (4), e (5), f (6), g (7), h (8), i (9), k (10), l (20), m (30), n (40), o (50), p (60), q (70), r (80), s (90), t (100), u (110), v (120), w (130), x (140), y (150), z (160)

Using this key, he demonstrated that "l'empereur Napoléon" added up to 666, although he had to add 5 for the *e* that was dropped from the *le*.[16] And for those who weren't convinced that either Louis or Napoleon was Antichrist, there was always Hitler. In this case, you let A equal 100, and added one number for each additional letter, so that you reached this happy result: H = 107, I = 108, T = 119, L = 111, E = 104, R = 117. Total = 666.[17] The rule is simple: Always start off with your conclusion, and work backwards until you come up with the number-letter equivalents that fit.

At any rate, three things stand out from the connection between revelation and the religious right. First, prophecy belief has continued to play a major role within the worldview of American Protestant fundamentalists – a group that remains a significant social and political force within the United States. Second, the fundamentalist-prophetic image of the future rejected secular notions of progress. On the contrary, the world was clearly going to hell in a handbasket, and it was hubris for humans to think they could rewrite the Divine Script. All you could do was try to save as many people as possible, through individual exertions and moral crusades against such evils as abortion, promiscuity, and homosexuality. And third, as Paul Boyer points out, there were hidden radical tendencies within this reactionary, intolerant, and often paranoid outlook. In their attack on consumerism and socioeconomic homogenization, the modern-day millenarians came up with "strikingly similar denunciations" to those "emanating from the left" – something neither side would feel comfortable about.[18]

Certainly, the religious right has had no monopoly on catastrophic images of the future. What Michael Barkun has called the "secular apocalyptic" strand in popular culture found early expression in Orson Welles' famous 1938 radio adaptation of H.G. Wells' *War of the Worlds,* when the Martians came a microbe away from destroying humankind and taking over the planet. The panic-stricken reaction was almost certainly linked to deep and wide anxieties about the nature of aerial warfare, which had been graphically demonstrated the year before at Guernica during the Spanish Civil War.

In more recent times, the movie industry has excelled in tapping into our increasingly well-founded fears about our fragility as a species. There have been innumerable space invasions, asteroids heading straight for us, diseases that have brought us to the brink of extinction, and cracks in the crust of the Earth that have threatened to rip the world apart. But we have always prevailed against impossible odds. We want and need reassurance, and box-office demands ensure that we get what we want. The *Titanic* can sink, but the Earth will always stay afloat.

The film of the *Titanic,* in fact, reflects a deep ambivalence in modern attitudes to technology. On the one hand, the ship's fate has become a symbolic warning against the arrogance of technology: the most advanced ocean liner in the world was sunk by an iceberg and did not carry enough lifeboats because it was supposed to be unsinkable. On the other hand, the film opened with impressive high-tech scenes of the ship on the ocean floor, and combined a syrupy love story with amazing special effects. Technological virtuosity became a means towards the end of telling a story about the dangers of technological hubris.

The same kind of tension appears in films about the future, which became increasingly pessimistic against the background of energy shortages, environmental anxieties, and nuclear brinkmanship during and after the 1970s. A classic example is *Blade Runner,* which was set in the Los Angeles of 2019. In a stunning opening sequence, helicopters and jets ferry people past gigantic advertisements to monolithic skyscrapers, over a pitiless and polluted city that is shrouded with perpetually falling acid rain. Biotechnology has progressed to the point where people can make robotic humanoid "replicants," some of whom are seeking revenge on their creators. The future is a technological nightmare, in which there are no traces of tenderness. The film stands as a stark warning about the consequences of a technologically driven world.

And yet, much of the film's appeal was itself technologically driven: not only the visual effects but the graphic depiction of futuristic violence kept the audiences coming. Moreover, the narrative structure of *Blade Runner* was traditional and even nostalgic. The mission to seek out and destroy the replicants was clearly modelled on the detective story genre of the 1940s.

A similar blend of the future and the past characterized *Road*

Warrior, which is essentially a cowboy-and-Indian film projected into the Australian outback in the aftermath of a nuclear war. Instead of Indians on horses we have Hells Angel–style gangs on motorbikes. And just as the Indians were presented in Hollywood as the Bad Guys, attacking the encircled wagon train of the Good Guys (who just happened to be invading their territory), the bikers were a bunch of sadistic thugs who threatened a community that had built itself around an oil well. A determined enough film critic might just possibly be able to interpret the film as a futuristic version of the Hobbesian state of nature. But *Road Warrior* was really little more than a thinly disguised excuse for gratuitous rape and violence, against the background of a weirdly improvised and supposedly thrilling technological combat between heroes and villains.

Whatever we make of these films, their picture of the future can hardly be described as happy, innocent, or optimistic – unless the assumption that there would be *any* kind of life after a nuclear war can be seen as a form of innocent optimism. Where *Blade Runner* brought us environmental degradation, and *Road Warrior* gave us post-nuclear hell, the film *12 Monkeys* presented an equally catastrophic future in which five billion people were killed in 1996 by an act of biological terrorism. The survivors have moved into high-tech underground shelters, where they eventually discover the means to travel backwards in time. In the year 2037 they send back a man with the mission of finding the virus in its pure form, before it mutated, so that their scientists can develop an antidote.

The man returns to 1996 to find the Army of the 12 Monkeys, which he believes is responsible for spreading the virus – a belief that stems from a misleading message sent to the future as a result of his own quest in the past. In fact, the virus will be unleashed by an apocalyptic scientist, whom we encounter mid way through the film, arguing that the Alarmists are right: "Surely there's very real and very convincing data that the planet cannot survive the excesses of the human race – proliferation of atomic devices, uncontrolled breeding habits, pollution of land, sea and air, the rape of the environment. In this context, isn't it obvious that Chicken Little represents the sane vision, and that homo sapiens' motto, 'Let's Go Shopping,' is the cry of the true lunatic?" The scientist spreads the virus to save the planet from the "excesses of the human race," and the man from the future winds up being shot by the police at the Philadelphia airport in front of his boyhood self. The young boy had unknowingly witnessed his own death.

It gets rather confusing once you start travelling backwards from the future – a point that was also made in a *Star Trek* episode written by Harlan Ellison, "The City on the Edge of Forever." Dr. McCoy was hurled back through time to Depression America and inadvertently changed history so that space travel never occurred, and – horror of horrors – the Starship *Enterprise* never existed. Kirk and Spock had to go in after him and stop him from saving the life of a peace activist (played by none other than Joan Collins) whose actions would have prevented America from entering the Second World War.

Such head-spinning logic was among the many targets in Mike Myers' parody *Austin Powers: The Spy Who Shagged Me*. Austin's mojo had been stolen, and Basil the Spymaster was sending him back to 1969 so he could retrieve it. "Wait a tick," says Austin. "Basil, if I travel back to 1969 and I was frozen in 1967, presumably I could go visit my frozen self. But, if I was still frozen in 1967, how could I have been unthawed in the '90s and travel back – oh no, I've gone cross-eyed." "I suggest you don't worry about this sort of thing," replies Basil, "and just enjoy yourself." And then, turning to the audience, he adds: "That goes for you all, too." "Yes," nods Austin in smiling agreement.

As the nuclear threat lifted, the path to the supposedly fateful year of 2000 became much less anxiety-ridden than it otherwise would have been, apart from some vague apprehensions about the Y2K bug. It is clear, though, that modern pessimism about the future rested on firm foundations. With nuclear weapons and the Cold War, it was impossible to live without the knowledge that everything we knew and loved could be totally and irrevocably destroyed in a matter of minutes. Everyone was walking in the shadow of the valley of death.

There were many possible reactions to this threat. People could support deterrence and learn to live with the balance of terror. They could build shelters and convince themselves that they had a fighting chance of survival. They could support the Strategic Defense Initiative, on the grounds that the promise of technology could negate its threat. They could campaign for nuclear disarmament. Or they could read the Bible, decide that nuclear war was the inevitable fulfilment of religious prophecy, and concentrate on individual salvation, to get that grandstand seat in the sky.

And if nuclear war didn't get humanity, there were plenty of other things out there that might. Growing evidence about the pollution of the planet, acid rain, global warming, and the depletion of the ozone layer all suggested that if the world did not end with a bang, it would end with a whimper. Add to this the emergence of international terrorism, and the potential to wreak enormous destruction through well-placed nuclear devices or biological warfare, and the future looked even grimmer. And all these threats operated in the context of a sexual and social revolution, which generated cynicism and apprehension as well as idealism and hope. On the left, the English historian E.P. Thompson could talk scathingly of the "revolting sons and daughters of the revolting bourgeoisie doing their revolting thing," while the Canadian Tory-Radical philosopher George Grant could lament a society that was driven by the "emancipation of the passions." On the right, religious fundamentalists, convinced that current events confirmed dire biblical prophecies, hunkered down for Armageddon.

No wonder, then, that there was a growing culture of catastrophe from the 1960s through to the 1990s and that faith in technology coexisted with fear of change. There was, after all, a lot to be afraid about.

· · ·

Among the myriad social changes that emerged during the late 1960s, none was more significant than the feminist movement – something that took the technocratic futurologists of postwar America completely by surprise. The "housewife of 2000," according to an illustration from *Popular Mechanics* in 1950, would happily be doing her daily housecleaning with a garden hose, since everything would now be made of plastic. Similarly, a General Electric promotional film, featuring the pre–Captain Kirk William Shatner, presented the housewife of the future enthusiastically embracing the latest revolution in kitchen technology. "The chic woman of the year 2000," speculated an article written for the *New York Times* Woman's Page, "may have live butterflies fluttering around her hairdo ... attracted by a specially scented hair spray. The same woman, according to predictions made at a cosmetic industry luncheon, will control her body measurements by reclining on a chaise longue with electronic bubbles that massage away problem areas ... She will have available silicones for filling in frown lines and wrinkles on aging faces." "Even in the year 2000," speculated one futurologist, "it may be more damaging [for young women] to be thought homely or lacking in sex appeal than to be stupid."[19]

It was precisely against this kind of stereotyping, and its accompanying economic, social, and political discrimination, that the "women's liberation" movement organized itself. Women should no longer derive their satisfaction from their contribution to the achievements of their husbands and sons, ran the message.

They must break out of the kitchen, establish their own self-worth as independent human beings, and assert the value of intelligence over "sex appeal." The point was not to fill in the "frown lines" with silicone, but to remove the reasons for the frowns in the first place.

Out of this movement came radical new visions of the future. For the previous fifty years, futuristic utopias had vanished from the literary map. During the 1970s the feminists brought them back. But these utopias were very different from their eighteenth- and nineteenth-century predecessors. For one thing, they rejected or qualified the earlier easy confidence in technology. On the contrary, technology was frequently associated with an aggressive and inherently male attempt to control the world. Among the results were the military-industrial complex, with all its "toys for the boys," and an environmental crisis that was deepening and widening. For another thing, feminist futuristic writing now rejected the religious ideology that had characterized the work of a nineteenth-century utopian such as Mary Griffith – something that was hardly surprising, given the derision and disdain with which Christian fundamentalists greeted the emergence of the "women's libbers."

As Nan Bowman Albinski has pointed out, the new feminist utopias generally took a holistic approach to nature, embraced sexual permissiveness, and replaced Christianity and materialism with new forms of spirituality and mysticism. They also transcended traditional gender roles: the women and men of the future would cooperate as equals at home and in the workplace. And, above all, women would now be able to think and act for themselves in an environment free from sexual oppression, family violence, and rape.

At the same time, though, feminist writers in the 1970s and 1980s remained acutely aware of darker possibilities. Given the backlash that their movement faced, it could hardly have been otherwise. One consequence was a tendency to combine both utopian and dystopian visions of the future in the same novel. In this way, the future-as-hope was sharply juxtaposed with the future-as-warning. Perhaps the most striking, and certainly the best-known, example of this new approach was Marge Piercy's *Woman on the Edge of Time,* published in 1977.

Piercy's story centres on Connie Ramos, a Mexican-American woman who smashes a wine jug into the face of an abusive pimp and is subsequently forced into a mental institution. Here she is contacted by Luciente, a visitor from the year 2137, who transports her in a dreamlike trance into the future. Luciente's future is very much like a post-hippy 1970s counter-culture folk festival writ large. It is certainly nothing like the one Connie expects to find: "She looked slowly around. She saw ... a river, little no-account buildings, [and] strange structures like long-legged birds with sails that turned in the wind ... No skyscrapers, no space-ports, no traffic jam in the sky. `You sure we went in the right direction? Into the future?'"[20] This was an ideal feminist future, in which men and women were in touch with their deepest emotions and were not afraid to express their innermost feelings. There were no big cities because "they didn't work." People travelled by foot or bicycle, hung their clothes on lines to dry, used solar and wind power, practised conservation and recycling, grew vegetables and raised chickens. At first Connie was reminded of her grand-parents' dirt-poor life back in Mexico. She soon realizes, though, that the people of 2137 have blended the best features of traditional tribal life with a humanistic approach to modern technology. Fully automated machines took all the drudgery out of work, leaving people with hours of leisure time "to talk, to study, to play, to love, to enjoy the river."[21]

The nuclear family had been superseded and gender boundaries had become blurred. Connie initially mistook Luciente for a man, and she later witnessed a man breastfeed a baby. Everyone practised free love, and the entire community took responsibility for the children, all of whom chose their own names. Embryos were grown in special laboratories, freeing women from the pain of childbirth and the stereotypical role of mother and wife. Luciente explained:

> It was part of women's long revolution. When we were breaking up all the old hierarchies. Finally there was that one thing we had to give up too, the only power we ever had, in return for no more power for anyone. The original production: the power to give birth. Cause as long as we were biologically enchained, we'd never be equal. And males never would be humanized to be loving and tender. So we all became mothers. Every child has three. To break the nuclear bonding.[22]

The children themselves inhabited an open sexual environment. They played sexual games, learned from each other, and came to regard sexual activities as a normal, natural, and healthy part of life. "Our notions of evil," explains one of Luciente's friends to a shocked Connie, "center around power and greed – taking from other people their food, their liberty, their health, their land, their customs, their pride. We don't find coupling bad unless it involves pain or is not invited."[23]

There are intriguing parallels here with Huxley's *Brave New World,* where embryos were hatched on a production line, sexual promiscuity was encouraged, and erotic play for children was compulsory. The connections even extend to genetic engineering, which was part of Luciente's future world, where there were lively debates between those who wanted to "breed for selected traits" and those who "don't think people can know objectively how people should become."[24]

In Piercy's utopia, as opposed to Huxley's dystopia, these things were intended to enhance freedom and harmony, and to create a kinder, gentler world. The hatching of embryos in laboratories would now liberate women and men from their sexual straitjacket. Sexual promiscuity was redefined as sexual openness, in which warm and tender feelings would flourish, and the sexual games of children were now part of the natural process. Feminist genetic engineering was entirely benevolent, racial differences were being obliterated through the mixing of genes, and cultural diversity was still encouraged and welcomed. Huxley had been humanized – or so Piercy would have us believe.

Unlike its eighteenth-century predecessors, Piercy's utopia was not a static society in which there were no longer any clashes of values or personalities. Luciente and her fellow-worker Bolivar did not like each other, and conflict-resolution techniques were not entirely successful in settling their differences. There were lively debates in town meetings about the local projects that needed to be undertaken. And there was still violent crime in 2137, although less so than in the past. Methods of dealing with such crime included various healing practices and self-atonement strategies. If these failed, and someone used violence a second time, the response was rapid and ruthless: "Second time someone used violence, we give up. We don't want to watch each other or imprison each other. We aren't willing to live with people who choose to use violence. We execute them."[25]

Here, then, we have Piercy's positive image of a compassionate, kind, and loving future, with a dash of capital punishment thrown in for good measure. Meanwhile, in Connie's world of 1976, she and her fellow mental patients are being treated like meat and subjected to brain- control experiments that involve the implantation of electrodes and mini-computers – an echo from the left of the fears we have encountered from the religious right. After an unsuccessful attempt to escape, Connie is forced to undergo remedial surgery. The doctors drill a hole in her skull, insert a needle, and implant a metal disk "that would rule her feelings like a thermostat": "Suddenly she thought that these men believed feeling itself a disease, something to be cut out like a rotten appendix. Cold, calculating, ambitious, believing themselves rational and superior, they chased the crouching female animal through the brain with a scalpel."[26]

When Connie next impels herself into the future, she finds herself in a very different world from that of Luciente. This was a world in which "everybody's implanted." Women had become objects of male pleasure and were biologically engineered to meet male specifications. Violent and pornographic holographs were the chief form of entertainment. The air was polluted, the streets were too dangerous for anyone to walk outside, and people got blasphemously high on a drug called Rapture.[29] Brain-control techniques were used to change behaviour and detect sedition. There were vast class differences and warring clans of "richies" who fought each other with genetically engineered fighters.

In this way, Piercy presents alternative futures, each of which appears as the logical conclusion of very different tendencies in the America of the 1970s – the post-hippy folk festival versus Eighth Avenue and Times Square. Luciente had already explained it to Connie: "Those of your time who fought hard for change, often they had myths that a revolution was inevitable. But nothing is! All things interlock. We are only one possible future. Do you grasp?" "Yours is a crux-time," Luciente continued. "Alternative universes coexist. Probabilities clash and possibilities wink out for ever."

And so we come back to the arrogance of the present: 1976 was a "crux-time," and the existence of Luciente's future world was contingent on the "revolution of the powerless" that was apparently beginning in America. That, it turns out, was the very reason that Luciente visited Connie in the first place – to enlist her in a struggle that would determine whether Luciente and her world would ever exist. As Connie is subjected to further electroshock therapy, the battle in her mind becomes increasingly blurred with the battle for the future. Because of her blackouts and long periods of unconsciousness, the doctors eventually removed her implant. As she recuperated, she realized that she must indeed join the struggle: "The war raged outside her body now, outside her skull, but the enemy would press on and violate her frontiers again as soon as they chose their next advance. She was at war."

Her first and last act of war was to put poison in the doctors' coffee: "I murdered them dead. Because *they* are the violence-prone. Theirs is the money and the power, theirs the poisons that slow the mind and dull the heart. Theirs are the powers of life and death. I killed them. Because it is war ... I'm a dead woman now too. I know it. But I did fight them. I'm not ashamed. I tried."[27] Without violent revolution, without a new Thirty Years' War, Times Square would take over the future. Only through armed struggle could the dream of Luciente become a reality. In this sense, at least, we are right back in the utopian mindset of the late eighteenth century – and look how splendidly that turned out.

Piercy, then, presented a polarized view of the future, in which either a feminist utopia or a misogynist dystopia must ultimately prevail. The war was already under way, there was no room for compromise, and the time for action was now – in the 1970s. But the attempt to transform gender relations, the battle between the Folk Festival and Times Square, had the potential to bring a third force into the field – the religious right. This was something that Piercy had not foreseen, but which had been anticipated as early as 1965 by Margaret Mead, in her musings about the future:

It is ... crucial to realize that ... radically new styles of behavior may engender counter-revolutions that may be ideological or religious in character. Under these circumstances the most intense efforts might be made to nullify the effect of innovations in life styles. The aim of such counter-revolutions, whatever their specific form, might well be to refocus attention on the home, limit sexual freedom, [and] curtail the individual development of women.[28]

By the late 1970s it was clear that precisely such a religious and ideological counter-revolution was gathering momentum. And it was against this background that Margaret Atwood in 1985 published her dystopian novel, *The Handmaid's Tale*.

The book describes the first years of the Republic of Gilead, a puritanical and patriarchal theocracy centred in Massachusetts, sometime in the "near future." It takes us into a totalitarian, misogynist, fundamentalist world whose leaders had copied CIA techniques of subversion and destabilization to launch a coup against the American government. In this new republic, Stalinist methods of control are linked to literalist interpretations of the Old Testament, spies are everywhere, opposition is ruthlessly repressed, and women are reduced to a state of degradation and slavery. The birthrate has declined, largely as a result of pandemic pollution, and procreation is at a premium.

Following scriptural precedents in the Book of Genesis, men whose wives cannot conceive (it is always the wives who are infertile) employ "handmaids" who function as substitute birth machines. The story is told through the words of one such handmaid, who has been stripped of her former identity and is now known as "Offred," meaning "of Fred," her current "Commander." There is also a hidden pun here: the handmaids wear red cloaks, along with white wings that function as veils. Offred wants to shake off the red clothes and everything they imply.

In the classic dystopian fashion, the rulers of Gilead created a society in which order is placed above freedom of choice. They were reacting against both the world of pornography and the world of feminism, and they were implementing their own kind of Christian utopia. On one of her carefully controlled walks, Offred thought about the days before the religious revolution:

> Women were not protected then.
>
> I remember the rules, rules that were never spelled out but that every woman knew: don't open your door to a stranger, even if he says he is the police. Make him slide his ID under the door. Don't stop on the road to help a motorist pretending to be in trouble. Keep the locks on and keep going. If anyone whistles, don't turn to look. Don't go into a laundromat, by yourself, at night ...
>
> Now we walk along the same street, in red pairs, and no man shouts obscenities at us, speaks to us, touches us. No one whistles.
>
> There is more than one kind of freedom, said Aunt Lydia. Freedom to and freedom from. In the days of anarchy, it was freedom to. Now you are being given freedom from. Don't underrate it.[29]

The aunts, such as Lydia, were the women who trained the handmaids, indoctrinating them in the ways of Gilead and imposing discipline with electric cattle prods. The handmaids had been reduced to the status of cows whose only function was to service the bulls.

In the old society, "freedom to" had produced Pornomarts, Feels on Wheels vans, and extreme violence against women. "Freedom from" was the backlash. Aunt Lydia would show the handmaids porno movies from the 1970s and 1980s:

> Women kneeling, sucking penises or guns, women tied up or chained or with dog collars around their necks, women hanging from trees, or upside-down, naked, with their legs held apart, women being raped, beaten up, killed. Once we had to

watch a woman being slowly cut into pieces, her fingers and breasts snipped off with garden shears, her stomach slit open and her intestines pulled out.

Consider the alternatives, said Aunt Lydia. You see what things used to be like? That was what they really thought of women, then. Her voice trembled with indignation.[30]

The feminists who opposed such things, Aunt Lydia explained, had some good ideas, but they were Godless and supported abortion. As such, they were really "unwomen." In using this word, Atwood was simultaneously reaching back to Orwell and obliquely attacking Canada's self-styled "Real Women" organization of the late 1970s and early 1980s, whose members attacked pornography, feminism, abortion, and atheism as symptoms of modern decadence.

By preventing freedom of choice and providing security, the Republic of Gilead claimed that it was releasing women from the intolerable anxieties of the permissive and competitive society. Before the revolution, Offred's Commander points out, women suffered the collective humiliation of singles bars, blind dates, and the meat market. Judging themselves by their sex appeal, they would starve themselves, pump silicone into their breasts, or change their faces with plastic surgery. And when they did marry, they were often abandoned by their husbands and left to raise their children on welfare. Under the new regime, all this uncertainty had been remedied: marriages were arranged, and women were fully supported and encouraged to "fulfil their biological destinies in peace."[31]

In effect, the exploitation of women in consumer capitalist society had been twisted into a justification for their enslavement in a totalitarian theocracy. And the enslavers turned out to be as hypocritical as those televangelists, like Jimmy Swaggart, who preached fire-and-brimstone sermons against the evils of pornography while soliciting the services of prostitutes. The leaders of Gilead had their own secret club where sex was freely available, and used dubious "laws" of Nature to justify their actions. It was all part of Nature's "procreational strategy," explained Offred's Commander.[32]

One of the central aims of Atwood's book was to demonstrate the dangers of underplaying or ignoring the growing power of the religious right in North America. The process through which the fundamentalists took over was gradual, subtle, and insidious. There were stories in the newspapers, but somehow they never seemed quite believable. Then, after the coup, the newspapers were censored or closed, Identipasses were issued, and the Pornomarts were shut down. Before long, women were forbidden to work, to own property, to read, or to be seen in public without veils. Gradually, the new order began to consolidate itself and its values even appeared normal: "Ordinary," said Aunt Lydia, "is what you are used to. This may not seem ordinary to you now, but after a time it will." Already, only a few years after the coup, the old society seemed part of "an unimaginably distant past."[33]

All manifestations of dissent were comprehensively crushed. Protesters were machine-gunned in the streets, and the enemies of the Republic were publicly executed in rituals known as "Men's Salvagings" – a combination of savagery and salvation. The victims included heretics such as Baptists and Catholics; "Gender Traitors," otherwise known as homosexuals or lesbians; and doctors who had performed abortions. Just as the state in *Nineteen Eighty-Four* had channelled repression into frenzied "Two Minutes Hate" sessions, the Republic of Gilead held "Particicutions," in which the handmaids tore convicted rapists apart with their bare hands. In fact, the so-called rapists were actually part of the resistance movement.

Like Orwell, Atwood constructed a terrifying image of the future from the materials of the present: "There was little that was

truly original with or indigenous to Gilead," remarks one character in the book; "its genius was synthesis." The Old Testament literalism of religious fundamentalists was combined with a variety
of other practices, ranging from the compulsory fertility programs
of Nicolae Ceausescu's Romania to the kind of political purgings
that occurred in the Philippines.

"I do not believe that the kind of society I describe necessarily
will arrive," Orwell had written of *Nineteen Eighty-Four,* "but I
believe ... that something resembling it *could* arrive."[35] The same
words apply to *The Handmaid's Tale.* To describe the book as
"paranoid," as one recent commentator has done, is to misunder-
stand the nature and function of dystopian literature. The whole
object of the exercise is to project dangerous and disturbing elements of our own time into the future, so that we may prevent
that future from happening. The cry of warning becomes a call for
action, and the call for action becomes an act of hope.

But, precisely because it is based on a synthesis of the present,
there is also a sense in which the projected future is already with
us. And in Atwood's case, the kind of totalitarian theocratic nightmare she describes has actually come to pass, although not in
America, and not through Christian forms of fundamentalism.
Instead, it has happened, and continues to happen, in the fundamentalist Islamic state of Afghanistan under the rule of the
Taliban, where women are prevented from working and from
owning property, are excluded from the educational system, are
denied access to hospitals, and are not allowed to be seen in public without veils. The fictional Republic of Gilead pales in comparison to the actual regime of the Taliban.

• • •

And so we enter the twenty-first century with a variety of conflicting images of the future. At the Epcot centre, described by
Walt Disney as a "living blueprint of the future," the new millen-

nium was ushered in (on the wrong date, in common with the rest of the Western world) by a towering star-topped wand waved over Spaceship *Earth* by the gigantic gloved hand of Mickey Mouse. "With themes of science and technology providing inspiration," Epcot celebrated the achievements of the present and invited the guests to "discover the exciting breakthroughs that lie ahead."[36] It was 1939 all over again.

Meanwhile, in Jerusalem, far from the sight of Mickey's enormous glove, a camera called the MessiahCam points silently at the Mount of Olives, giving updated photographs every thirty seconds, so that when the Messiah returns, you can witness it on the Web. Eight million Americans continue to believe that the Second Coming will occur in their own lifetime.

Within the world of astrology and New Age culture, prophets of doom still ply their trade. After Y2K, the new date for disaster was May 5, 2000, when Mercury, Venus, Mars, Jupiter, and Saturn were aligned with Earth for the first time in 6000 years, somehow triggering a New Ice Age. The next one to watch for is September 17, 2001, when the secret meaning of the Great Pyramid at Giza will be revealed and the world will stop.

While Walt Disney carries on the tradition of technological utopianism, while religious fundamentalists still wait for the Second Coming, and while the New Age meets the Ice Age, feminist visions of the future continue to oscillate between hope and fear. In recent years, though, the pendulum has swung more in the direction of cautious optimism, and even a veteran "victim-feminist" like Andrea Dworkin believes that "patriarchy is dying a slow, slow death."[37] Whether women's rights can be sustained in the face of Christian, Islamic, and Judaic fundamentalism remains to be seen. The speculative prognostications of Margaret Mead and the warning cry of Margaret Atwood seem particularly relevant to conditions in the Third World.

In our own time, all the past portraits of the future, from the religious and folkloric to the secular and rational, from the utopian to the dystopian, have become jumbled together in a confusing canvas of clashing colours. We are large, and beneath an apparently homogenous exterior we contain multitudes and continue to contradict ourselves. And perhaps this, rather than any single, overriding vision of the future, is the enduring feature of the human condition. Perhaps, in the end, it was Woody Allen who got it right: "I have seen the future, and it is very much like the present, only longer."[38]

· 8 ·

PREDICTIONS

NINE TIMES OUT OF TEN, it has been said, people stumble across truth in the resolute pursuit of error. So it is with predictions: if you make enough of them, some are bound to come true in the end. Obviously, some outcomes are more likely than others. If you organized a hockey match between the Toronto Maple Leafs and the St. Alban's Boys' and Girls' Club under-twelve team, it would not take a genius to forecast who would win. Even here, though, nothing is absolutely certain, especially with the Maple Leafs. Using the same logic of probabilities, who could possibly have foreseen that the Canadian soccer team would have won the Gold Cup in 2000? Certainly not the manager, the players, the fans, the other teams in the competition, the people who wrote the program notes, or the bookmakers who offered odds of a hundred to one against.

Still, the fact remains that some things are more likely to happen than others. People who smoke heavily will probably remain more at risk of dying from heart disease than those who do not. Anyone who walks blindfolded across a six-lane highway is highly likely to get hit. The insurance industry is based on a sophisticated statistical analysis of probabilities and possibilities, and it appears to work well enough. From here, it would seem a short step to developing a science of probabilities that would forecast the future with a reasonable degree of accuracy.

This was certainly the dream of those eighteenth- and nineteenth-century mathematicians and scientists who substituted reason for religion as the key to understanding the future. Condorcet led the way, and his fellow countryman Pierre Simon Laplace followed in his footsteps. If a man could discover "all the forces animating nature and the relative positions of the beings in nature," Laplace wrote, if "his intelligence were sufficiently capacious to analyze these data," and if he could work out a formula for "the movements of the largest bodies of the universe and those of the smallest atom," then the path to the future would be clear: "Nothing would be uncertain for him: the future as well as the past would be present to his eyes."[1]

The dream has proven remarkably persistent and seductive. One person's intelligence alone, it became clear, was not "sufficiently capacious" for such an enormous task. But suppose you could get whole groups of people working together on the project, assisted by computers: all kinds of breakthroughs might then be possible. That is exactly what was tried in the United States during the 1950s and 1960s.

General Electric blazed the trail, with a small army of scientists, engineers, economists, and sociologists who were paid seven million dollars a year to look into the future. The University of Illinois ran a "computerized exploration of the year 2000."[2] Other research institutes fed a series of political, social, and economic variables into their computers, like ingredients in a recipe, and studied what might happen when the variables were mixed in different ways. In 1965 the American Academy of Arts and Sciences brought together around thirty leading intellectuals from a variety of disciplines to discuss the relative merits of extrapolation, forecasting models, cybernetic models, and "Delphi techniques" (in which "experts" functioned as oracles) in speculating about the "alternative futures" facing America as it moved towards the year 2000.

It all sounded very impressive, and the sociological language employed by such intellectuals was certainly sophisticated enough to impress and overawe the wondering multitude. Now that we have actually reached the year 2000, let us see how these scientific futurologists actually fared.

There were quite a few successes. For one thing, they got the world's population right: just as they expected, it doubled from three to six billion between 1965 and 2000. For another, they accurately predicted many aspects of the communications revolution: small, user-friendly computers would be everywhere, they said, and increasing numbers of people would use this technology to work in their own homes. In the year 2000, they argued, information retrieval systems would transmit the entire contents of libraries and educational institutions to individual households. Thanks to communications satellites, people throughout the world would be talking to each other at low cost; thanks to "facsimile broadcasts," documents would be duplicated instead of distributed.

The futurologists also anticipated increasing automation in traditional assembly-line industries and the growth of large-scale mechanized agriculture at the expense of small farms. They correctly argued that cars would become safer, and suggested that they would be guided electronically to their destination – something that is just beginning. And they were right about medical advances in organ transplants, the use of genetic engineering in agriculture, and the development of drugs that would make people happy, motivate the lethargic, and stimulate the sexually challenged. All in all, it seems like a pretty good track record: welcome to the world of Prozac, Viagra, personal computers, fax machines, instant information, and the Internet.

However, when you bring in all the other predictions, the gap between their expectations and our reality grows wider and wider. Take, for example, the question of leisure. In the year 2000, according to the futurologists of the 1960s, we would have so much free time on our hands that people would actually be paid not to work. It seemed to make perfect sense. In the 1960s only 40 per cent of America's population worked outside the home. Given increased automation and higher productivity, it was argued, this figure could only fall, and would eventually level out at around 10 per cent. More and more of our time would be taken up with hobbies, sports, and entertainment. The families of 2000 would watch free-standing, three-dimensional home movies in their living rooms, and spend many hours talking to and looking at each other on their videophones. The principal psychological problems of 2000, it was widely believed, would stem not from too much stress, but from too much boredom.

Nor would there be any poverty in the year 2000, at least in America. Technological advances would make everyone independently wealthy and significantly reduce class divisions. The increasing complexity of society and the growing need for long-term planning would mean an expanded role for government. "Resistance to high income taxes will become less and less desperate," predicted Karl Deutsch, "because people do not really mind giving up marginal proportions of their income if their income is high enough."[3] Lots of free time, an independently wealthy population, greater economic equality, more government, and a general acceptance of high income taxes – How familiar does this sound?

And then there were the robots. No self-respecting housewife in the year 2000 would be without one. "By the year 2000," asserted the chairman of the United States Atomic Energy Commission, "housewives ... will probably have a robot `maid' ... shaped like a box [with] one large eye on the top, several arms and hands, and long narrow pads on each side for moving about."[4] In retrospect, it seems that he had been watching too many episodes of *Lost in Space*. Nor was he alone: the same kind of ideas were circulating in British universities, along with speculations about robots who cut the lawn, took out the garbage, vacuumed the floor, and did the dishes.

When it came to travel, the projected world of 2000 was equally chimerical. Intercontinental ballistic rockets would take you anywhere on Earth in under forty minutes; underground trains would shoot along at close to a thousand kilometres an hour; hovercrafts would be replacing automobiles as the preferred mode of transportation. Men and women would have not only landed on the Moon, but started to colonize it as well. By the year 2000 the first children would have been born on the Moon and astronauts would have set foot on Mars.

Anything that could be done, it was argued, would be done. The "great lesson of our age," wrote Arthur C. Clarke, was that "if something is possible in theory, and no fundamental scientific laws oppose its realization, then sooner or later it will be achieved."[5] There was, it seemed to the futurologists of the mid-1960s, no limit to progress: money was no object, energy was no problem, and natural resources were inexhaustible.

"We will have fusion power long before our oil and coal run out," believed Clarke, "and will be able to draw fuel from the sea in virtually unlimited quantities."[6] A dozen nuclear power stations would supply all America's electrical needs by 2000, according to General Electric's Technical Management Planning Organization, or TEMPO. Every home would have its own nuclear generator, others believed – not exactly a comforting thought. The sea would supply not only fuel but also food: the Rand Corporation's Delphi predictions envisaged frogmen farmers spending months under water, harvesting seaweed that would eventually be chemically reprocessed to simulate steak or hamburgers.

All this would take place against the context of weather control and environmental engineering. The possibility of global warming wasn't even on the radar screens. Instead, the scientific regulation of the climate would solve all kinds of problems. In the Los Angeles of 2000, an enormous nuclear power station would be built on Mount Wilson, overlooking the city. The heat that the station generated would be directed into the atmosphere and would raise the inversion layer over the city to 19,000 feet, taking the smog with it. Meanwhile, sea winds would be drawn into the space below, bringing a gentle rain that would irrigate the desert and turn it into fertile land. Mega-technology would create a new Californian Garden of Eden.

And there we have it: the scientific predictions of the mid-1960s about the year 2000 were sometimes right on the money, but more often spectacularly wrong. If most of us are batting at 100 when it comes to the future, the scientific futurologists have at best succeeded in getting their average up to around 333. Note, too, that their prognostications focused on the technological future, and that social and political change has proved even harder to predict. How many people in 1965 could possibly have foreseen the feminist revolution or the collapse of the Soviet Union? How many realistic observers could have anticipated the end of apartheid in South Africa? What economist could have predicted that, in 2000, the per capita gross national product of Ireland would exceed that of Britain?

With this in mind, it is worth considering some of the musings that are being made in our time about the character of the twenty-first century. In 1999 *The Times Higher Educational Supplement* brought together "thirty of the world's distinguished minds" and published their thoughts on the future in a book entitled *Predictions*. To some extent, the results are reminiscent of the scientific speculations of the1960s. As the editor, Sian Griffiths, pointed out, the possibilities include:

Children genetically engineered to resist new and deadly viruses, the creation of "bionic" people capable of understanding thoughts without the necessity of language and a solution, finally, to the riddle of human consciousness. We will create life in our labs and send it out to thrive on hostile planets, elect female governments to put an end to war and teach schoolchildren how to manage their emotions just as today we teach them English and Maths.[7]

But there have also been significant changes in the content and tone of our contemporary predictions. In particular, the wide-eyed optimism that characterized so many of the scientific predictions of 1965 has now been tempered by a significant degree of caution and concern.

A good example of the mixture of hope and fear can be found in the crucial area of "gene therapy" and takes us right back into the world of eugenics. During the mid-1960s biologists such as Hudson Hoagland believed that "genetic intervention" would be sufficiently advanced by 2000 to prevent diseases from occurring and to enable humankind to control its own evolution. All in all, this was taken to be a Good Thing: parents could not only ensure healthy children but determine the gender, abilities, and psychological characteristics of their offspring.

Now, in 2000, the Human Genome Project is well on the way to developing a "gene-based treatment for every disease." According to French Anderson, it will have revolutionized the practice of medicine within the next thirty years. On balance, he welcomes this advance as a means of stopping the terrible suffering associated with hereditary illnesses. But he also recognizes the immense potential for the misuse and abuse of such technology: "In the name of minor 'improvements' that we see as conveniences," he writes, "we might start using human genetic engineering to attempt to 'improve' ourselves – and our children."

For many scientists, such as Stephen Jay Gould and his colleagues on the Council for Responsible Genetics, the dangers are so great that the entire project should be scrapped: "Say No to Designer Children!!!" ran one of their recent broadsides. And, as Anderson also recognizes, the combination of "gene therapy" with our propensity for ethnic hatred has truly terrifying implications. His answer is to "develop an informed society which recognizes the dangers of genetic engineering and prevents misuses of the technology before it is too late."[9] Whether this precaution is sufficient remains very much an open question. Our general historical record on such matters, however, would point strongly towards pessimism.

Along with the caution and concern, some of the contributors to *Predictions* cast doubt on the entire nature of the enterprise itself. "It is hard to contemplate a request for predictions for the coming century," responded Noam Chomsky, "without serious reservations. The record of prediction in human affairs has not been inspiring, even short-range; nor in the sciences ... Perhaps the most plausible prediction is that any prediction about serious matters is likely to be off the mark, except by accident" – to which one can only say Amen. Similarly, Umberto Eco declined to make any predictions and pointed out the paradox of the plane: "At one time it seemed most logical that you had to be lighter than air in order to fly in the sky – but then it turned out that you had to be heavier than air to fly more efficiently." "The moral of the story," he continued, "is that in both philosophy and the sciences you must be very careful not to fall in love with your own airship."[10]

Even Jonathan Weiner, who wrote the introduction to *Predictions,* shared this scepticism. "Whether any of the specific predictions ... will come true," he commented, "is impossible to say. Guessing the fates of any single one of the predictions in this book is like guessing the path of the bottle in the ocean, or the fate of any one of the millions of species that grow and jostle on the tree of life."[11]

Very true, but it rather makes you wonder why the book was written in the first place. The whole idea of forecasting the future is fraught with so many problems and perils that it is not worth pursuing. Still, the idea of speculating about where we might be going, how we feel and think about such directions, and what we might do to change or continue our course is not only healthy but essential to our survival and development as a species. It is in this spirit, together with a sense of humility, an awareness of complexity, a deep distrust of utopian solutions, and a sceptical attitude towards apocalyptic scenarios, that we should, in my view, approach the unknown world of the future.

• • •

Nevertheless, prophecies and predictions continue to speak to deeply felt human needs. They offer meaning and direction where there is uncertainty, hope in the midst of despair, warnings where there may be danger, and answers where there is anxiety. For these reasons, it is reasonably safe to predict that predictions will be around for as long as humans continue to inhabit the planet. It is also reasonably safe to predict that most of these predictions will be wrong – these "reasonably safe" predictions being the exceptions that prove the rule. And if this is the case, then prophets and prognosticators will have a lot of explaining ahead of them. I will conclude, then, with a few helpful hints for aspiring augurs – a kind of user's guide for prophets with losses.

To begin with, you can avoid a lot of potential trouble by being as vague and ambiguous as possible when actually making your predictions. Like a good politician, you should steer well clear of specifics. If you must insist on giving dates, you should ensure that they are open to a variety of different interpretations. Follow the example of Nostradamus, an acknowledged master in the field. The end of the world, he wrote, would occur when Easter Monday fell on April 25. During the early seventeenth century, this prediction was taken to signify the year 1666. When nothing happened, it was relatively easy to change the date to 1734, the next point of convergence, followed by 1886 and 1943. The next year in line is 2038: Nostradamus is still going strong. All potential dates should, of course, be outside your own lifespan – that way, recriminations are easier to deal with.

As we have seen, the best way to make your prophecies foolproof is simply to cheat. The trick here is to make it look as if you have prophesied events that have already happened. This is what Daniel did for religious purposes, what eighteenth-century Irish revolutionaries did for political purposes, and what con-men like Richard Head and Charles Hindley did (through the medium of Mother Shipton) for crass commercial considerations. As a short-term strategy, this approach can be extremely effective; in the long term, though, the chances are that you'll be found out. Again, as long as you aren't too concerned about your posthumous reputation, that need not be a problem.

But what if you've already committed yourself and events have proven you wrong? What do you do when prophecies fail? One course of action is to admit the mistake, apologize, and move on. Another, more common approach is to admit the mistake, revise the figures, and come up with a new date, preferably in the distant future. A third is to ignore the failure and simply switch from one apocalyptic scenario to another. This is the model adopted by the syndicated radio host Art Bell. Before January 1, 2000, he whipped up a frenzy of fear that the Y2K bug would usher in Armageddon. When nothing happened, he moved without so much as a backwards glance into equally alarmist prophecies about the Coming Global Superstorm. It didn't do him any harm; his program remains the most popular overnight radio show in North America.

If this appears too crass, a more sophisticated approach has been to revise, reinterpret, or reconstruct the meaning of the original prophecy. This has been the preferred option of religious systems that have rested at least in part on apocalyptic foundations. The classic success story, in this respect, is Christianity. Despite, or possibly because of, the perpetual postponement of the Second Coming, the early Christians managed to attract impressive numbers of followers. Here was the heart of the problem: Jesus had supposedly said that the Second Coming would take place in the lifetime of his listeners. They had all died, and, if the Second Coming had occurred, no one had noticed. Explanations were needed, and fast.

Various lines of defence emerged: Jesus had never actually uttered these words; Mark and Matthew had misunderstood his meaning; his words were not to be taken literally; only God knew the time of the Second Coming. More generally, the shift towards an allegorical reading of biblical prophecies proved to be an effective way of wriggling out of an awkward situation – all the more so because it implicitly flattered the sophistication of modern believers by contrasting their higher understanding with the primitive literalism of their predecessors. And for those who continued to believe in the Second Coming, it was simply a matter of waiting and watching, whether or not they believed it was actually possible to read the signs of the times.

In more recent times, the experience of Jehovah's Witnesses confirms the view that repeated prophetic failures can be overcome, provided the right strategy is followed. Founded in the 1870s by Charles Taze Russell, Jehovah's Witnesses believed that the Second Coming had already occurred and that the gathering of the 144,000 elect, as described in Revelation 7:4, was already under way. God's living saints, Russell predicted, would all assume spiritual form in 1878. When nothing happened, the deadline was extended to 1881, and then to 1914, and then to 1918, and then to 1925, and then to 1975. The pattern is familiar enough. What was special about Jehovah's Witnesses, though, was their ability to keep bouncing back – and even to expand in the teeth of such a disastrous prophetic record.

Central to their repeated recovery was the ingenious way in which apparent failure was retrospectively reinterpreted as partial success. After the confusion and disappointment that followed each unfulfilled prophecy, the leaders came to the conclusion that God was actually working according to a kind of invisible instalment plan. Although nothing *seemed* to have happened in 1878, they argued, it was really the year in which God had withdrawn his favour from all the other Christian churches. And although 1881 *appeared* uneventful, it was the year after which all the saints who died would be immediately transformed into spiritual beings.

The beauty was that such arguments were impossible to prove or disprove. But for those who preferred at least the semblance of empirical evidence, it was a happy coincidence that the next prophetic date coincided with the outbreak of the First World War. Although the Second Coming had still not happened, there could be no doubt that 1914 was a significant date in world history. It was, Jehovah's Witnesses decided, all part of God's Great Instalment Plan: 1914 was now seen as the year when God withdrew his benevolence from the Christian nations. This time, there was no shortage of proof.

And so it went: 1925 and 1975 passed by, and still the world stubbornly refused to stop. Finally, over a hundred years after their formation, Jehovah's Witnesses decided that it just might be better not to pinpoint the date after all. True, the end of the world had been delayed, but it could happen at any time, and Jehovah's Witnesses had to prepare themselves for that glorious day. Accordingly, the movement continued to flourish in anticipation of a future that was always almost there, but not quite.[12]

Prophetic failures, then, are not necessarily fatal and can even coexist with the continuing expansion of a religious movement or the increasing popularity of a radio show. This is also true of astrology, which has weathered many unfavourable conjunctions and continues to thrive. After all, the law of averages suggests that some predictions will come true – and the occasional astrological success is more likely to be remembered and remarked upon than the frequent failures. Besides, astrologers traditionally had two very effective escape routes. The first was to bring God into the equation and argue that the prediction would have come true, except that divine intervention threw everything out of kilter. And the second was to maintain that heavenly bodies influenced but did not actually determine the future. Once this position was accepted, errors became relatively easy to explain. At any rate, astrology is still alive and well, and its house remains very much in the ascendant.[13]

If all else fails, your predictions have repeatedly been proven false, and you cannot convince anyone that your original prophecies have been misunderstood, there is one last line of recourse for the truly desperate – to insist that the prophecies have actually come true, despite all appearances to the contrary. From this perspective, the problem lies with our perceptions of reality, rather than the prediction itself. The classic example comes from Poland in the seventeenth century. At the royal court, a prophet solemnly informed the queen that Louis XIII and Urban VIII would destroy the "Mahometan Empire." But the queen knew something that the prophet did not: Louis and Urban had recently died. She did not hesitate to apprise him of that information. "Pretended *facts*," replied the prophet, without missing a beat, "are never to be set in competition with unquestionable Predictions."[14]

It is the last refuge, not only of prophets, but of all theorists whose brilliant intellectual constructs do not work in practice.

When in doubt, embrace the notion of "false consciousness," insist you are right, and blame any difficulties on what passes for reality. The frightening thing is that it sometimes works.

• • •

And finally, a few words about Elvis Presley and the End of the World. In Rob Reiner's film *This is Spinal Tap,* the members of a fictitious rock band stand above Elvis' grave at Graceland, singing "Heartbreak Hotel" appropriately off-key. "Gives you a sense of perspective," says one of them, staring at the grave. "Too much fucking perspective if you ask me," replies another. Here, according to scientists George Bowen and Lee Ann Willson, is "too much fucking perspective" on the fate of our planet.

Eventually, they say, the Sun will expand into a Red Giant and pull the Earth closer and closer into its orbit. The oceans and the atmosphere will boil away, and global warming will increase to around 2000 degrees Celsius. We won't have to go to the Moon; the Moon will come to us, crashing down from a great height and at a great speed. A new atmosphere will form, consisting of vaporized rock. The sky will turn a beautiful deep red, but no one will be around to enjoy the view. And then the Earth will be swallowed up by the Sun, and our little place in the universe will be no more.[15]

This will occur approximately five billion years from now. Until then, though, anything can happen.

NOTES

CHAPTER 1: PROPHETIC FALLACIES

[1] Cicero, "On Divination," in CD Yonge, ed, *The Treatises of M.T. Cicero* (London 1892), 141.

[2] [Joseph Lomas Towers], *Illustrations of Prophecy* (London 1796), 1.

[3] Ibid., 82.

[4] Book of Daniel 7:8; Book of Revelation 12:1.

[5] Mark 13:32.

[6] This was the view of Arnold of Vilanova, a leading thirteenth-century prophetic writer, as discussed in Harold Lee, Marjorie Reeves, and Giulio Silano, *Western Mediterranean Prophecy: The School of Joachim of Fiore and the Fourteenth-Century Breviloquium* (Toronto 1989), 33.

[7] This was the view of Edgar Whisenant, a leading twentieth-century prophetic writer, as discussed in Paul Boyer, *When Time Shall Be No More: Prophecy Belief in Modern American Culture* (Cambridge, Mass 1992), 130.

[8] Thomas Paine, "The Age of Reason," in Philip S Foner, ed., *The Life and Major Writings of Thomas Paine* (New York 1948), 1: 475–77, 510–11, 554, 561–62.

[9] David A Wilson, *Paine and Cobbett: The Transatlantic Connection* (Montreal 1988), 154–55, 172, 182–83, 188.

[10] Thomas Malthus, *An Essay on the Principle of Population* (1798; Oxford 1993, edited with an introduction by Geoffrey Gilbert), 61.

[11] Cited in Eugen Weber, *Apocalypses: Prophecies, Cults, and Millennial Beliefs through the Ages* (Toronto 1999), 239.

[12] Quoted in EH Carr, *What Is History?* (Harmondsworth 1964), 21.

[13] Book of Nahum, 2:3–4.

[14] Edmund Collins, quoted in Carl Berger, *The Sense of Power: Studies in the Ideas of Canadian Imperialism, 1867–1914* (1970; Toronto 1976), 114n.

[15] Bernie Ward, *Nostradamus: The Man Who Saw Tomorrow* (New York 1997), 50.

[16] John Beresford to Lord Auckland, in William Beresford, ed, *The Correspondence of the Right Hon. John Beresford* (London 1854), 2:128.

[17] Quoted in David Miller, "Presbyterianism and 'Modernization' in Ulster," *Past and Present* 80 (1978): 83–84.

[18] *Dictionary of National Biography* (1917; Oxford 1964), 18:119.

[19] John Tillinghast, *Knowledge of the Times* (London 1654).

[20] Quoted in Donald Weinstein, *Savonarola and Florence: Prophecy and Patriotism in the Renaissance* (Princeton 1970), 288.

[21] John Allan, quoted in Gordon Stewart and George Rawlyk, *A People Highly Favoured of God* (Toronto 1972), 75.

[22] Ibid., 154–92; see especially 159, 165–66, 175.

[23] Boyer, *When Time Shall Be No More*, 84–87.

[24] BS Capp, *The Fifth-Monarchy Men: A Study in Seventeenth-Century English Millenarianism* (London 1972), 42–43.

[25] Francis Dobbs, *Memoirs of Francis Dobbs, Esq* (Dublin 1800), 11, 41–47.

[26] Book of Ezekiel 38:22, 39:18.

[27] James 2:13.

[28] Quoted in *The Illuminator, or Looking-Glass of the Times* (London 1797), 14–15.

[29] Boyer, *When Time Shall Be No More*, 278.

[30] Christopher Hill, *Antichrist in Seventeenth-Century England* (London 1971), 107.

[31] Barbara Newman, "Hildegard of Bingen: Visions and Validation," *Church History* 54 (June 1985): 174.

[32] Geoffrey of Monmouth, *The History of the Kings of Britain*, trans Lewis Thorpe (1136; Harmondsworth 1966), 196.

[33] Quoted in WHG Armytage, *Yesterday's Tomorrows: A Historical Survey of Future Societies* (Toronto 1968), 36.

[34] Quoted in EP Thompson, *The Making of the English Working Class* (Harmondsworth 1968), 17.

[35] Bruce Elliott, *Irish Migrants in the Canadas: A New Approach* (Kingston and Montreal 1988), 6.

[36] Thomas Jefferson to William Short, January 3, 1793, in John Catanzariti, ed, *The Papers of Thomas Jefferson* (Princeton 1992), 25:14.

[37] Wolfe Tone to Thomas Russell, October 25, 1795, Sirr Papers, Trinity College, Dublin, 860/2/13-15.

[38] Quoted in Jenny Graham, *Revolutionary in Exile: The Emigration of Joseph Priestley to America, 1794–1804,* in *Transactions of the American Philosophical Society* 85, 2 (1995): 103.

[39] Edmund Burke to Adrien-Jean-François Duport, March 29, 1790, in Thomas Copeland, ed, *The Correspondence of Edmund Burke* (Cambridge 1967), 6:109.

[40] Quoted in Armytage, *Yesterday's Tomorrows,* 14.

Chapter 2: The Age of the Spirit

[1] Matthew 16:28; see also Mark 13:24–31.

[2] Gregory, Bishop of Tours, *History of the Franks,* trans Ernest Brehaut (New York 1965), 244–45.

[3] James F Kenney ed, *The Sources for the Early History of Ireland: An Introduction and Guide* (New York 1929), 750; see also Whitley Stokes, "Adamnan's Second Vision," *Revue Celtique* (1891): 420–43.

[4] See CG Coulton, *Life in the Middle Ages* (1910; Cambridge 1961),1:1–7.

[5] The best source for medieval millenarianism in general is Norman Cohn, *The Pursuit of the Millennium: Revolutionary Millenarians and Mystical Anarchists of the Middle Ages* (1957; London 1969).

[6] For an excellent overview of Joachim's influence, see Marjorie Reeves, *Joachim of Fiore and the Prophetic Future* (London 1976).

[7] Quoted in Bernard McGinn, *The Calabrian Abbot: Joachim of Fiore in the History of Western Thought* (New York 1985), 22.

[8] Quoted in Gordon Leff, *Heresy in the Later Middle Ages: The Relation of Heterodoxy to Dissent, c 1250–c. 1450* (Manchester 1967), 72. For the sake of clarity and consistency, I have substituted the word "period" for "age" in Leff's translation.

[9] This sketch of Joachim's outlook is drawn mainly from Margaret Reeves and Warwick Gould, *Joachim of Fiore and the Myth of the Eternal Evangel in the Nineteenth Century* (Oxford 1987); Marjorie Reeves and Beatrice Hirsch-

Reich, *The Figurae of Joachim of Fiore* (Oxford 1972); and Leff, *Heresy in the Later Middle Ages.*

[10] Daniel 12:12.

[11] Revelation 13:3.

[12] Quoted in Cohn, *Pursuit of the Millennium,* 121, 122; for Cohn's general discussion of these issues, see 108–26.

[13] This discussion is indebted to Leff, *Heresy in the Later Middle Ages,* 5–64.

[14] Ibid., 70–81; Reeves and Gould, *Joachim of Fiore and the Myth of the Eternal Evangel,* 8.

[15] Harold Lee, Marjorie Reeves, and Giulio Silano, *Western Mediterranean Prophecy: The School of Joachim of Fiore and the Fourteenth-Century Breviloquium* (Toronto 1989), 23–26.

[16] Cohn, *Pursuit of the Millennium,* 94–98.

[17] Reeves, *Joachim of Fiore and the Prophetic Future,* 50.

[18] Leff, *Heresy in the Later Middle Ages,* 193; Reeves, *Joachim of Fiore and the Prophetic Future,* 48–49.

[19] Quoted in Lee, Reeves, and Silano, *Western Mediterranean Prophecy,* 60.

[20] Leff, *Heresy in the Later Middle Ages,* 215.

[21] 2 Corinthians 3:17.

[22] Quoted in Cohn, *Pursuit of the Millennium,* 156.

[23] Quoted ibid, 152.

[24] Quoted in Howard Kaminsky, "The Free Spirit in the Hussite Revolution," in Sylvia Thrupp, ed, *Millennial Dreams in Action: Studies in Revolutionary Religious Movements* (New York 1970), 170; see also Cohn, *Pursuit of the Millennium,* 212.

[25] Quoted in Kaminsky, "The Free Spirit in the Hussite Revolution," 180–81.

[26] Quoted in Cohn, *Pursuit of the Millennium,* 182.

[27] For a useful discussion of "models" of the millennium, see Michael Barkun, *Disaster and the Millennium* (New Haven 1974).

[28] Boyer, *When Time Shall Be No More,* 60–61.

[29] Barkun, *Disaster and the Millennium,* 168–70; the following account is based on the breathtaking narrative in Cohn, *Pursuit of the Millennium,* 252–80.

Chapter 3: The Future in Folklore

[1] Peter Laslett, *The World We Have Lost* (1965; London 1971), 134.

[2] Eric Kerridge, *The Farmers of Old England* (London 1973), 22.

[3] Kevin Danaher, *The Year in Ireland: Irish Calendar Customs* (Dublin 1972), 161–62.

[4] Keith Thomas, *Religion and the Decline of Magic* (London 1971), 31.

[5] Alwyn and Brinley Rees, *Celtic Heritage: Ancient Tradition in Ireland and Wales* (1961; London 1973), 83–94.

[6] Ann Ross, *The Folklore of the Scottish Highlands* (London 1976), 134–38.

[7] Quoted in Rees, *Celtic Heritage*, 168; see also Máire MacNeill, *The Festival of Lughnasa: A Study of the Survival of the Celtic Festival of the Beginning of Harvest* (Dublin 1982).

[8] Ross, *Folklore of the Scottish Highlands*, 139.

[9] James Joyce, "Clay," in *Dubliners* (1916; Harmondsworth 1976), 104–5.

[10] WG Wood-Martin, *Traces of the Elder Faiths of Ireland* (1902; Port Washington, NY 1971), 2:267.

[11] Donald Akenson, *Between Two Revolutions: Islandmagee, County Antrim, 1798–1920* (Port Credit, Ont: 1979), 142–43; Paul Boyer and Stephen Nissenbaum, *Salem Possessed: The Social Origins of Witchcraft* (Cambridge, Mass. 1974), 1.

[12] Eleanor Hull, *Folklore of the British Isles* (London 1928), 111–12.

[13] Wood-Martin, *Traces of the Elder Faiths*, 1:297.

[14] Ibid., 1:295–96.

[15] Donal O'Sullivan, *Carolan: The Life, Times and Music of an Irish Harper* (London 1958), 1:118.

[16] Wood-Martin, *Traces of the Elder Faiths*, 2:222.

[17] Hull, *Folklore of the British Isles*, 106–7; T Gwynn Jones, *Welsh Folklore and Folk-Custom* (London 1930), 113.

[18] Rees, *Celtic Heritage*, 341; "The Hour of Death," in Sean O' Sullivan, ed, *Folktales of Ireland* (Chicago 1966), 165.

[19] See Patricia Lysaght, *The Banshee: The Irish Supernatural Death-Messenger* (Dun Laoighaire 1986).

[20] Jones, *Welsh Folklore and Folk-Custom*, 108–11.

[21] Thomas, *Religion and the Decline of Magic,* 237–40; Richard Godbeer, *The Devil's Dominion: Magic and Religion in Early New England* (New York 1992); Donald Harman Akenson, *Being Had: Historians, Evidence, and the Irish in North America* (Port Credit, Ont 1985), 4–9.

[22] Rees, *Celtic Heritage,* 192–94.

[23] W Elliot Woodward, *Records of Salem Witchcraft* (1864; Roxbury, Mass. 1969), 2:62.

[24] Personal interview with historian Jane Kamensky, 1992; see also Carol F Karlsen, *The Devil in the Shape of a Woman: Witchcraft in Colonial New England* (New York 1987).

[25] Woodward, *Records of Salem Witchcraft,* 1:246–47.

[26] Boyer and Nissenbaum, *Salem Possessed,* 9.

[28] Thomas, *Religion and the Decline of Magic,* 296, 333; Gerald of Wales, *The History and Topography of Ireland* (Harmondsworth 1982), 59.

[28] Thomas, *Religion and the Decline of Magic,* 314–15.

[29] Ibid., 327–28.

[30] Phyllis Deane, *The First Industrial Revolution* (Cambridge 1965), 227–28.

[31] Harry Rusche, "*Merlini Anglici:* Astrology and Propaganda from 1644 to 1651," *English Historical Review* 80 (1965): 324.

[32] Ibid., 330.

[33] Thomas, *Religion and the Decline of Magic,* 286, 294, 298, 413.

[34] Jonathan Swift, *Bickerstaff Papers and Pamphlets on the Church,* ed Herbert Davis (Oxford 1957), 141–46, 154, 159–62, 220–25.

[35] Quoted in John R Millburn, *Benjamin Martin: Author, Instrument-Maker and "Country Showman"* (Leyden 1976), 41.

[36] Nick Hornby, *Fever Pitch* (London 1992), 111.

CHAPTER 4: REVOLUTION AND REVELATION

[1] Thomas Paine, "Age of Reason," in Philip S Foner, ed, *The Complete Writings of Thomas Paine* (New York 1945), 1:496.

[2] Paine, "Rights of Man, Part the Second," in Foner, *Complete Writings,* 1:453–54. I have corrected Foner's typographical errors.

3 Paine, "Rights of Man, Part the First," in Foner, *Complete Writings,* 1:344.

4 Paine, "Common Sense," in Foner, *Complete Writings,* 1:45.

5 See JH Stewart, ed, *A Documentary Survey of the French Revolution* (Toronto 1951), 286–88.

6 Paine, "Rights of Man, Part the First," in Foner, *Complete Writings,* 1:341–42; see also Hannah Arendt, *On Revolution* (1963; Harmondsworth 1973), 43–46.

7 "Declaration of the Dublin Society of United Irishmen," quoted in Marianne Elliott, *Partners in Revolution: The United Irishmen and France* (New Haven 1982), 23.

8 Matthew 24:32–33.

9 James A Leith, *Media and Revolution: Moulding a New Citizenry in France during the Terror* (Toronto 1968).

10 Ebenezer Baldwin, *The Duty of Rejoicing under Calamities and Afflictions* (New York 1776), 38.

11 Ibid., 39–40.

12 BS Capp, *The Fifth Monarchy Men: A Study in Seventeenth-Century English Millenarianism* (London 1972), 232; Revelation 11:3.

13 Keith Thomas, *Religion and the Decline of Magic* (London 1971), 133–34, 144.

14 Capp, *Fifth Monarchy Men,* 29; Revelation 19:16.

15 Thomas, *Religion and the Decline of Magic,* 137.

16 George Wither, *Britain's Remembrancer* (London 1628), 241–42, 254–55, 277.

17 Capp, *Fifth Monarchy Men,* 38; Christopher Hill, *Antichrist in Seventeenth-Century England* (London 1971), 81–82.

18 Thomas Brightman, *The Revelation of St John Illustrated* (London 1644), frontispiece, 162, 712.

19 Christopher Hill, "John Reeve and the Origins of Muggletonianism," in Ann Williams, ed, *Prophecy and Millenarianism: Essays in Honour of Marjorie Reeves* (Bungay, Suffolk 1980), 308.

20 Capp, *Fifth Monarchy Men,* 42–43; Hill, *Antichrist in Seventeenth-Century England,* 79.

21 Abiezer Coppe, *A Fiery Flying Roll* (London 1649), ii–iv, 1, 4, 8–9.

[22] Hill, "John Reeve and the Origins of Muggletonianism," 307–33; Hill, *Antichrist in Seventeenth-Century England*, 132–33.

[23] Hill, *Antichrist in Seventeenth-Century England*, 110, 116–17, 121.

[24] Daniel 7:18.

[25] Capp, *Fifth Monarchy Men*, 76–82, 131–55.

[26] Ibid., 102, 192; Daniel 12:11; Revelation 11:3. The day-year connection was derived from Numbers 14:34: "And the number of the days in which ye searched the land, even forty days, each day for a year, shall ye bear your iniquities, even forty years, and ye shall know my breach of promise."

[27] Alan Heimert, *Religion and the American Mind from the Great Awakening to the Revolution* (Cambridge, Mass 1966), 82, 325.

[28] Revelation 12:1–17; 13:2.

[29] Samuel Sherwood, *The Church's Flight into the Wilderness* (New York 1776), 30, 33.

[30] Ibid., 49.

[31] Eric Foner, *Tom Paine and Revolutionary America* (New York 1976), 114–15.

[32] Stephen A Marini, *Radical Sects of Revolutionary New England* (Cambridge, Mass. 1982), 46–48.

[33] *Prophecies of the Rev Christopher Love: Who Was Beheaded on Tower-Hill, London, on The Twenty-Second Day of August 1651, and His Last Words on the Scaffold* (Boston 1794), 7; Ruth H Bloch, *Visionary Republic: Millennial Themes in American Thought, 1756–1800* (Cambridge, Mass.: 1985), 25.

[34] See, for example, Samuel Hopkins, *Treatise on the Millennium* (Boston 1793), and *Characteristics in the Prophecies Applicable to, and Descriptive of, the Power and Duration of the French Republic* (New York 1798).

[35] David Austin, *The Millennial Door Thrown Open* (East Windsor 1799), 26–32.

[36] Thomas Birch, *The Obligation upon Christians, and Especially Ministers to Be Exemplary in Their Lives* (Belfast 1794), 29–31, and *Seemingly Experimental Religion* (Washington, Penn 1806), 7–8; *Washington Reporter*, 26 November 1810; David A. Wilson, *United Irishmen, United States: Immigrant Radicals in the Early Republic* (Ithaca 1998), 112–32.

[37] Joyce Appleby, *Capitalism and a New Social Order: The Republican Vision of the 1790s* (New York 1984), 79–105; Paine, *Rights of Man*, in Foner, *Complete Writings*, 1:251–52.

38 Rationalis, "Remarks, which Are Supposed Will Be Made in This Kingdom, by Two North American Travellers in the Year One Thousand Nine Hundred and Forty-Four," *The Literary Register, Or, Weekly Miscellany* (London 1769), 98–99.

39 Ibid., 98.

40 Thomas Hardy, *The Patriot* (Edinburgh 1793), 52–53.

41 Drew R McCoy, *The Elusive Republic: Political Economy in Republican America* (New York 1982), 130–31, 170–72, 255–59.

42 Joseph Priestley, *The Present State of Europe Compared with Antient Prophecies* (London 1794), 28.

43 James Bicheno, *The Signs of the Times* (London 1793), ii.

44 *The Illuminator, or Looking-Glass of the Times* (London 1797), 8–10, 28; *Jurieu's Accomplishment of the Scripture Prophecies* (London 1793).

45 Robert Fleming, *Apocalyptical Key: An Extraordinary Discourse on the Rise and Fall of the Papacy* (1701; London 1793), 52–61.

46 [Joseph Lomas Towers], *Illustrations of Prophecy* (London 1796), iv–vi, xiii–xix, 82–83.

47 Bicheno, *Signs of the Times,* 6–9; Priestley, *Present State of Europe,* 45–48.

48 [Towers], *Illustrations of Prophecy,* 761–62.

49 J.F.C. Harrison, *The Second Coming: Popular Millenarianism, 1780–1850* (London 1979), 58; Richard Brothers, *A Revealed Knowledge of the Prophecies and Times* (London 1794; Philadelphia 1795), 65.

50 Brothers, *Revealed Knowledge,* 50–52, 56.

51 Ibid., 63–64.

52 John Binns, *Recollections of the Life of John Binns* (Philadelphia 1854), 47–49

53 Ibid., 48; Bloch, *Visionary Republic,* 164.

54 Binns, *Recollections,* 50–51.

55 This account is drawn from Harrison, *Second Coming,* 88–104.

56 Edmund Burke, *Reflections on the Revolution in France* (1790; Harmondsworth 1969), 342.

CHAPTER 5: UTOPIA

[1] See, for example, Mary Lefkowitz, *Not Out of Africa: How Afrocentrism Became an Excuse to Teach Myth as History* (New York 1996).

[2] RG Thwaites, ed, *The Jesuit Relations and Allied Documents* (Cleveland 1896–1901), 44:297; *Anthologia Hibernica* 2 (July 1793): 1.

[3] Francis Bacon, "New Atlantis," in Richard Foster Jones, ed, *Francis Bacon: Essays, Advancement of Learning, New Atlantis, and Other Pieces* (New York 1937), 480–88.

[4] Ibid., 490.

[5] [John Lithgow], "Equality – A Political Romance" (1802); reprinted as *Equality: Or, A History of Lithconia* (Philadelphia 1947), 5, 62, 75–76, 84.

[6] Ibid., 10–11.

[7] Ibid., 23–24, 53.

[8] See Gregory Claeys, *Utopias of the British Enlightenment* (Cambridge 1994).

[9] Samuel Madden, *Memoirs of the Twentieth Century: Being Original Letters of State under George the Sixth* (1733; New York 1972), 3.

[10] Ibid., 23–26, 47, 259–60; WHG Armytage, *Yesterday's Tomorrows: A Historical Survey of Future Societies* (Toronto 1968), 19.

[11] Anon, *The Reign of George VI, 1900–1925* (1763; London 1972), 100, 104.

[12] Ibid., xxviii.

[13] Louis-Sebastian Mercier, *L'An 2440* (Paris 1771) The book was translated into English under the title *Memoirs of the Year Two Thousand Five Hundred* (1772; New York 1974), and all quotations are from this edition. The spy's remarks are in Robert Darnton, *The Literary Underground of the Old Regime* (Cambridge, Mass. 1982), 26.

[14] Mercier, *Memoirs,* 1:vi–vii, 5–7.

[15] Ibid., 1:30, 34; 2:120, 125, 131–32.

[16] Ibid., 2:175.

[17] Ibid., 1:49, 182–83.

[18] Ibid., 1:140.

[19] Ibid., 1:153.

[20] Ibid., 1: 76.

[21] Ibid., 1:73–74; 2:3, 5–7, 28, 31–33.

[22] Ibid., 1:58–59.

[23] Ibid., 1: 95, 109, 113.

[24] Ibid., 1:26; 2:154, 161.

[25] Ibid., 152–53.

[26] Ibid., 1:171, 208; 2:213–15, 235–36.

[27] Saint-Just, quoted in Christopher Hibbert, *The French Revolution* (Harmondsworth 1982), 268.

[28] Comte de Volney, *The Ruins: Or a Survey of the Revolutions of Empires* (1791; New York 1796), 107–9.

[29] Ibid., 111.

[30] Ibid., 112–17.

[31] Armytage, *Yesterday's Tomorrows,* 29.

[32] Christopher Hill, *Antichrist in Seventeenth-Century England* (London 1971), 25–26.

[33] Marquis de Condorcet, "Outlines of a Historical View of the Progress of the Human Mind," in Frank E Manuel and Fritzie P Manuel, eds, *French Utopias: An Anthology of Ideal Societies* (New York 1967), 194–215.

[34] Mary Griffith, *Camperdown: Or, News from Our Neighbourhood* (Philadelphia 1836), republished as *Three Hundred Years Hence* (Boston 1975), 49–51.

[35] Ibid., 55–56.

[36] Ibid., 72–75, 99, 119–21.

[37] Ibid., 98–102, 116; see also Linda K Kerber, "The Republican Mother: Women and the Enlightenment – An American Perspective," *American Quarterly* 27 (1976): 187–205; Jan Lewis, "The Republican Wife: Virtue and Seduction in the Early Republic," *William and Mary Quarterly* 44 (October 1987): 689–721.

[38] Griffith, *Three Hundred Years Hence,* 57–60, 67, 71, 114–15.

[39] This theme is developed in Nan Bowman Albinski, *Women's Utopias in British and American Fiction* (New York 1988), 17–24.

[40] Edward Bellamy, *Looking Backward, 2000–1887* (1887; Boston 1926), 10–18.

[41] Ibid., 56, 62–63.

[42] Ibid., 131.

[43] Ibid., 98, 128, 199.

[44] Ibid., 256–65.

[45] Ibid., 267–68.

[46] Quoted in Armytage, *Yesterday's Tomorrows,* 49, 63.

[47] HG Wells, *A Modern Utopia* (1905; Lincoln, Nebraska 1967), 136, 141–43, 147.

[48] Ibid., 183–84, 268–69.

[49] HG Wells, *Men Like Gods* (1923; London 1976), 64.

[50] Ibid., 72–74; Wells, *Modern Utopia,* 231.

[51] Wells, *Men Like Gods,* 205.

CHAPTER 6: SERPENTS IN THE GARDEN

[1] George Orwell, *Nineteen Eighty-Four* (1949; Harmondsworth 1990), 280.

[2] Jules Verne, *Paris in the Twentieth Century* (New York 1996), 26, 131, 136, 157.

[3] Ibid., 14.

[4] Ibid., 30, 53.

[5] Ibid., 88, 92.

[6] Ibid., 78.

[7] Ibid., 177–85.

[8] Ibid., xxv.

[9] Jules Verne, "Eternal Adam," in Sam Moskovitz, *Masterpieces of Science Fiction* (Cleveland and New York 1966), 169–206.

[10] HG Wells, *The Time Machine* (1895; New York 1983), 66, 93.

[11] Ibid., 65.

[12] Ibid., 93–98.

[13] Wells, *Modern Utopia,* 73, 91, 155.

[14] Ibid., 103, 187–88, 194.

[15] HG Wells, *The World Set Free: A Story of Mankind* (London 1914), 31, 34,

44–45.

[16] Ibid., 73–74, 77.

[17] Quoted in WHG Armytage, *Yesterday's Tomorrows: A Historical Survey of Future Societies* (Toronto 1968), 23.

[18] Wells, *World Set Free*, 88–89.

[19] Ibid., 95–103.

[20] Ibid., 130, 137.

[21] Ibid., 212, 222–23, 229–30, 233.

[22] Ibid., 234; [Joseph Lomas Towers], *Illustrations of Prophecy* (London 1796), 732, 762.

[23] HG Wells, *Men Like Gods* (1923; London 1976), 14, 63, 221–22.

[24] Yevgeny Zamyatin, *We* (1923; New York 1987), 2.

[25] Ibid., 13, 55.

[26] Ibid., 21–22.

[27] Ibid., 12, 33, 82, 102.

[28] Ibid., 1, 53.

[29] Ibid., 35.

[30] Ibid., 2, 8, 22, 27.

[31] Ibid., 32, 77.

[32] Ibid., 56, 61, 89.

[33] Ibid., 232.

[34] Ayn Rand, *Anthem* (1938; New York 1995), 94.

[35] Ibid., 100–1.

[36] Ibid., 104–5.

[37] Wells, *Modern Utopia*, 266.

[38] Aldous Huxley, *Brave New World* (1932; London 1985), 10, 13.

[39] Marquis de Sade, "Philosophy in the Bedroom," in Frank E Manuel and Fritzie P Manuel, eds, *French Utopias: An Anthology of Ideal Societies* (New York 1967), 226.

[40] Huxley, *Brave New World*, 14.

[41] Ibid., 51.

[42] Ibid., 177.

[43] Ibid., 188–90.

[44] Ibid., 183–84.

[45] Ibid., 192.

[46] Ibid., 14.

[47] See David Bradshaw, "Introduction," *Brave New World* (London 1994)

[48] George Woodcock, *Orwell's Message: 1984 and the Present* (Madeira Park, BC 1984), 1, 101.

[49] Quoted ibid., 79.

[50] George Orwell, *The Road to Wigan Pier* (1937; Harmondsworth 1972), 203; Woodcock, *Orwell's Message,* 83.

[51] Orwell, *Road to Wigan Pier,* 166.

[52] Orwell, *Nineteen Eighty-Four,* 267, 275–76.

[53] Ibid., 279.

[54] Ibid., 4–5, 65, 279.

[55] Ibid., 139.

[56] Ibid., 13–19.

[57] Ibid., 277.

[58] Ibid., 55–56, 154.

[59] Ibid., 72.

[60] Ibid., 74–75.

[61] Ibid., 267.

CHAPTER 7: THE AMBIVALENT FUTURE

[1] Quoted in Nan Bowman Albinski, *Women's Utopias in British and American Fiction* (New York 1988), 163.

[2] Josiah Wedgwood to Thomas Bentley, October 9, 1766, in A Finer and G Savage, eds, *The Selected Letters of Josiah Wedgwood* (London 1965), 44.

[3] Thomas Paine, "Utility of This Work Evinced," and "To the Public,"

Pennsylvania Magazine, January 1775; Alexis de Tocqueville, *Democracy in America* (1840; New York 1981), 368.

⁴ Joseph J Corn and Brian Horrigan, *Yesterday's Tomorrows: Past Visions of the American Future* (New York 1984), 49. The following discussion is deeply indebted to this excellent work.

⁵ Quoted ibid., 101.

⁶ Ibid., 11.

⁷ Quoted in Paul Boyer, *When Time Shall Be No More: Prophecy Belief in Modern American Culture* (Cambridge, Mass 1992), 106–7. This book is the source of my general discussion of contemporary American apocalypticism.

⁸ Ibid., 125.

⁹ II Peter 3:10; Zechariah 14:12; Revelation 16:9.

¹⁰ Quoted in Boyer, *When Time Shall Be No More,* 140.

¹¹ Quoted ibid., 136.

¹² Ibid., 162.

¹³ II Timothy 3: 1–4, 6, 13.

¹⁴ Leviticus 20:13 The death penalty was also recommended for adultery, incest, bestiality, and cursing your parents.

¹⁵ Boyer, *When Time Shall Be No More,* 283.

¹⁶ James Bicheno, *The Signs of the Times* (London 1793), 76–77; Leo Tolstoy, *War and Peace* (Harmondsworth 1978), 788–89.

¹⁷ Boyer, *When Time Shall Be No More,* 108.

¹⁸ Ibid., 289.

¹⁹ Daniel Bell, ed, *Toward the Year 2000: Work in Progress* (Boston 1967), 2, 274.

²⁰ Marge Piercy, *Woman on the Edge of Time* (1977; New York 1983), 60

²¹ Ibid., 60, 120.

²² Ibid., 97.

²³ Ibid., 131.

²⁴ Ibid., 219–20.

²⁵ Ibid., 202.

[26] Ibid., 276.

[27] Ibid., 169–70, 283, 331, 370.

[28] Margaret Mead, "The Life Cycle and Its Variations: The Division of Roles," in Bell, ed, *Toward the Year 2000,* 242.

[29] Margaret Atwood, *The Handmaid's Tale* (Toronto 1985), 34.

[30] Ibid., 128.

[31] Ibid., 231.

[32] Ibid., 249.

[33] Ibid., 43, 94.

[34] Ibid., 319.

[35] Quoted in George Woodcock, *Orwell's Message: 1984 and the Present* (Madeira Park, BC 1984), 2.

[36] "Walt Disney Millennium Celebration," Walt Disney World Web site, 2.

[37] Andrea Dworkin, "A New Jerusalem for Women," in Sian Griffiths, ed, *Predictions* (Oxford 1999), 94.

[38] Quoted in Griffiths, ed, *Predictions,* 234.

CHAPTER 8: PREDICTIONS

[1] Quoted in WHG Armytage, *Yesterday's Tomorrows: A Historical Survey of Future Societies* (Toronto 1968), 31.

[2] Daniel Bell, ed, *Toward the Year 2000: Work in Progress* (Boston 1967); "The Futurists: Looking Toward A.D. 2000," *Time,* February 25, 1966; "2000: the year of spare-part humans, instant politics," Toronto *Globe and Mail,* January 31, 1966.

[3] Quoted in Bell, ed, *Toward the Year 2000,* 25.

[4] Quoted in "The Futurists."

[5] Arthur C Clarke, *Profiles of the Future: An Inquiry into the Limits of the Possible* (1963; New York 1967), 116.

[6] Ibid., 142–43.

[7] Sian Griffiths, ed, *Predictions* (Oxford 1999), ix.

[8] W French Anderson, "Gene Therapies," ibid., 19–20.

[9] Ibid., 20.

[10] Noam Chomsky, "Language Design," and Umberto Eco, "Never Fall in Love with Your Own Airship," ibid., 30, 105.

[11] Ibid., xxi.

[12] Joseph F Zygmunt, "Prophetic Failure and Chiliastic Identity: The Case of Jehovah's Witnesses," *American Journal of Sociology* 75 (1970): 926–48.

[13] Keith Thomas, *Religion and the Decline of Magic* (London 1971), 335–36.

[14] Quoted in Samuel Madden, *Memoirs of the Twentieth Century: Being Original Letters of State under George the Sixth* (1733; New York 1972), 518.

[15] "To the ends of the earth," *The Economist,* February 26, 2000.